TROTSKY

Leon Trotsky has aroused strong passions, and historians love and hate him in equal measure. This new biography provides a full account of his political life, based upon a wealth of primary sources, including previously unpublished material.

Ian D. Thatcher paints a new picture of Trotsky's standing in Russian and world history. Key myths about Trotsky's heroic work as a revolutionary, especially in Russia's first revolution of 1905 and the Russian Civil War, are thrown into question. Although Trotsky had a limited understanding of crucial contemporary events such as Hitler's rise to power, he was an important thinker and politician, not least as a trenchant critic of Stalin's version of communism.

This study provides a clear and accessible introduction to Trotsky's life and thought for anyone interested in twentieth-century Russian and world history.

Ian D. Thatcher lectures in Modern Russian History at the University of Leicester. His previous publications include *Leon Trotsky and World War One* (2000) and *Regime and Society in Twentieth-Century Russia* (1999).

ROUTLEDGE HISTORICAL BIOGRAPHIES

SERIES EDITOR: ROBERT PEARCE

Routledge Historical Biographies provide engaging, readable and academically credible biographies written from an explicitly historical perspective. These concise and accessible accounts will bring important historical figures to life for students and general readers alike.

In the same series:

TROTSKY

Ian D. Thatcher

Routledge
Taylor & Francis Group

LONDON AND NEW YORK

3/7/13
Lan
gift

First published 2003
by Routledge
11 New Fetter Lane, London EC4P 4EE

Simultaneously published in the USA and Canada
by Routledge
29 West 35th Street, New York, NY 10001

Routledge is an imprint of the Taylor & Francis Group

© 2003 Ian D. Thatcher

Typeset in Garamond and Scala Sans by Taylor & Francis Books Ltd
Printed and bound in Great Britain by TJ International Ltd, Padstow,
Cornwall

All rights reserved. No part of this book may be reprinted or
reproduced or utilised in any form or by any electronic,
mechanical, or other means, now known or hereafter
invented, including photocopying and recording, or in any
information storage or retrieval system, without permission in
writing from the publishers.

British Library Cataloguing in Publication Data
A catalogue record for this book is available from the British Library

Library of Congress Cataloging in Publication Data
Thatcher, Ian D.
Trotsky / Ian D. Thatcher
Includes bibliographical references and index.
1. Trotsky, Leon, 1879–1940. 2. Revolutionaries–Soviet
Union–Biography. 3. Statesmen–Soviet Union–Biography. I. Title.
DK254.T6 T5 2002
947.084'092–dc21

ISBN 0–415–23250–3 (hbk)
ISBN 0–415–23251–1 (pbk)

CONTENTS

PLATES

All illustrations © David King Collection

Acknowledgements

The completion of this book was made possible by a semester of study leave granted by the University of Leicester and a six-month Research Fellowship awarded by the Leverhulme Trust. James D. White and Robert B. McKean read and commented upon a draft manuscript. Thanks are also due to Geoffrey Swain, Robert Pearce, and Vicky Peters and Sünje Redies of Routledge. Any errors are the responsibility of the author.

CHRONOLOGY

	Personal	*Political*	*General*
1879	Birth of Trotsky		
1896		Trotsky joins his first revolutionary group	
1898		Trotsky is arrested for revolutionary activities and exiled to Siberia	
1899	Trotsky marries his first wife, Alexandra Sokolovskaya, also a revolutionary		
1900	Birth of Trotsky's daughter, Zinaida		
1902	Birth of a second daughter, Nina	Escapes from exile and leaves Russia	
1903	Meets his second wife, Natalia Sedova	Attends the Russian Social Democratic and Labour Party's (RSDLP) Second Congress and witnesses the split between Martov and Lenin	
1905: January			Bloody Sunday marks the start of a year of Revolution in Russia
October			Tsar Nicholas II grants a Duma, or parliament
December		Trotsky briefly becomes President of the St Petersburg Soviet	
1906	Birth of first son, Lev	Stands trial with other members of the Soviet	
1907		Flees Siberian exile to live abroad	

	Personal	Political	General
1908	Settles in Vienna; birth of second son, Sergei		
1912–14		Works as war correspondent during the Balkan wars	
1914	Moves to neutral Switzerland; moves to Paris	Works on the internationalist newspaper, *Our Word*	Outbreak of World War One
1916	Expelled from France to Spain		
1917: January	Arrives in New York		
February			Nicholas II abdicates
May	Arrives in Russia		
August		Joins the Bolsheviks	
September		Trotsky becomes chairman of the Petrograd Soviet	
October		Organises the October Revolution; becomes the People's Commissar for Foreign Affairs	
1918: January		Heads the peace negotiations with Germany at Brest-Litovsk; resigns as People's Commissar for Foreign Affairs	
March		Appointed People's Commissar for Military and Naval Affairs	Russian Civil War begins
November			End of World War One
1919			Third International founded
1920			Russian Civil War ends; Russo-Polish War

	Personal	Political	General
1921			Kronstadt Uprising; New Economic Policy (NEP) adopted
1922			Stalin becomes General Secretary
1923: October		Sends letter to the Central Committee outlining his disagreements with current policy	
1924			Death of Lenin
1925		Removed as head of Military and Naval Affairs	
1926		Removed from the Politburo	
1927: October		Removed from the Central Committee	
November		Expelled from the Bolshevik Party	
1928: January		Sent to Alma-Ata, Kazakhstan	
June	Death of daughter, Nina, from TB		
July–September			Sixth Congress of the Third International
1929		Deported to Turkey; launches the *Bulletin of the Opposition*	Five-Year Plans begin in USSR
1930		Publishes autobiography, *My Life*; foundation of an International Left Opposition in Paris	
1931		Publishes *History of the Russian Revolution*	
1933	Death of daughter, Zinaida, from suicide; leaves Turkey for France		Hitler becomes Chancellor of Germany

	Personal	Political	General
1934			USSR joins the League of Nations
1935	Moves to Norway		Seventh Congress of the Third International
1936	Leaves Norway for Mexico	Completes *The Revolution Betrayed*	Moscow Show Trials; Spanish Civil War begins
1937	Death of son, Sergei, in Moscow trials		
1938	Death of son, Lev, following operations	Foundation of the Fourth International	
1939			Spanish Civil War ends; Soviet–German Pact of Non-Aggression; start of World War Two
1940	Death, following assassination attempt		

INTRODUCTION

The political life of L.D. Trotsky (1879–1940) is a biographer's delight. It includes a rise from village obscurity to seizing power in the capital of Russia; a fall in the struggle to be Lenin's successor; and a lengthy period of exile in which current and past events were analysed in numerous publications. The last period was to be cut short by a vicious assassination, in which an ice-pick was twice inserted into the victim's skull. If this was not enough, it is a life filled with irony, heroism and tragedy, in which personal fortunes and misfortunes intersect with great historical moments, including World War One, the collapse of Tsarism, Hitler's rise to power, the Purges in the USSR and the failure of the Spanish Republic. Of all the leaders of the Russian Revolution, Trotsky's life is undoubtedly the most fascinating. No other Bolshevik shares his history of opposition, support for and then opposition to Bolshevism. No other Bolshevik attempted to found a new, Fourth International. No other Bolshevik wrote about his life as Trotsky did, even arranging the sale of his personal papers to Harvard University. Little wonder, then, that Trotsky has been represented in movies (by, amongst others, Richard Burton), has appeared in literature (in, for example, Anthony Burgess' *End of the World News*) and has even featured in popular song (most famously in 'No More Heroes' by The Stranglers).

Trotsky's actions, as commentator and participant, have also aroused great controversy. He is admired and vilified in equal measure. All too often, however, have the political passions of the biographer determined the nature of the biography. Trotsky's life cries out for a more dispassionate study. This is one of the chief aims of the present political life.

Before we begin our account, however, it is important to review how Trotsky's life has been presented by previous studies. An examination of their strengths and weaknesses will also help to throw into relief how the current book hopes to shed fresh light on an already much examined life.

EARLY WRITINGS: SOVIET AND NON-SOVIET

Given the widely conflicting opinions of Trotsky and his fame as a Marxist, it is as well to remember that at one time his name was little known. Indeed, before the October Revolution Trotsky, like other Bolsheviks, was familiar only to a relatively small circle of revolutionaries and radicals. One of the many tasks of the newly proclaimed Bolshevik regime was to explain who its members were, and the history of their relations in the pre-revolutionary era. There were several means by which the lives of the People's Commissars were publicised.

To begin with, the Soviet government utilised the resources of the state. Trotsky became more widely known through the use of posters, film and other propaganda, as well as numerous newspaper articles lauding his achievements. Second, biographies of key figures in the Cabinet were commissioned. These were often written in a simple style, with photographs, for easy consumption by a wide audience, presumably to include party members, schoolchildren and members of the public. B. Volnyi, for example, researched brief biographies of twelve of the leading Bolsheviks, none longer than five or six pages. Although each mini-biography was listed alphabetically, Trotsky emerges as the leading figure, most notably for his role in organising the October Revolution and for building the Red Army. Third, the leaders' writings were published in impressive-looking selected and collected works. These had a scholarly appearance, with introductions and numerous footnotes. Fourth, members of the government would write character sketches of one another.

These official publications were largely complimentary to Trotsky. In the footnotes to the first edition of Lenin's collected works, for example, he is celebrated as the author of the theory of permanent revolution. On the first anniversary of the October Revolution, in the official daily newspaper *Truth*, none other than Joseph Stalin applauded Trotsky for organising the seizure of power. However, Trotsky was not painted in one colour. Zinoviev's collected works, for example, mentioned the disputes between Trotsky and Lenin of World War One, even if some of the harsher comments of the time were cut. Trotsky's colleagues were not reticent in mentioning the negative as well as the positive aspects of his character. In a memoir published in 1919, for example, A. Lunacharsky praised Trotsky for his talents as an orator and as a man of revolutionary action, but also pointed out his arrogance and disregard for the feelings of others, qualities that often left him friendless and without allies in the party. Lunacharsky also contrasted Lenin and Trotsky as thinkers. If Lenin was flexible and creative, Trotsky was orthodox and mechanical.

The images of Trotsky typical of early Soviet publications were supplemented and, in some cases, challenged by works issued abroad, written variously by visitors to Soviet Russia, by those who had once known Trotsky and were now keen to produce their own portraits, and by analysts interested in Russian affairs. Some of these reached wide audiences, for publishers were eager to print first-hand accounts of the Bolshevik experiment. In the reminiscences of the sculptress Claire Sheridan, for example, Trotsky is remembered as a punctual, hardworking, excessively polite and charming subject. Sheridan, whose artistic talents were stretched by this particular commission, was pleased that her bust of Trotsky captured a man so 'adored'. For Sheridan,

> [Trotsky] has come into his own and has unconsciously developed a new individuality. He has the manner and ease of a man born to a great position; he has become a statesman, a ruler, a leader. But if Trotsky were not Trotsky, and the world had never heard of him, one would still appreciate his very brilliant mind. The reason I have found him so much more difficult to do than I expected, is on account of his triple personality. He is the cultured, well-read man, he is the vituperative fiery politician, and he can be the mischievous laughing schoolboy with the dimple in his cheek. All these three I have seen in turn, and have had to converge them into a clay interpretation.[1]

Other early accounts of Trotsky published in the West, particularly those in Russian, remained obscure. This is to be regretted as they often contain valuable insights and comments. Books on Trotsky by G. Ziv and M. Smolensky, for example, were published in New York and Berlin in 1921. Ziv and Smolensky approach their topic with different intentions. Ziv was writing a memoir, based upon an acquaintance with Trotsky that began in the revolutionary circles of southern Russia in 1896. Smolensky was contributing to a publisher's series of history of political thought. It is uncertain whether he ever knew Trotsky personally. Such differences in genre notwithstanding, these books are interesting when juxtaposed, for they contain conflicting views of Trotsky.

Ziv's book must be approached with some caution. This is partly because, as the introduction admits, there were long periods in which the author and Trotsky did not meet. Furthermore, the memoir is particularly unsympathetic to the Bolshevik Revolution and to what is considered to be Trotsky's excessive use of violence in its defence. Nevertheless, Ziv's memoirs are of tremendous importance because they are the only first-hand account of Trotsky's early political activities, highlighting Trotsky's strengths and weaknesses as a politician. Moreover, the memoir was produced before the power struggle that followed Lenin's death; it is not a work of hindsight. Trotsky's chief attributes, as seen by Ziv, were a desire and talent for action combined with complete devotion to the revolutionary cause. It was these characteristics that made Trotsky of such value to the socialist movement, whether in running the small Southern Workers' Russian Union of the late 1890s, or in organising various newspapers and taking on leading roles in the great events of 1905 and 1917. In these senses, it is argued that Trotsky was always a Bolshevik 'by nature'. However, according to Ziv, Trotsky rose to the top with only a surface understanding of events. A lack of discipline required for consistent and serious study, evident even in his schoolwork, rendered Trotsky incapable of profound political analysis. His theoretical work, from his first attempts to write a treatise on the Masons and a Marxist novel to later tracts on the Duma and the outbreak of World War One, were, for Ziv, largely vacuous, full of bombastic phrases but devoid of real content. Moreover, Trotsky's weaknesses as a thinker were surpassed only by his failings as a human being. Trotsky's arrogance, his need to be acknowledged as superior, placed demands on his friends that few could bear. Most became enemies. As the practitioner of Bolshevism *par excellence*, Trotsky had won his place in history, but Ziv does not perceive any constructive political future for his subject.

Smolensky's conclusions differ sharply from those of Ziv and Lunacharsky. According to Smolensky, not only was Trotsky equal to Lenin as a theoretician, but Trotsky's Marxism was much more inventive than Lenin's orthodox approach. If Lenin's works are full of dry citations, Trotsky leaves classic texts behind, displaying instead a penchant for the analysis of living social forces. For Smolensky, Trotsky's method gave him the acumen, as early as 1905–6, to predict the future outcome of the Russian Revolution with great accuracy. Thus, for example, the peasantry's inability to play an independent political role, the leadership position that the proletariat would occupy, and the difficulties and dangers of a socialist revolution in a backward country, were all discussed intelligently by Trotsky well in advance of 1917. Smolensky also devotes much attention to Trotsky's writings after the revolution, most notably *Terrorism and Communism*, Trotsky's riposte to the critique of Karl Kautsky, the famous German socialist leader, of the anti-democratic aspects of Bolshevism. Smolensky interprets this debate as a clash of competing trends in Marxism, one evolutionary and democratic (Kautsky), the other revolutionary and unapologetically undemocratic (Trotsky). That the task of defending Bolshevism from its major socialist opponent fell to Trotsky was testimony, for Smolensky, of Trotsky's stature as a thinker. How long, asks Smolensky, could Lenin have survived in power without Trotsky? For Trotsky was not only the major source of ideological support, but also the leading man of action. In rushing from front to front, organising and inspiring, it was Trotsky who was responsible for the Red victory in the Civil War. In only one respect does Smolensky detract from the praise heaped upon Trotsky. *Pace* Lunacharsky, whose memoirs he mentions specifically, Smolensky does not consider Trotsky the greatest orator of the day.

THE STRUGGLE FOR POWER AND THE DEVELOPMENT OF STALINIST HISTORIOGRAPHY

By 1921, then, one could claim that the main competing interpretations of Trotsky's life were already in place – this some two decades before his death. However, positive voices in the USSR were soon to be censored as a consequence of Trotsky's fate in the power struggles of the

1920s. In these battles historical topics played no small role. A key moment in the introduction of questions of history in the struggle for power was a discussion that arose in 1924. The starting-point was the publication of volume three of Trotsky's collected works. This volume gathered Trotsky's writings of 1917, to which he added a new introduction, the essay 'Lessons of October' (1924).

For Trotsky, the main lesson that revolutionaries should take from a study of 1917 was that a revolutionary party headed by a determined leadership was the vital precondition for the success of a socialist attempt on power. If the leadership erred, by choosing the wrong moment to act or by adopting reformist tactics when revolution was the order of the day, for example, all would be lost. This had been revealed most recently, for Trotsky, when poor leadership had let the opportunity for revolution slip by in Bulgaria, Hungary and, most importantly, Germany. Even in Russia in 1917 it was not guaranteed that Bolshevism would find the right course, for, as Trotsky points out in some detail, there was tremendous resistance among prominent Bolsheviks to the idea of a Bolshevik-led seizure of power. Most notably, Kamenev and Zinoviev had acted as Mensheviks, arguing that Russia was ready for a democratic revolution only, and that the Bolsheviks should remain a party of revolutionary opposition. It took pressure from Lenin to ensure that a defeatist policy was not thrust upon the party. It is in this sense that Trotsky argues that the October Revolution would not have happened without Lenin. However, according to Trotsky even Lenin, for the most part in hiding, made mistakes. Chief among these were preferring Moscow over Petrograd as the starting place for the assumption of power, and thinking that a seizure of power would be obstructed if it was linked to the convocation of the Second Congress of Soviets. Although Trotsky does not mention himself by name, it is made clear that it was the Military-Revolutionary Committee, which Trotsky chaired, that was responsible for the smooth transfer of power to the Bolsheviks.

Trotsky claimed that he was revisiting the experience of 1917 to help foreign comrades carry out their own Octobers, and not to draw any current political advantage for himself. It is, however, hard to avoid precisely this conclusion. After all, Trotsky states that the ultimate test of a leadership is how it acts in a revolutionary situation. From Trotsky's account of 1917 only he emerges with honour. If in 1924 one accepted the arguments of 'Lessons of October', then only one man could replace the now dead Lenin, namely Leon Trotsky. It is perfectly understandable, then, that having been accused of the sins of Menshevism in 1917, Trotsky's colleagues sought to refute his 'Lessons of October'. This they did in a series of speeches and articles, which were then gathered together and published in Russian and in translations in book form.[2]

Leading Bolsheviks (including Kamenev, Stalin, Zinoviev and Bukharin) and key representatives from the Communist International (the Comintern) and the Communist Youth League (the Komsomol) argued that Trotsky's essay was not a genuine history of the October Revolution. If one consulted the key documents of the time and a growing supply of memoir literature, for example, Trotsky's detractors claimed that one would discover how far his memory had painted a distorted picture. Most notably, Trotsky had minimised the roles played by Lenin and the Bolshevik Party and had exaggerated his own contribution. It was, for example, wrong to claim that in 1917 there was a long and sustained battle between a Lenin seeking to rearm the party with Trotsky's theory of permanent revolution and a right-Menshevik faction within Bolshevik ranks. In actual fact Lenin's analysis of the events of 1917 grew out of a long-held theory of the Russian Revolution. Once Lenin had convinced colleagues of the correctness of his developing strategy, the party acted in a unified way to guarantee victory. In this process neither Lenin nor the party was in any way influenced by Trotsky or Trotskyism.

Indeed, the anti-Trotsky case continues, the whole history of Leninism and Bolshevism before and after 1917 was one of opposition to Trotskyism. Unfortunately, Trotsky had failed to realise that he was only effective in 1917 because he acted under the guidance of the Bolshevik Party. Indeed, Trotsky had never fully understood the implications of joining the Bolshevik Party. He had not made a full commitment to becoming a Bolshevik. If he had, then he would have produced a very different history. Trotsky would, for example, have admitted his past and recent theoretical, as well as organisational, errors. Only in this way would youth understand the proper relationship between Leninism and Trotskyism, and how to avoid the sins of the latter. 'Lessons of October' was an attempt by Trotsky to replace Leninism with Trotskyism. This, however, the Bolshevik Party would not allow him to achieve. The leadership understood the dangers of Trotskyism, revealed in Trotsky's underestimation of the importance of the peasantry, and in his mistaken policies during the peace negotiations with Germany, in the debate over the trade unions and on the issue of currency reform.

Although the prospect of repressive measures against Trotsky was rejected, a call was made for a propaganda war against Trotskyism. It was pointed out, however, that such a campaign should not be directed at Trotsky personally. The party recognised his skills, but only by being protected from the pitfalls in his own theories could comrade Trotsky contribute to the cause of Leninism.

In 1924, then, two conflicting versions of Trotsky's relationship to Bolshevism were established within the Russian Communist Party. With Trotsky in the minority, support was both needed and rare. Some of his friends did come to his aid. In 1926 the leading American communist and frequent visitor to Moscow Max Eastman, for example, published a portrait of the young Trotsky. This placed Lenin above Trotsky, the latter lacking the former's maturity and depth of thought. When Trotsky opposed Lenin at the Second Congress of 1903, Eastman claims, it was largely out of innocence and hurt feelings. Lenin, however, was able to see beyond this and, despite a parting that was to last for many years, continued to appreciate Trotsky's abilities, not least a bravery and devotion to socialism. It was these qualities that Lenin was to call upon in 1917 when he welcomed Trotsky back into the fold. None other than Lenin's widow, Krupskaya, confirmed Lenin's longstanding esteem for Trotsky in a (reproduced) note sent to Trotsky within a week of Lenin's death. Lenin, Eastman concluded, always believed in Trotsky.

Although it was a passionate and heartfelt account, Eastman's book only appeared abroad. It made little impact on developments in Russia. In 1927 an official encyclopedia of the revolution was published. The essay on Trotsky, by V. Nevsky, is pervaded by references to Trotsky's anti-party activities, for which he paid the ultimate price, expulsion from the party. However, Nevsky does not present a one-sided tale of continuous hostility between Trotsky and Bolshevism. He points out that there were attempts at reconciliation (in 1907 and 1909, for example) and concedes that in 1917 Trotsky played a leading role in preparing the October Revolution. Such concessions became increasingly rare as Trotsky was sent into internal exile and then expelled from the USSR. In 1931 Stalin sent a letter to the editorial board of the journal *Proletarian Revolution* calling for the lid to be closed on certain historical questions. Subsequently the infamous textbook on party history, the *Short Course* (1939), confined Trotsky and Trotskyism to the dustbin of history as an anti-party, petty-bourgeois tendency. This was to set the agenda for Soviet writings on Trotsky for several decades to come.

TROTSKY ON TROTSKY

As Stalin was tightening his grip on the writing of history in the USSR, Trotsky responded, quite naturally, by taking up his pen. He wrote about his own life, producing one of the most important sources for future students of Trotsky. The 'attempt at an autobiography' (the subtitle of *My Life*, 1929) was made in very special circumstances, a context that left a deep mark on the work itself. Trotsky was aware of this and made no attempt to hide this fact from his readers. Produced in exile, the memoir, he states candidly, would not have existed had he not fallen from power. Given recent events, his autobiography could be nothing other than polemical. It was an opportunity to defend himself and attack others, along lines set by the debates and accusations of the internal party wrangles of the 1920s.

Above all, Trotsky wanted to prove that the best of all Leninists was Trotsky himself. This image is constructed in several ways. The disagreements of the pre-revolutionary years are minimised. Those of the period 1914–17, for example, are largely omitted. Second, the disputes with Lenin that are admitted (principally over the nature of a forthcoming Russian revolution and whether a party of the Leninist type was needed) are turned to Trotsky's advantage. The process of arriving at Leninism through a period of inner resistance made of Trotsky, we are told, a better Leninist. The ultimate proof of this is the fact that in 1917 only Lenin and Trotsky, working independently of one another, concluded that the bourgeois-democratic Provisional Government had to be overthrown and all power given to the Soviets. Third, N. Krupskaya and M. Gorky, amongst others, are cited to show that in the post-revolutionary years Lenin retained only the highest regard for Trotsky. Old and current battles were forgotten to such an extent that Lenin wanted Trotsky to succeed him as head of the Soviet state. This is clear, claims Trotsky, from a reading of Lenin's Testament, as well as from Lenin's desire for an alliance with Trotsky to remove Stalin. Fourth, Lenin and Trotsky were joined not only as creative thinkers in the Marxist tradition, but as individuals. In their work habits, for instance, both insisted upon order and thoroughness. Neither liked petty intrigue or small talk. All issues were viewed from the standpoint of revolutionary morality, and comradely relations were maintained despite occasional differences of opinion. Little wonder, then, that Lenin is presented as turning first of all to Trotsky as a sounding-board for ideas, exchanging secret notes during government meetings. Little surprise, then, that all the best elements in the Bolshevik Party gather around Trotsky, wanting to serve in the ministries he headed.

The main target of attack was, of course, Joseph Stalin. Stalin is belittled in many ways, as a person and as a revolutionary. In the period February to April 1917, for example, Trotsky claims that Stalin acted as the worst sort of Menshevik, proclaiming partnership between Soviet and Provisional Government. This was the nonsense that Lenin had to overcome, most notably in the April Theses, before the October Revolution could be staged, an event for which Stalin did nothing. This record, continues Trotsky, was sustained post-1917. Unable to undertake constructive work, Stalin, revealing his true self, used his idle hands to cause mischief in military, party and nationality affairs. Little wonder then that all the worst, most corrupt elements in the party sought friendship with Stalin. When Lenin woke up to this state of affairs he broke off personal relations with Stalin and sought the bloc with Trotsky.

The Lenin–Trotsky alliance, however, was not able to achieve anything of great value. Lenin was to die before it was really cemented. Nevertheless, given the stark contrast between the 'good' Trotsky and the 'bad' Stalin, it is natural to wonder why Stalin was able to win the battle of succession. This question also troubled Trotsky, who offered several reasons for Stalin's success. To begin with, Lenin came to learn of Stalin's devious character and penchant for intrigue relatively late. Before 1917, Trotsky claims, Lenin barely knew Stalin. Stalin was appointed General Secretary of the Communist Party in 1922 against Lenin's will, even though the post was considered a minor one. Once in post, however, Stalin used powers of appointment to good advantage, removing Trotsky's followers and promoting his own. With Lenin dead, Trotsky doubted whether he could muster the forces to overcome Stalin's stranglehold on the party. The Politburo, for example, bar Trotsky, was committed to the anti-Trotsky campaign. Trotsky was increasingly denied access to information; he was even misinformed about the date of Lenin's funeral so as to keep him from returning to Moscow. Second, Trotsky lacked the inner resources for a naked battle for power. This was partly because the thought of openly trying to take on the master's mantle was abhorrent to him, and partly because of a mysterious and recurring illness that struck at key moments. The decisive factor identified by Trotsky as dooming him to defeat, however, was a reaction within the revolution itself. If Trotsky had risen to the top on the revolution's tidal wave, its ebbing, typified above all by the failure of revolution in Germany in 1923, signalled his downfall.

There are many problematic aspects of Trotsky's *My Life*. It draws upon sources in a highly selective manner, taking care to refer only to those that confirm the author's view of events. Lunacharsky, for example, is quoted when he praised Trotsky but his critique of Trotsky's arrogance and vanity is ignored. At no point does Trotsky discuss his use of sources and how his 'life' differs from the existing literature, most notably the portrait painted by Ziv. Trotsky is very careful to show his concern for historical truth, in particular the need to correct the falsifications of the past typical of the anti-Trotsky campaign. At several points he refers to documents kept secret in the USSR because of praise for Trotsky contained in them. However, Trotsky does not confront the possibility that he also used the past for political purposes. Was the essay 'Lessons of October' (1924), for example, an attempt by Trotsky to use history to promote his own candidacy for leader? After all, much of the muckraking into the past subsequently condemned by Trotsky was written as a response to 'Lessons of October'. But Trotsky is not keen to consider his own responsibility for generating this aspect of the power struggle.

In some instances the interpretations seem contradictory or not very convincing. If Trotsky lost to Stalin because the revolution itself went into decline, for example, why does Trotsky claim that he could have defeated Stalin if he had acted more boldly in 1923? Even later, in 1926–7, we are told that the revolutionary spirit was still sufficiently strong for the majority of workers in Moscow and Leningrad to support the Left Opposition. It seems as though revolutionary decline is invoked to explain defeat and revolutionary spirit is recalled to show that Trotsky was the real popular hero of the revolution, that his ideas had a resonance in society, that ultimately victory would be on his side. But the exact correlation of forces between 'decline' and 'spirit' at specific points in time is never fully explained and, for this reader, the primacy of 'social causation' in explaining Trotsky's defeat is thrown into doubt. The portrait of Stalin is somewhat contradictory. That Stalin backed Trotsky against Lenin over how best to defend Petrograd in the Russian Civil War shows that Stalin was not always the Lenin-automaton Trotsky claims him to have been. Finally, it is not clear why Trotsky was left with no alternative but to continue with his travels after he had been told by Stalin that he would miss Lenin's funeral by one day. Surely a better political instinct would have told him to return to Moscow post-haste?

Such issues notwithstanding, one cannot but be impressed by *My Life*. There are wonderful descriptions of Trotsky's transition from child to adult, most notably how he came to associate the countryside with backwardness and brutality, and the town with culture and good manners. One cannot imagine Stalin writing with similar ease about his formative experiences, including his first encounters with adult sexuality and sexual liaisons. There are also fascinating insights into how business was conducted in the first sessions of the Soviet government, the Sovnarkom, of how Lenin acted as chairman and of the disputes that raged in the Cabinet over military strategy in the Civil War. The picture of power bases being constructed through appointment and patronage, with the Secretariat as the key political office, offered a powerful model for interpreting the Soviet political system. As a memoir, *My Life* has exerted a tremendous influence on subsequent historians of this period. Isaac Deutscher, for example, finds it as honest an account as can be expected, and often relies upon it for a factual version of events. Indeed, the leitmotif of Deutscher's trilogy − that of Trotsky as prophet − is taken straight out of *My Life*, in which Trotsky's talent as a Marxist is illustrated through the power of his predictions. *My Life* has been accepted as the main source for biographers, some of whom have accomplished little more than rewriting it on a new canvas. To this extent Trotsky more than achieved the aims he set for himself.

TROTSKYISTS AND TROTSKY

Following Trotsky's death it fell first of all to his political allies to defend his life. Obituaries produced by Trotskyists, for example that by

James T. Farrell, lauded Trotsky's intellectual and personal qualities. Trotsky, Farrell tells us, was not only capable of profound and prophetic political analyses, but would also devote 'as much care and thought to a letter to an unknown worker as he would to an article directed against a famous figure. ... In his personal relations he was simple and charming – a man of singular grace.'[3] Such brief obituary notices were soon followed by more substantial memoirs. Trotsky's widow, Natalia Sedova, wrote an early example of this genre. She was aided by Victor Serge, a left-revolutionary of long standing. Together they elaborated the picture of Trotsky presented in the Trotskyist obituaries, but on a much larger scale. From his school days to his death, Sedova and Serge see Trotsky as promoting justice and democracy from a socialist perspective. Above all, they stress Trotsky's humanistic aspirations. For example, Trotsky resorted to violence only when absolutely necessary. He sought power not for himself, but so that the workers could be liberated. Indeed, Trotsky was a medium rather than an independent political actor; his political presence derived from his ability to express the mood and demands of the masses. Through tireless and modest efforts, in the spirit of open and honest exchanges with colleagues, Trotsky embodied all that was best in the Russian socialist movement. His banishment, Serge and Sedova claim, 'sealed the total collapse of morale inside the Bolshevik Party'.[4]

Apart from obituary notices and memoirs, the Trotskyist movement has also contributed in other ways to protecting Trotsky's reputation. Pathfinder Press is probably the most famous of the Trotskyist imprints that have published a broad selection of Trotsky's oeuvre, including the multi-volume *Writings*, covering the period from 1929 onwards. Numerous primers on Trotsky's main ideas and a host of biographies have also been written. Some of these are of little value, being mostly works of hagiography. The most recent biographical study, in four volumes (1989–93), of this school of thought belongs to the late Tony Cliff, a longstanding British Trotskyist. His efforts contain the flaws typical of this genre. Most annoying is Cliff's tendency to reproduce long passages from Trotsky, either as evidence for a particular view of Trotsky's actions or as uncritical acceptance of Trotsky's analysis of events. Furthermore, Cliff avoids a serious discussion of Trotsky's works, preferring simple flattery. Without offering any elaboration or justification, for example, Cliff describes Trotsky's five-volume *How the*

Revolution Armed as 'a rich combination of broad historical sweep, originality, innovation and attention to the details of army life'.[5] The final volume of Cliff's study concludes with a message for the party faithful, rather than a considered evaluation:

> Present and future generations of Marxists will carry the revolutionary flame left to us by Lenin, Luxemburg and Trotsky. ... The last six decades belonged to Stalin. The coming decades will belong to Lenin, Luxemburg and Trotsky. We owe a massive debt to Trotsky. Without his opposition to the Stalinist bureaucracy, without his internationalism, the tradition of 'socialism from below', the identification of socialism with the self-activity of the working class, would not have survived.[6]

Cliff's biography is unlikely to have a wide public audience or to make much of an impact in academia. This cannot be said of the most influential of the Trotsky biographers within the Trotskyist tradition, Isaac Deutscher. His trilogy on Trotsky (1954–63) was not only published by the highly reputable Oxford University Press, it was also the first serious account of Trotsky the thinker and Trotsky the man. Having gone through many editions, Deutscher's work has remained the basic text on Trotsky's life for several generations of undergraduates and general readers. When the present author was studying for his first degree, Deutscher was recommended as summer reading, not only as a text of great historical sweep, but also because it would be fun. It would read, I was told, as a boy's own adventure story. This is worth recalling as it gives an indication of the attractions, as well as the weaknesses, of Deutscher's tomes.

At a general level, Deutscher sets out to prove that Trotsky's achievements should not be linked to his political fortunes. Indeed, Trotsky's great strengths, chiefly intellectual honesty and clear and cogent political prognoses, were unaffected by the outcomes of political struggles. Throughout his life Trotsky remained what he was, simply, in Deutscher's words, 'one of the most outstanding revolutionary leaders of all times, outstanding as fighter, thinker, and martyr'.[7] Deutscher's work abounds with instances in which Trotsky saw further and deeper than those around him. A long list includes: predicting the course of the

Russian Revolution; being the first Bolshevik of real influence and stature to take up the cause of the oppressed nationalities and highlighting the need for greater democracy in the Bolshevik Party; understanding the importance of freedom of criticism in the arts and science; identifying the dangers of neo-NEP (New Economic Policy) and calling for socialist planning in industry and in agriculture; and, finally, pointing out how best to guard against the victory of Fascism in the Europe of the 1930s. The final two instalments of Deutscher's biography were published as Khrushchev was grappling with the problems of de-Stalinisation in the USSR. In this context, Deutscher contrasts a Soviet elite acting out of the 'narrowest motives of self-defence',[8] incapable of a full analysis of Stalinism, with Trotsky's profound insights into that self-same phenomenon.

If Trotsky had any weaknesses, Deutscher identifies two. First, the theory of permanent revolution was flawed. At its heart lay a piece of wishful thinking, namely that a revolution in Russia would be repeated in Europe, if not across the globe. In the event, the Russian Revolution remained isolated and therefore likely to degenerate as it foundered on the bedrock of Russia's poverty. It is interesting, however, that Deutscher blames this illusion not on a flaw in Trotsky's thinking, but on history with a capital 'H':

> [I]t may be wondered whether Lenin and Trotsky would have acted as they did ... if they had taken a soberer view of the international revolution and foreseen that in the course of decades their example would not be imitated in any other country. A speculative question of this sort cannot be answered. The fact was that the whole dynamic of Russian history was impelling them, their party, and their country towards this revolution, and that they needed a world-embracing hope to embrace a world-shaking deed. History produced the great illusion and planted it and cultivated it in the brains of the most soberly realistic leaders when she needed the motive power of illusion to further her own work.[9]

For Deutscher, the second major misconception held by Trotsky was the notion that he could found a Fourth International in conditions clearly unfavourable to the socialist cause in general and to Trotskyism in particular. Indeed, the Polish delegation at the founding Congress of the Fourth International pointed out the real obstacles that would prevent the new organisation winning support amongst the workers, as turned out to be the case. In a footnote Deutscher admits that the author of the Polish protests was none other than Deutscher himself. His biographical study therefore became an arena to continue his debate with Trotsky.

Deutscher's trilogy was a great achievement and an important landmark in the development of Trotsky studies. It cannot, however, stand as the final word. Apart from disagreements with particular interpretations – not to mention the appearance of thirty to forty years of new research that inevitably places old issues in a new light – its shortcomings as a work of history should not be overlooked. First and foremost is the uncritical or one-sided use of sources. For example, too often Deutscher relies on *My Life* or official publications as evidence. The problem of bias is insufficiently addressed. Furthermore, Deutscher happily cites Ziv to Trotsky's advantage but does not mention any of Ziv's negative evaluations. Second, there is the serious issue of invention, moments at which Deutscher simply puts thoughts into his subjects' heads for which there is no evidence. The following passage, which compares the disputes amongst the Bolsheviks over the peace with Germany with a dilemma faced by the Paris Commune over whether to wage a revolutionary war, and if so against whom, is typical of numerous acts of invention:

> Trotsky, who so often looked at the Russian Revolution through the prism of the French, must have been aware of this analogy. ... He must have seen himself as acting a role potentially reminiscent of Danton's, while Lenin's part was similar to Robespierre's. It was as if the shadow of the guillotine had for a moment interposed itself between him and Lenin. ... This consideration was decisive in Trotsky's eyes. In order to banish the shadow of the guillotine he made an extraordinary sacrifice of principle and personal ambition.[10]

No doubt Deutscher could be defended from this attack with reference to biographer's licence. Without question, such diversions into fiction make Deutscher an easy and gripping read, adding a sense of drama and dramatic effect. However, such passages do detract from the work's sta-

tus as a history, and as historians we must approach Deutscher both crit-
ically and with caution.

TROTSKY AND ACADEME

Outside the Trotskyist movement there emerged a large body of scholarly interest in Trotsky. This mirrored the expansion of higher education
in the post-World War Two era and a high level of commitment to
Soviet studies given the on-going Cold War. Opinion in the universi-
ties, as elsewhere, divided into pro- and anti-Trotsky schools, although
as a general rule Trotsky is held in lower regard as a thinker in academic
circles. There are numerous studies that point out the contradictions or
pitfalls in his thought. In a critical evaluation of Trotsky's analysis of
bureaucracy under Stalin, for example, David Lovell concludes that
Trotsky developed only a 'cursory understanding of bureaucracy and its
role' and that 'there are good reasons for doubting that Trotsky's was a
thoroughgoing alternative to Stalin's rule'.[11] In a three-volume investigation of nineteenth- and twentieth-century Marxism, the Polish
scholar L. Kolakowski dismisses Trotsky's politics as 'an unhappy mixture of unfulfilled prophecies, fantastic illusions, false diagnoses, and
unfounded hopes'.[12] For Kolakowski, Lenin and Trotsky brought the
Russian people only 'sheer physical force, the fear of imprisonment,
physical injury and death'.[13] The academic who has given us the most
sustained scrutiny of Trotsky's thought, Baruch Knei-Paz, begins his
book by claiming that, 'Trotsky's "ideas and aims" were "betrayed" not
so much by others – as he was prone to believe – as by the contradictions of his own intellectual preconceptions.'[14]

Of course in this brief introductory chapter the whole range of scholarly studies on Trotsky cannot be examined. The most important contributions will be drawn upon where appropriate in subsequent chapters.
There is one study, however, that merits special attention here, for it is
partly in comparison with it that the current work will be judged. In
1978 Knei-Paz's monumental (600-odd page) account of Trotsky's social
and political thought was published by Oxford University Press. For
that publishing house Knei-Paz no doubt offered the perfect companion
volume to Deutscher's biography. What need the present work given
the ready availability of this powerful combination? Reference has
already been made to the flaws in Deutscher's work. Knei-Paz made

several errors of judgement in how he conceived his study. A chronological approach was rejected, as was an attempt to place Trotsky in his proper context, covering the debates with opponents and so on. These decisions were taken so as to enable an exposition and critical scrutiny of Trotsky's thought 'in the round'. This may have been achieved but, if so, it was at a cost, most notably the overlooking of important elements in Trotsky's thinking. There is nothing, for example, in Knei-Paz's study on Trotsky's musings on the pre-1917 Russian parliament, the Duma, and almost nothing on his conceptions of a United States of Europe and a Federation of Balkan republics. A reader would also find it hard to appreciate the development of Trotsky's ideas. The methodology of *this* book, in contrast, is self-consciously chronological, seeking to place Trotsky in the broader context of his intellectual milieu.

THE RE-EMERGENCE OF TROTSKY STUDIES IN THE USSR

Stalin's death in March 1953 opened up the possibility of a re-evaluation of the history of the revolution, including Trotsky's role and his relationship to Lenin and Bolshevism. This was to be a long and tortuous process. Of all of Stalin's victims, it is understandable that Trotsky would come near the end of the list of those to be considered for rehabilitation. After all, how could the Communist Party of the Soviet Union (CPSU) allow disinterested study of Trotsky without addressing Trotsky's critique of Soviet bureaucratisation? Furthermore, what of the small, but vociferous, Trotskyist movement calling for the workers of the USSR to stage a political revolt to put the USSR back on the path of world revolution? Historical investigation of Trotsky could lead to another contemporary communist heresy that an already beleaguered CPSU could well do without. However, once Khrushchev embarked upon even limited de-Stalinisation, Soviet historians did turn their attention to Trotsky. An interest was rekindled that survived during the era of reaction of Brezhnev's rule. Here the official view of Trotsky is well summarised in the titles of works such as *Trotskyism is the Enemy of Leninism* (Political Literature, Moscow, 1968). Nevertheless, counter-images and voices would bubble to the surface, noted, for example, in some positive representations of Trotsky in the Russian literature of the late 1960s and in the researches of several Soviet historians. These trends were allowed much more freedom of expression in the debates that raged around Trotsky during Mikhail Gorbachev's brief reign of 1985–91.

It was never Gorbachev's intention to restore Trotsky to the party. Gorbachev was much more interested in Lenin's and Bukharin's supposed market socialism. It was Lenin and Bukharin, not Trotsky, who were the officially approved historical precedents for and heroes of Gorbachev's reconstruction, or *perestroika*, of Soviet socialism. However, a civil rehabilitation of Trotsky undoubtedly occurred, as an initial small spate of articles and minor reprints of his articles snowballed into a veritable Soviet Trotsky industry.

Although no new or original contributions were made to our understanding of Trotsky, it was exciting to chart the emergence of a genuine plurality of views amongst Soviet historians and publicists around Trotsky's historical significance. Russian nationalists were critical of what they perceived as Trotsky's promotion of Western values. In a roundtable discussion of Trotsky's *The Revolution Betrayed*, for example, Yu.V. Emel'yanov claimed that 'almost everything in Russia's history aroused disgust in Trotsky'.[15] Longstanding party historians met the demand for a more honest evaluation of the past by conceding that Trotsky had served the Bolshevik Revolution in positive ways, but limited these instances to when Trotsky had followed Lenin. This interpretation is particularly evident in the officially sanctioned writings of N.A. Vasetskii, who wrote on Trotsky more than any other historian during the Gorbachev era. There was also, however, a smaller pro-Trotsky school of historical thought, whose leading light was the late Vadim Rogovin. Rogovin *et al.* defended Trotsky's creative, intellectual and socialist credentials, seeing Trotsky as a real democratic-socialist alternative to Stalin. Finally, market-inspired anti-Bolshevik thinkers rejected Trotsky along with the Russian Revolution. In a particularly harsh critique of Bolshevik tutelage of his country, Alexander Tsipko described the leading Bolsheviks, including Trotsky, as variously 'ill, stupid or criminals'.[16]

TROTSKY STUDIES AFTER THE CRASH

The collapse of communism in the USSR and Eastern Europe should enable us to produce accounts of Trotsky's life and thought that do not follow the fault-lines of the Cold War. This is partly because, as more sources are made available, we should have firmer grounds to judge how well Trotsky understood events, and partly as a result of a de-ideologisation of the topic. Such an agenda was beyond the first biographies of Trotsky written by Russian scholars post-1991.

Well-established members of the former Soviet academic elite N.A. Vasetskii and D. Volkogonov had the advantage of a long acquaintance with restricted sources. They lacked the training, however, to write biographies based upon good historical practice. Political considerations, not an honest evaluation of documents, were uppermost in their minds. Both see the ideas and policies associated with Trotsky himself as misconceived, especially the theory of permanent revolution. It was, they argue, with this theory in mind that Trotsky was prepared to betray Russia's best interests with his 'no war, no peace' strategy adopted for the peace negotiations at Brest-Litovsk. Neither conceives the USSR as likely to have been a radically different society had Trotsky instead of Stalin become the post-Lenin leader of the CPSU. After all, they argue that in politics and morals Trotsky shared Stalin's love of force, while in his Five-Year Plans the latter put the former's economic prejudices into practice. Although they reason from different assumptions – Vasetskii distinguishing between a 'good' Lenin and a 'bad' Stalin and Trotsky, Volkogonov linking Lenin, Stalin and Trotsky as theorists of totalitarianism – their negative view of Trotsky has long been extant. Vasetskii and Volkogonov can simply be added to a long-standing tradition.

CONCLUSION

The main developments in Trotsky studies and their respective strengths and weaknesses should by now be clear. Although much of interest has been written, no single study has yet approached Trotsky's life with the basic question of 'what was Trotsky writing and doing at a particular time and why' as the defining research issue. For the most part eschewing a chronological approach, biographers have written their lives with the outcome of Trotsky's life telescoped into its very beginnings. Little wonder, then, that biographies have been overly concerned with Trotsky's relations with Lenin, even if the actual context did not justify this bias. Our aim is to restore the balance by focusing upon the broader context, to understand the dilemmas faced by Trotsky in their full measure. By also being the first general account to re-examine Trotsky's writings against the background of (primarily Western) research of recent decades, we should also be better able to evaluate the extent of his contributions to our understanding of late nineteenth- and early twentieth-century history.

1

THE YOUNG REVOLUTIONARY, 1879–1907

The main source of our knowledge about Trotsky's early life is the version set out in the autobiography of the late 1920s, *My Life*. He was born in 1879 in the village of Yanovka in the south of the Ukraine, the third child of David and Anneta Bronstein. By his own account, the young Lev Bronstein, or Leon Trotsky as he came to be known, did not experience any particular hardship. The family was comfortably off and prospering. There was a maid and a cook to help with the domestic chores. The boy Trotsky was a loved and favoured son. His parents set great store by education. Eventually they arranged for Leon to stay with relatives in the town of Odessa so that he could enjoy a better schooling. We cannot be certain how far Trotsky projected the political beliefs he subsequently acquired onto his younger self. He did claim, however, that as a boy he was conscious of his father's unjust exploitation of poorer neighbours and that in school he defended the weak from attack. He even noted that the skirmishes at school offered lessons for the more consequential political conflicts of his future, with 'the talebearers and the envious at one pole, the frank, courageous boys at the other, and the neutral, vacillating mass in the middle'.[1]

FIRST POLITICAL STEPS

When Trotsky was coming of age as a young man, opposition to tsarism was divided into several schools of thought, including nationalist, socialist, populist and liberal. These trends were not necessarily easily demarcated, and anyone new to opposition politics would be open to many possible influences. Political choices would no doubt be made partly by accident, depending upon location and circumstance, upon peers and what literature came one's way in a regime of censorship. It is not clear exactly when Trotsky considered himself a Marxist. His first political acts consisted of reading illegal literature and discussing it with a small circle of associates, and taking part in the so-called Southern Russian Workers' Union (SRWU), which had a brief existence from April 1897 to January 1898. Despite its grand-sounding name, the SRWU was no more than a small body composed mainly of student activist intellectuals similar to the young Trotsky. It was as a member of this organisation that he underwent his first arrest and journey into internal exile in Siberia. From there he wrote an account of the SRWU, which appeared in a pamphlet on the workers' movement in Odessa and Nikolaev, published in Geneva in 1900. This is an interesting source, in which Trotsky identifies the opportunities and difficulties of socialist agitation in provincial Russia.

Trotsky considers Nikolaev to have been ripe for the formation of the SRWU for several reasons. Most notably, thanks to investment from state and foreign capital, the town's factory working class had mushroomed in size from under 1,000 in 1896 to over 5,500 in 1897. Although modern scholarship points out that the Russian working class was not in the main located in large factories, what struck the young Trotsky was precisely the larger industrial plants. It was here, he argued, that the workforce was younger and enjoyed higher literacy levels, a hopeful combination for a revolutionary activist. This early impression left a lasting mark on Trotsky's outlook that always favoured the large factories as the best breeding ground for socialism. Trotsky claims that, unfortunately, it was beyond the material and physical means of the SRWU to satisfy the undoubted desires of the workers for an education in socialism. Most disruptive of all was infiltration by the police, which eventually accounted for the arrest of the leading organisers and the closure of the SRWU. Nevertheless, despite its small scale and quick disappearance, Trotsky's involvement in the SRWU gave him important practical experience, from collecting dues to dividing money amongst strike funds, mutual self-help schemes and the building of libraries, from conducting education circles to writing propaganda. From these tasks he drew important conclusions about how socialists should organise and act in inhospitable Russian conditions.

The best way to reach the workers, Trotsky advised, was through good propaganda, especially the production of a regular newspaper. The majority of its coverage should be dedicated to local issues of real relevance to the readership. Only after contact and trust had been built up in this way could more abstract concepts of exploitation be raised. Socialists should also learn how to write brief and understandable leaflets for distribution at the factories over specific grievances. These were also useful in creating bridges over which the workers could be led from particular conflicts to the general principles of Marxism. As well as focusing upon bread-and-butter issues, Trotsky stressed the need to entertain the workers. Irony, amusing illustrations, stories, poems and songs should all be integral elements of socialist journalism. Beyond this, Trotsky touched upon other topics socialist literature should cover. Given the problems of police surveillance and arrests, he recommended that a manual be produced advising comrades how to identify police spies and listing the rights comrades would have should they fall victim to the oppressive tsarist regime. Recounting the events that led up to the demise of the SRWU, Trotsky warned against excessive centralisation of workers' organisations. The SRWU was made up of a series of local cells, each of no more than twenty-five members and each having its own committee of five office-holders: cashier, bookkeeper, secretary and two deputies. The members would meet twice each week to discuss their cell's progress and activities. Linking the cells to a central committee created nothing, according to Trotsky, but trouble. Once the central committee was compromised and its assets seized, for example, all activities were brought to an abrupt end. A system of independent and isolated cells, answering local needs and questions through their own printing presses or hectographs, was the most sensible method to ensure continuity of action even if one cell was arrested.

Soon after dispatching his essay on the SRWU, Trotsky was engaged as a correspondent of a newspaper published in Irkutsk. The *Eastern Review* was widely read amongst the local population, including the colony of political prisoners. We do not know how Trotsky was co-opted, but his contributions afforded him a chance to expand his journalistic portfolio. No longer was he writing simple copy for a humble audience. Now he set out to impress with his erudition in classic and contemporary literature and philosophy, commenting and criticising from a Marxist perspective.

Trotsky, for example, exposes the Norwegian dramatist Ibsen as a timid critic of bourgeois society. Sickened by its hypocrisy and restrictions, Ibsen was nevertheless unable to think beyond bourgeois categories:

> Ibsen starts with individuality and returns to it. He resolves – or tries to resolve – every social problem within the bounds of individual spirit. He widens and deepens this flexible individual spirit to super-human dimensions (*Brand*) without even touching on social conditions.[2]

Several of Trotsky's essays are concerned with the relationship between art and economic and social progress. Although an enemy of bourgeois exploitation, Trotsky welcomed the spread of capitalism into the dark and ignorant countryside (the poverty of peasant life was a frequent topic of his journalism). Machines more than unspoiled nature, he declared, contain the beauty that inspires great art. Nor, he explained in another contribution, should artists worry that the increasing power of man over nature was rendering the 'thick novel' of pre-industrial society obsolete. Rather the novel had to adapt to new conditions, even if, in certain respects, it was being superseded by the contemporary short story:

> Life becomes more complicated, it becomes richer ... and literature is forced not to reject old forms for embodying creativity, but rather to create new ones. The novel survives as a social frame for all the beauties and horrors of life that look at us in isolated images and scenes in the pages of sketches and essays. ... The novel fascinates us for its wide social scope, while the short story achieves the same effect, but with the energy of a psychological blow. But if the novel is dead as a mandatory form, with all its ritual of chapters, parts, prologues and epilogues, it lives on nevertheless as a modern Iliad, as a poem of Reality. So, the novel is dead: long live the novel![3]

Not all of Trotsky's essays were easy to digest. An attack on metaphysical thinkers writing in the journal *Questions of Philosophy*, for example, contains numerous contorted sentences, in which clarity of meaning is lost. However, such excursions were typical of a young man who was not modest in outlook or in viewpoint. An ambitious writer, one who did not hide his dislike of barren lands, Trotsky resolved upon an escape from his Siberian exile. Leaving a wife and children behind, he took flight along a path that was to lead him to Western Europe, with its ranks of local and émigré socialists.

TROTSKY AND ÉMIGRÉ POLITICS, 1902–4

Trotsky entered the world of émigré politics at a particularly important time for Russian social democracy. The movement's First Congress had been held in Minsk in 1898, but this had turned into a largely decorative affair as its participants were quickly arrested. Since then there had been debates over how best to further the cause but no follow-up congress. The party programme and the form of its organisation needed to be clarified. By 1902 several groups and leading individuals were planning the convocation of a new congress. Chief amongst these were the editors of the newspaper *The Spark*. This had begun publication in December 1900. For V.I. Lenin, producing and distributing *The Spark* was the means to assert orthodoxy in theory and to build up a network of agents answerable to a centralised leadership under his control. This view of a centralised, professional operation, which Lenin saw as the ideal model for the political party to follow, was much at odds with the loosely connected body of locally based cells favoured by Trotsky after his work in the SRWU. For Lenin, however, Trotsky's suggestions would have smacked of the amateurish, parochial outlook characteristic of the so-called sin of *kustarnichestvo* (amateurish work).

When Trotsky met Lenin at his London home in 1902 it is not clear to what extent Trotsky had abandoned his former views. He was, however, invited to contribute articles to *The Spark*. Beginning in November 1902, the topics Trotsky addressed focused on events in Russia. Employing an ironic humour that was to become his trademark as a revolutionary journalist, Trotsky exposed the evils and contradictions of the tsarist system of government, from a corrupt and oppressive Ministry of Internal Affairs to a bankrupt foreign policy in the Balkans. Trotsky's target audience was social democrats and workers, whom he warned of the dangers of liberal opposition tactics of within-system reform, and of the obvious flaws in the regime's attempts to fool the workers to take part in officially sponsored 'Zubatov' trade unions, so called after the police chief who thought that they could be used to channel the workers' discontent into less harmful pursuits.

As is clear from their private correspondence, *The Spark*'s working editors, chiefly Lenin and Yu. Martov, were so impressed by Trotsky's talents and energy that in the spring of 1903 Lenin proposed that Trotsky be invited to join the editorial board.[4] Martov, who in turn urged co-editor and leading theorist Pavel Akselrod to give his support, warmly welcomed this suggestion.[5] Unfortunately for Trotsky a unanimous vote was required and G. Plekhanov, the 'father of Russian Marxism', had sufficient doubts about the young prodigy to have the decision delayed until after the Second Congress, now set for July–August 1903. But in the meantime Trotsky had guaranteed for himself a seat at the congress as the representative of the Siberian Union, a social democratic organisation that Trotsky had joined in his first exile. The already high esteem in which Lenin and Martov held him would also ensure that his voice would be heard. When the Congress actually convened, the 24-year-old Trotsky emerged as an active participant.

A brief glance at the protocols reveals that Trotsky spoke at thirty out of the Second Congress's thirty-seven sessions. Of course not all of his interventions are worth noting; often they were attempts to keep discussions moving by drawing attention to already agreed rules of practice, or were tabled improvements clarifying resolutions. At other points, particularly when defending the concept of a dictatorship of the proletariat and the party's agrarian programme, Trotsky emerged as a bulwark of Marxist orthodoxy against revisionism. However, even minor interjections are testimony to Trotsky's level of commitment, as he and his comrades grappled with complex matters of party organisation. Issues surrounding the role of the large and successful Jewish socialist organisation, the Bund, and rival definitions of party membership proved to be the most contentious of all the topics debated.

Trotsky recognised the special part played by the Bund in conducting socialist propaganda amongst the Russian Empire's Jewish proletariat, but he was not prepared to accept the Bund's desire that the autonomous status it had been granted at the First Congress be reaffirmed. This would only make sense, Trotsky reasoned, if the Russian

Social Democratic and Labour Party (RSDLP) was to adopt a federal rather than a preferred unitary structure. However, there were limits to how far Trotsky was prepared to push the notion of control from a leading central body. He raised objections if he thought that too much power was being taken away from local committees that should be to 'greater or lesser degrees independent units'. The most famous example of this is when the Congress debated Lenin's demand for stricter control from above over who should count as a party member against Martov's looser formulation. In supporting Martov, Trotsky was concerned that Lenin was using unproductive means to achieve dubious ends. It was Lenin's intention, according to Trotsky, that a powerful Central Committee should oversee the movement, rooting out 'opportunism' or beliefs that were considered not fully Marxist. However, he objected, no Central Committee could know and vet each and every party member and, furthermore, no rule, however watertight, could guard against opportunism. Did Lenin and his backers, chiefly Plekhanov, not know that opportunism had deeper causes? The debates around this issue did not produce a compromise resolution. Further sessions were marked by struggles between followers of the so-called 'hard' (Lenin) and 'soft' (Martov) factions as the functions and make-up of the party's chief offices of Council, Central Committee and the editorial board of the party newspaper were discussed. The Congress ended with division and hurt feelings. Lenin's supporters adopted the name 'majoritarians' ('Bolsheviks'), their opponents accepting the title of 'minoritarians' ('Mensheviks').

As the delegate of the Siberian Union Trotsky produced his reflections on the Congress soon after its conclusion. These circulated in rough draft before being polished for publication by the party printing presses in Geneva. Although Trotsky did not want readers to lose sight of the Congress's achievements, the bulk of his essay was given over to explaining divisions and disappointments. In part, he felt that too much had been expected of the Congress. Evidently several delegates did not realise that there were objective limits to what any congress could achieve. After all, resolutions could only be effective to the extent that they reflected reality; they could not in and of themselves mould reality. Trotsky illustrated this point with reference to the Bund's behaviour. Because it had stood alone, acting and growing at a time when the RSDLP as such did not exist, nationalist and separatist ideology had naturally taken hold of its leaders. The Bund would return to the general fold only after unification of Jewish and other workers had occurred from below and not because of a congress resolution from above.

Similarly, continued Trotsky, comrade Lenin, having lost a sense of reality, had played the most disruptive role out of all the delegates at the Congress. By this Trotsky meant that Lenin had become so fixated on the 'metaphysical' task of rooting out opportunism that he had ignored the way central bodies and local organisations actually interacted. Both served as well as advised each other as complex practical issues were confronted. There was simply no clear line of authority; this varied from central to local bodies depending upon circumstances. Indeed, warned Trotsky, Lenin's centralism would not only ensure Lenin's personal dictatorship over the party, but also a downgrading of everyday concerns. In this way the whole concept of centralism would be thrown into disrepute and the RSDLP would lose any influence it had amongst the workers. Trotsky recalled the experience of the French Revolution to show why Lenin's model of the party, although intended to defeat opportunism, would reap only destruction. Casting Lenin in the role of Robespierre, Trotsky argued that:

> Too many hopes are placed on a party 'government' ... a regime that begins by expelling some of the best party workers promises too many executions and too little good. It inevitably leads to disappointments that could prove disastrous not only for Robespierre and the helots of centralism, but also for the idea of a single fighting party organisation. Then the masters of the situation will be the social democratic opportunistic 'Thermodorians' and the doors of the party will be thrown wide open.[6]

Fortunately for Trotsky, Lenin did not enjoy a complete victory at and following the Second Congress. Lenin's formulation for party membership had not entered the statutes, for example, and he lost control of *The Spark*. Trotsky was thus able to continue as one of its regular correspondents. His post-Congress journalism was full of the prospect of political change in Russia. Commentators, domestic and foreign, from high conservatives to timid liberals, he pointed out, seemed to agree that an irrational tsarist order could not survive for long. Even patriots expected trouble if the recently declared war with Japan did not go well. Trotsky, of course, was most concerned that at a time of uncertainty social democrats should draw maximum political capital. Russia's new political regime would depend on who led the transition. Either (illiberal) liberals seeking agreement with the old order would produce minimal change or social democrats in co-operation with the workers would ensure a radical break with the past in establishing a more just and equitable society.

Time and again Trotsky returned to what he saw as the fundamental differences that divided liberals and social democrats, warning readers to beware liberal cowardice and rotten compromises. For example, regarding reform of the country's political system, the liberals demanded a consultative assembly and a franchise limited by educational and social restrictions. Only social democrats sought a sovereign parliament based upon equal, universal, direct and secret suffrage. In making such points Trotsky highlighted what he saw as the flaws in the works of classic liberal thinkers, arguing, for instance, that J.S. Mill wrote about politics without a class analysis of power. Any party, such as the peasant Socialist Revolutionaries, who approved tactical alliances with the liberals was, for Trotsky, a traitor to the revolutionary cause. Although Trotsky thought that the decisive battles of the forthcoming political upheavals would be fought in the towns, he stressed the importance of social democrats winning influence in the countryside. In welcoming the prospect of revolution, Trotsky looked back to the great events of 1789 and 1848, portraying the revolutionaries of those years as embodying the highest of human qualities. A socialist revolution would also be a safe revolution in which women and children would not be harmed as they walked the streets.

While Trotsky emerges as a revolutionary journalist of undoubted talent, not every socialist was pleased with Trotsky's articles in *The Spark*. Plekhanov, for example, was upset that his friends accepted Trotsky's submissions. The contributions from Trotsky's pen that most angered Plekhanov were those that touched upon party organisation and tactics. Trotsky's insistence that the most important section of the movement was an 'autonomously-acting proletariat' and not intellectuals at the 'organisational summit'[7] was taken personally by Plekhanov as a direct affront, lowering *The Spark*'s high standards. Akselrod defended Trotsky, informing Plekhanov that the editors published Trotsky's work not to offend Plekhanov but because they agreed with its conclusions.

Furthermore, Akselrod could not see anything in Trotsky's journalism directed at Plekhanov personally.[8] If the root cause of Plekhanov's invective against Trotsky was the political falling-out between the two before and after the Second Congress, Plekhanov could not have been pleased with Trotsky's major pamphlet of 1904, *Our Political Tasks*. Here Trotsky returned to the themes raised in his 'Siberian Report', but in greater detail.

In large part, *Our Political Tasks* was written as a reply to Lenin's brochure *One Step Forwards, Two Steps Back* (1904). *One Step* is a lengthy essay, in which Lenin in his best pedantic style rebuffed the critics of his views on party organisation and defended his behaviour and tactics at the Second Congress. For Lenin, the Second Congress was significant in that the RSDLP had split into Bolshevik-revolutionary and Menshevik-opportunist wings. In this battle, particularly in the discussion of how to define a party member, Trotsky had spoken 'like an opportunist'.[9] Trotsky was not convinced by the 'arguments' contained in Lenin's 'boring book'. He saw no reason to change his earlier evaluation of 'Maximilien' (after Robespierre, responsible for the Reign of Terror in the French Revolution) Lenin as dictator-in-waiting. If anything, Trotsky stepped up the attack on Lenin.

Lenin, claimed Trotsky, had displayed a 'poverty of thinking' and 'bureaucratic and "Jacobin" organisational prejudices'. He was, for instance, carrying a conviction of theoretical correctness typical of the early *Spark*'s programme against ideological revisionism amongst the intelligentsia into a new era that demanded agitation in the working class. To follow Lenin's methods would, according to Trotsky, result in the pretence of political work devoid of any meaningful content. Instead of encouraging the workers to become an active, autonomous and conscious element in their own right, for example, Lenin was absorbed with an organisational fetishism that substituted itself for the working class. Rather than produce effective propaganda to raise the workers in battle against tsarism and the bourgeoisie, Lenin concentrated on expelling opportunists from his ranks, creating committees that had no contact with real workers. This was so disastrous because the success of the forthcoming Russian Revolution, in which the proletariat would still be obliged to play the role of an 'opposition party', would be determined not by the presence of a theoretically pure social democracy existing in paper statutes only, but by the extent to which an active and independent proletariat was pressurising the liberal bourgeoisie for a 'free Russia'. Unfortunately Lenin did not seem to understand that 'the proletarian theory of political development cannot substitute for a politically developed proletariat'. It was in the midst of this polemic against Lenin's 'substitutionism' that Trotsky was to make one of his most famous remarks, seen as a prediction of the fate of the Bolshevik Party post-1917:

> In the internal politics of the Party [Lenin's] methods lead ... to the Party organisation 'substituting' itself for the Party, the Central Committee substituting itself for the Party organisation, and finally the dictator substituting himself for the Central Committee.[10]

Whatever the prophetic value of this statement, at the time Lenin was unimpressed with Trotsky's new work. In letters sent to supporters in Russia, for example, he declared that Trotsky had emerged as the Mensheviks' chief provocateur, describing him in particularly unflattering terms as the 'balalaika-Trotsky'.[11] Lenin was most upset by what he saw as Trotsky's distortions of recent party history. It was wrong, for example, to declare that the early editions of *The Spark* were intended for 'bourgeois ideologues' cut off from the masses. It was also blatantly unfair to present Lenin as a bureaucratic renegade. Trotsky's relations with Lenin were definitely at a low point. Here, at least, Trotsky was not alone. Trotsky's analysis of the dictatorial dangers contained in Lenin's concept of the party was shared by, amongst others, Polish and German comrades, including Rosa Luxemburg and Karl Kautsky.

It would be wrong to conclude from the polemics against Lenin, however, that in 1904 Trotsky was part of a coherent Menshevik faction opposing the Bolsheviks. Harmony did not reign in Menshevik ranks. Although it is difficult to trace the full nature of the disagreements from the fragments of correspondence that survive, it is clear that by the autumn of 1904 Trotsky was disgruntled with Menshevik colleagues over several issues. He clashed, for example, with T. Dan's 'organisational confusion', and disagreed with Martov's and Axelrod's more positive evaluations of the potential for political alliances with liberals in an anti-tsarist coalition. Trotsky threatened to give up as a correspondent for *The Spark* and to resign from the Mensheviks. He even left the

Menshevik nucleus in Geneva and went to Munich, the starting-point of his collaboration with another émigré, A.L. Helphand (Parvus). Martov had to exert all of his talents as a party diplomat to pacify Trotsky and keep him on board.[12] The threads that still tied Trotsky to the Menshevik camp would be tested, however, as social turmoil in Russia threatened to reach revolutionary proportions and Trotsky's thought took on new directions.

TROTSKY IN 1905

In 1905 foreign correspondents rushed to Russia to report on a system in crisis. Strikes in the towns, unrest in the countryside, liberal professionals demanding a more active role for society in putting matters right, protest from the nationalities, a difficult military campaign and the occasional mutiny in the armed forces were all aspects of this troublesome time for tsarism. Opportunities also opened up for revolutionaries to return to Russia to join the fight. In 1904 Trotsky had demanded that social democrats produce effective propaganda to enable the proletariat to do battle and to learn and grow stronger from any defeats. After January 1905, as the regime stumbled against the social uproar caused by 'Bloody Sunday', in which armed detachments shot, killed and maimed unarmed workers taking a petition to Tsar Nicholas II, Trotsky could put his own advice to the test by entering the fray. The year 1905 was to be an important turning-point in Trotsky's political life as practitioner, theorist and part-historian of the Russian Revolution. Let us examine each in turn.

1905: Trotsky as revolutionary

Returning to his homeland, Trotsky was to gain invaluable experience of revolution, working primarily as a revolutionary journalist in the fire of events. He wrote tirelessly for newspapers and journals, including *The Spark*, the Menshevik broadsheet *The Beginning* and the bulletin of the Soviet of Workers' Deputies, a body of elected workers' representatives and social democrat activists that acquired a certain prominence and influence in October and November 1905. His articles covered events from a Marxist perspective. In a clear and aggressive style, Trotsky demolished any hope of meaningful reform coming from the tsarist regime. Particularly galling for Trotsky was the notion that in promising a consultative assembly Nicholas II had consented to the main demands of the revolution. Such assemblies might satisfy the propertied classes that would dominate them, but they in no sense answered the needs of the working class. In an open letter to the leading liberal Professor Milyukov, for example, Trotsky explained that a real political change occurs only when 'the material means of armed supremacy pass from the hands of absolutism into the hands of the people'.[13] By 'the people', Trotsky of course meant ordinary workers and peasants.

As an urban-based activist it is understandable that Trotsky considered the town proletariat to be his most immediate and important target audience. He did, nevertheless, on several occasions address specifically peasant concerns. In these articles he tried to convince the peasants that they were still in all essentials in a state of serfdom. The so-called Emancipation of the 1860s had done little to free them. Indeed, one could claim that the peasants had experienced further impoverishment; the keywords of their life were 'grief and suffering'. To overcome this state of affairs Trotsky urged the peasants to several acts. First, they had to stop believing in the goodness of the tsar. Was it not clear to them that their gracious lord was on the side of the landowners? Second, they should become aware of the slogans and actions of the urban proletariat, and follow their true brothers in demanding an end to oppression and genuine popular democracy in the form of a Constituent Assembly. Third, the peasants should educate themselves in the advantages of socialism by joining up with the social democrats. The Socialist Revolutionaries were mistaken in thinking that a redistribution of land within capitalism could solve the peasants' land-hunger. Finally, each village should contact its conscripts in the army and encourage the peasant soldiers to abandon the war with Japan and to ignore orders to shoot strikers. Only a worker–peasant alliance in this form could guarantee the revolution's victory.

Acting amongst the workers, Trotsky not only propagated the programme and slogans of revolutionary social democracy, he also became more intimately involved in the strike movement. In this instance his main efforts were exerted as a socialist member of the St Petersburg Soviet, for which he wrote numerous proclamations. Trotsky urged the workers to develop the strike as a weapon to win not just economic demands, chiefly the eight-hour working day without any loss of earnings. It should also be used for political purposes, for example to protest against the imposition of martial law in Poland or the passing of excessively repressive sentences on mutinous sailors. In both instances, however, Trotsky was keen for the workers to know the limits of what could be achieved via strikes, especially if they were limited to one industrial sector or to the capital. The biggest mistake, for Trotsky, was to expect too much of strike activity when the odds were still stacked in the factory owners' favour. He was never afraid of calling off a strike when he thought that this was in the workers' best interests. Trotsky was well aware of how lacking the workers still were in organisation and military might. But he reasoned that time was on the workers' side. They could only become stronger. In the meantime they should take heart from the disruption caused and concessions already won by withdrawing their labour. The tsar, for example, would not have conceded even a consultative Duma had it not been for the workers' strikes. The workers should also prepare for the decisive battles of the future by joining the RSDLP, seeking a wider union of forces with brother soldiers and peasants, and demanding the formation of a people's militia.

It is difficult to gauge the exact influence that Trotsky had upon the course of the 1905 Revolution. We have no way of knowing how many people were affected by his journalism. It is unlikely that his words reached many peasants. He simply lacked connections with the villages, and there was not a mass distribution of his appeals to the peasantry. Even in the capital, his main stomping-ground, he did not create or found any specific institution or faction. He was not, for example, the guiding force behind the emergence of the Soviet of Workers' Deputies, even though he may subsequently have been, as one participant records, 'the unchallenged leader of the Mensheviks in the Petersburg Soviet'.[14] In late 1905 Trotsky was arrested as a member, not the leader, of the Soviet. In the memoirs of the prime minister of the day, Count Witte, Trotsky does not merit a mention. Witte can only call to mind Khrustalev-Nosar as first elected leader of the Soviet.[15] His memory may have altered, of course, had he lived to write his memoirs after the Bolshevik Revolution instead of completing them in 1912, but this only confirms the limited impression Trotsky made at the time on the popular consciousness. And in any case Trotsky himself admits that, despite the Soviet's existence, it was often local trade unions or factories that took initiatives, the Soviet then reacting to events by offering its support. In this process 'politicals' like Trotsky performed a subsidiary role.

If Trotsky did not have a great impact on 1905, 1905 did have a great impact on him. In 1905 he was able to witness the workers acting spontaneously and independently. Although victory was not attained in 1905, Trotsky had hope for the future. And 1905 also cemented Trotsky's reputation as a revolutionary, even if to a limited audience. His performances in the meetings of the Soviet showed his oratorical talents. In resolving issues of whether to continue, extend or call a halt to strikes Trotsky's recommendations carried some weight.[16] Some socialists came to identify Trotsky with the Soviet and blamed him for the Soviet's 'excessive' radicalism, which in their estimation served only to push the authorities into arrests and closure.[17] But whatever criticisms were laid at his door and however his role may have been exaggerated, henceforth Trotsky could be guaranteed a hearing amongst social democrats, even if he was not sufficiently powerful to be an acknowledged general leader. He certainly emerged from 1905 with an identity of his own and a proven capacity for independent action.

1905: Trotsky as theoretician and historian

Following the revolution's defeat Trotsky had time to reflect upon the broader meaning of 1905. In several books, including *Our Revolution* (1906) and *1905* (1909), Trotsky discussed the significance of 1905 in theoretical and part-historical terms. To questions that had long troubled Russian socialists – what form would a Russian revolution take?; would Tsarism be replaced by a bourgeois-capitalist or socialist regime? – Trotsky answered with 'permanent revolution'. Although many books and articles have been written probing the meaning and profundity of this concept, its basic propositions, which Trotsky developed from late 1904 onwards, can be summarised quite easily.

According to Trotsky, the course of Russian history and the structure of its contemporary class relations meant that the key actor in the coming Russian Revolution would be the proletariat. In a long history of struggle for survival against the more powerful economies of the West, the Russian state had been forced to grow and defend itself partly through excessive exploitation of the country's scattered population and resources, and partly via foreign loans on the international money markets. This process had produced a state standing above society and opposed to it. But the forces of opposition were weak. An impoverished peasantry was incapable of playing an independent political role, and an underdeveloped indigenous bourgeoisie, as Peter Struve had pointed out in the 1898 Manifesto of the RSDLP, was timid and cowardly. However, Russian industrialisation of the recent decades had brought into existence a small but powerful working class. Concentrated in large factories that utilised the latest technology, the workers had forged the most up-to-date methods of class struggle as they battled against poor working conditions and political oppression. Having a strategic importance that far outweighed their percentage of the country's population, the workers were the only truly revolutionary class able to overthrow tsarism. Once in power, however, Trotsky emphasised that a workers' government would introduce socialism, including state control of the national economy. Such measures, as well as increasingly being opposed by the petty-bourgeois prejudices of Russia's peasants, would also bring forth the hostility of the international bourgeoisie, anxious, amongst other things, to protect the interest payable on loans made to the tsarist regime. In this context, a workers' regime in Russia could survive only if socialist revolutions, and hence sympathetic regimes, occurred in advanced Western Europe. Fortunately, the workers of Russia could be optimistic about the prospects of European-wide revolution. This would be a strong possibility, partly because of an already evident heightening of class tensions in Western Europe, but also because West European workers would take the side of Russian comrades should the international bourgeoisie seek to crush a Russian revolution.

A Russian revolution was therefore 'permanent' in two senses for Trotsky. First, there would be no lengthy period or historical stage separating tsarist Russia from socialism. Second, a socialist revolution in Russia would not seek to confine itself to its national borders, but would try to extend itself internationally. Only when socialism was established across the globe would the 'permanent' revolution come to an end.

There are several ways in which we can evaluate Trotsky's political programme of permanent revolution. We can ask, for example, how original it was in conception. Certainly several of its elements were in common circulation. Apart from the co-operation with Parvus, who edited and introduced some of Trotsky's writings of the time, Trotsky also mentioned several instances in which his ideas, even if in embryo, could be found in Kautsky's earlier works. Furthermore, the weakness and cowardice of the Russian bourgeoisie had been noted by, amongst others, Peter Struve at the First Congress of the RSDLP. The separation of the Russian state from society, so that the two stood opposed to one another in a hostile relationship, was a feature of the Russian liberal Professor Milyukov's writings on contemporary Russia. The notion that the revolution would pass quickly, or 'in permanence', from its bourgeois stage to socialism could also be read in the publications of the peasant-based Socialist Revolutionaries.[18] Finally, the dependence of a Russian revolution for its success upon socialist revolution in the more advanced Western Europe was also a condition set by Marx and Engels in the 1882 'Preface' to the second Russian edition of the *Communist Manifesto*. However, there was undoubted originality in the way in which Trotsky synthesised these currents to form a unique outlook. Previous propositions were transformed beyond recognition. For example, Marx and Engels had assumed that the social relations contained in the village commune (*obshchina*) offered Russia a chance to bypass capitalism. Trotsky, on the other hand, saw nothing in the countryside as a model for progressive change. Indeed, he assumed that, after an initial period of gratitude to the workers for the overthrow of feudalism, there would be serious peasant resistance to socialism.

We can credit Trotsky, then, with a furtile and original mind. His analysis provides a fruitful starting-point for discussion about the nature of Russian history and the prospects for revolution. Certainly, Trotsky himself did not subsequently feel the need to renounce or significantly modify the main tenets of permanent revolution. The propositions associated with permanent revolution, from the view of the peculiarities of Russian historical development to the class analysis of the driving forces of the Russian and international revolutions, were to remain with Trotsky, despite future additions, reformulations and even (as we shall soon see) the odd retreat, for the rest of his life.

A second question of interest is how Trotsky's contemporaries responded to permanent revolution. Did permanent revolution create theoretical allies or enemies for Trotsky? At the high points of the revolution it is true that several Marxists seemed to become infected with aspects of permanent revolution. In the first half of 1905, for example,

Luxemburg and Kautsky referred to the need for 'permanent revolution' in analyses of Russian events. In September 1905 Lenin wrote that 'from the democratic revolution we shall at once ... begin to pass to the socialist revolution. We stand for uninterrupted revolution. We shall not stop halfway.'[19] The Mensheviks A.S. Martynov and Martov, in separate articles, admitted that the Russian proletariat might be forced to seize power because of the weakness of Russian liberals. In this event, a workers' government in Russia, which could not survive in isolation, would do its utmost to spread revolution to the West. From abroad, Akselrod, who placed much more emphasis on the leading role of the bourgeoisie in a bourgeois revolution and advocated alliances between workers and professionals in opposition to tsarism, worried that Martov and others were allowing *The Beginning* to fall under the spell of permanent revolution. However, when the 'conditions of revolutionary madness',[20] as Trotsky called them, had died down most of the above returned to their previous negative evaluations of permanent revolution. Several comrades, including Rosa Luxemburg, for example, agreed with the German socialist Franz Mehring's arguments that the Russian workers could not leap from tsarist oppression to socialism. In a revolution that would remain bourgeois the most that could be achieved were the very important rights of suffrage, association, freedom of speech and publication, and better working conditions, all of which would help the movement to build for the eventual goal of socialism. Martov returned to the general Menshevik fold and to his earlier viewpoint that an immediate seizure of power by the working class was not possible. The present goal, in which the workers would remain in revolutionary opposition, helping the bourgeoisie where appropriate, was the establishment of a bourgeois-democratic republic. Lenin's concession to 'permanent revolution' proved to be a very fleeting aberration. A more typical response on the nature of current events is the rebuff to Parvus and Trotsky contained in an essay of April 1905. Here Lenin rejects the 'be more revolutionary than anyone else' approach of the 'windbag Trotsky'. A sober assessment revealed that there could be no workers' government until the workers were a conscious majority of Russia's population and that 'the objective logic of historical development' posed a democratic, not socialist, revolution as the task of the day.[21] Permanent revolution not only marked a new stage in Trotsky's thinking; it also set him apart – increasing a sense of uniqueness and isolation – from other currents in Russian social democracy.

A final method of evaluating Trotsky's formulation of permanent revolution is to ask how its prognoses stand up against the mass of research which historians have carried out into Late Imperial Russia. Did Trotsky have a sensible estimation of the class forces and the general march of history, notwithstanding the objections of his contemporary critics? To begin with, we can note the substantial overlap between Trotsky's analysis of the late tsarist economy and the findings of economic historians. Both highlight, for example, the coexistence of the most modern and outdated forms of production. In this picture, the advanced sectors of the economy are concentrated in foreign-owned and state-supported capital industries (railway-building, output for the armed forces, etc.), the more backward elements predominate in the agricultural sector, a large proportion of which aimed at nothing more than self-sufficiency.[22] Much historical research would also concur with Trotsky's view that tsarism was heading for a revolutionary crisis. Robert B. McKean, a distinguished historian who has devoted much of his career to the question of 'Whither Imperial Russia', for example, doubts whether tsarism could have evolved into a stable, constitutional monarchy. The reasons for this pessimism fit well into Trotsky's analysis of Russia's social instability. McKean also identifies a bourgeoisie that, despite the undoubted growth of a professional middle class, remained relatively small and divided between sectional interests, factors that fatally undermined its political weight. Furthermore, the tsar did not adequately address the undoubted difficulties faced by peasants and workers, both of whom were alienated from the regime. The government's Great-Power ambitions also promised to undermine its stability, not least because of the shortcomings of the armed forces.[23]

If Trotsky's broad analysis of Late Imperial Russia's future fate has much to commend itself, what of his narrower account of 1905? Here, again, one can find several themes common to Trotsky's work of the time and subsequent histories. Let us take, for instance, the issue of why tsarism survived the onslaught of 1905. In answer, both Trotsky and one of the most recent and detailed investigations of 1905 highlight the facts that the armed forces remained loyal to Nicholas II, and that protest in urban and rural settings did not unify into one coherent opposition.[24] Trotsky's awareness of opposition taking different forms in varying regional and occupational settings is also reflected in subsequent scholarly studies. This is true, above all, of case studies of urban and rural unrest. Here Trotsky's point that factory and plant workers, especially metalworkers and printworkers, were in the vanguard of labour protest is echoed in the works of labour historians.[25] Similarly, the forms of peasant protest identified by Trotsky – from evicting landlords to seizure of land and grain, from a refusal to pay land rents to ignoring the military draft – are still to be found in modern textbook accounts.[26] Furthermore, Trotsky's suggestion that peasant uprisings took on features peculiar to the local environment, with Saratov being a centre of particularly violent outbursts and radical politics, has been confirmed by regional studies of peasant behaviour in 1905.[27] Trotsky was also a keen observer of the Russian bourgeoisie, including its intra-class tensions. He notes, for example, the differences between the Moscow textile owners and the Petersburg metallurgists. The former, he contends, were more independent of the state and therefore more overtly critical of the tsar. The topic of the pre-revolutionary Russian bourgeoisie remains under-researched, although some historians have supported, if unconsciously, Trotsky's interesting asides.[28] As well as offering insights into the class and occupational bases of protest, Trotsky also concerned himself with ethnic tensions, in particular violence against the Jews in pogroms. Here the role of alcohol, rumour, encouragement from the anti-Semitic press and other nationalist organisations, including tacit approval from the police and army, feature in Trotsky's and more recent accounts.[29]

The largest flaw in Trotsky's conception of 1905 may well be in his understanding of peasant behaviour. However nuanced his analysis of peasant protests, and however much he emphasised the importance of peasant opposition for a mortal blow to tsarism, Trotsky appreciated the peasants only to the extent that they displayed 'proletarian characteristics'. Thus, peasant conscripts could not possibly have led rebellions in the army, the responsibility, according to Trotsky, of advanced worker recruits. Furthermore, for Trotsky uprisings in villages remained 'confused and chaotic' until they adopted urban-based political forms of councils, executive committees and general, preferably socialist, political slogans, as exemplified above all in the formation of the so-called Peasant Unions.[30] While such statements are understandable given Trotsky's Marxist prejudices against Russian backwardness, they do run counter to recent work that has taken a more sympathetic view of peasant life. Such studies present Russian peasants as far from dull and stupid. David Moon, for example, argues that peasants were rational and creative, and that the peasants' way of life – and strategies in its defence – makes perfect sense once one understands their circumstances.[31] It is because Trotsky lacked such an understanding, one could claim, that he underestimated the extent of peasant opposition to his planned post-revolutionary modernisation and enlightenment campaigns, and overestimated what a workers' government could achieve in the countryside by controlling the state. However, this dilemma in its extreme form was not evident to Trotsky in 1905 and we will return to it in later chapters. At this stage it is impressive that Trotsky's theoretical and part-historical analyses of 1905 have been largely confirmed by more recent scholarship.

POST-REVOLUTIONARY POLITICS, 1906–7

Almost the whole of 1906 was to be spent by Trotsky in jail, awaiting trial. However, these were not barren months. Supplied with books and newspapers, he was able to keep abreast of the latest developments in the party and in the country. The resulting commentaries were published by the party's printing presses, enabling us to follow Trotsky's political thoughts in prison. Two issues were uppermost in his mind. First, how should socialists respond to the announced elections of a Duma (parliament) and, second, what form of party organisation could best further the union of social democrats and the working class?

Nicholas II may have survived the upheavals of 1905, but he had granted a Duma. The method of election set out in the Law of 11 December 1905 was not as simple as many would have liked. There were several electoral streams, or curia, defined by place of residence and social class, with excessive weight being given to the propertied groups. Members of the Duma were not to be elected directly, but from meetings of electors. There were numerous opportunities for government intervention, and electoral irregularities were not uncommon. The Duma itself was not to be as powerful as many had demanded. It could not, for example, hold ministers to account. As before, ministers were appointed and dismissed by the tsar. However, the elections to the First Duma, held in 1906, offered previously denied chances for political agitation amongst a highly motivated electorate.[32] The Mensheviks encouraged social democrats to participate in the elections amongst the workers' curia, seeing this as an opportunity to further socialist propaganda. The Bolsheviks argued that to take part was to condone a far from democratic process. A boycott would send the appropriate dismissive message to the regime.

Trotsky also favoured a boycott of the elections to the First Duma. This, he thought, was the best tactic to protest against the lack of democratic rights allotted to the Duma by the tsar. Participation in the elections, from standing as a candidate to voting, would signify tacit approval. A boycott, however, Trotsky reasoned, did not mean adopting a passive or dismissive attitude to the Duma. A boycott was simply the best means of criticising the way the Duma was being elected, and the best tactic to rally the masses to the calls for equal electoral rights and a ministry responsible to the people. Furthermore, a boycott would not exclude the Duma from becoming a focal point of social democratic agitation. If and when the Duma actually convened, social democrats would highlight any deficiencies in its workings; or if, despite all expectations, the Duma emerged as a radical body, social democracy would support it, irrespective of how it was elected.

The First Duma was too radical for the regime's liking and was dissolved after a mere two months' existence. In the light of the conflict between the Duma and the tsar, and the political excitement that developed around these events, Trotsky soon became an advocate of full participation in the elections to the Second Duma, scheduled for February 1907. For Trotsky, the elections were worth serious consideration since they afforded socialists several opportunities. First, the programme of revolutionary social democracy could be propagated on an all-Russia scale. Although Trotsky admitted that the workers' curia was the most valuable to the social democrats, he argued that agitation should be undertaken in all curia and party candidates put forward wherever possible. Moreover, Trotsky stated, agitation should not overlook the disenfranchised. After all, social democrats sought to take socialism to the masses, who for the most part were not allowed into the official polls. The organisation of unofficial polls would allow social democratic deputies to claim a constituency larger than that of any other Duma member. Second, given that the Duma had developed into an arena of struggle between various sections of the elite, social democrats could expose and exploit these frictions. In this context, Trotsky thought it admissible, in cases where there was no chance of winning, for social democrats to support a relatively more left-wing candidate – a liberal Cadet over a conservative Octobrist, a peasant Trudovik over a liberal Cadet, and so on. This was not, he pointed out, simply opting for a 'lesser evil'. This 'lesser evil' would at all stages be subject to criticism and if elected to the Duma would no doubt expose his political bankruptcy. Trotsky insisted that in order to be seen as the only political party willing to keep its promises, social democrats had to avoid the sort of unity and platforms with other groups to attain a 'sovereign Duma' urged by Plekhanov. Only under full independence of programme and tactics would the RSDLP gain for itself a parliamentary fraction worthy of support, and also the fraction the backing of the proletariat.

Trotsky's writings on the Duma campaigns reveal the interest he took in the development of Russian parliamentarianism.[33] Ultimately he demanded not the tsar's Duma, but a Constituent Assembly elected on a four-tail suffrage (direct, equal, universal, secret). The most he expected from a radical Duma is that it would act as a 'caretaker regime', organising elections to a Constituent Assembly. It would be the Constituent Assembly, under a workers' majority, that would fully democratise Russian society, guaranteeing freedom of the press, an elected judiciary and people's militia, and so on. Trotsky made it clear that this would not be a dictatorship of the proletariat; and nor could it be, since the next stage of Russia's development was to be a democratic republic as a precursor to socialism. In this context he stated that Russian social democracy

> cannot jump ... over the natural phases of political evolution; it cannot pass through history in accordance with an abridged textbook or a summary which it itself has composed. ... The country is faced with the task of democratic renovation ... our responsibility in relation to it is not only to *demonstrate theoretically* that it is a limited task, but also, and above all to *excel in it in practice.*[34]

This seems to conflict with permanent revolution, in which Russia, guided by the workers, could jump over a historical stage. Trotsky does not seem to have been aware of this possible contradiction in his thought.

However actively Russian social democracy participated in the elections to the Duma, it was impossible for it to achieve a majority of deputies. Some socialist theorists argued that, given the shortcomings of the Duma, social democrats could nevertheless take advantage of the more open politics, with its competing programmes and debate, to re-establish the RSDLP on a new basis. Akselrod, for example, suggested that there was now a potential for the socialist movement to take giant strides forward if a broad workers' or labour congress were convened. This idea arose out of a concern that the intelligentsia was exerting too much influence over the RSDLP. However, before the workers could come to dominate in the party they would have to be aroused politically. For Akselrod, the solution lay in encouraging workers on the ground to agitate for a workers' congress, an institution in which workers' representatives would debate the leading issues of the day. Once a workers' congress had an agreed socialist agenda the RSDLP would merge with it to create a genuinely mass-based party. Of course Akselrod was aware that this would not be a smooth process, not least because the authorities could well ban the meeting of a workers' congress. Nevertheless he continued to propagandise the idea as a means of furthering the independent activity of the working class and of bringing the party and the working class closer together.[35]

In a letter to Akselrod of September 1906 Trotsky gave highly qualified support to the idea of a workers' congress. He conceded that, like the non-party Soviet of Workers' Deputies, a non-party workers' congress could be an important medium for bringing the RSDLP into closer contact with the advanced workers. However, Trotsky clearly rejected the notion that the RSDLP could be recreated via a workers' congress. He reserved his most biting criticism for comrades such as Yu. Larin, who argued that a workers' congress could lead to an RSDLP of almost one million members, organised as an open party on a West European model. Larin's hopes not only ignored the fact that West European conditions did not apply in Russia; if realised, for Trotsky they could also destroy all that was healthy in the RSDLP. Instead of an organisation that had taken a leading role in 1905, one would have a loose, ill-defined body, in which the initiative of the 'genuinely socialist elements' would be 'held back' by the 'political primitiveness of the broad masses'.

At the hub of the dispute over how much could be achieved by a workers' congress lay conflicting evaluations of the current state of the

RSDLP. The advocates of the workers' congress hoped that it would heal the divisions in the party and make of it a genuine working-class organisation. Trotsky, despite admitting that the congresses and central committees of the RSDLP were filled with intellectuals, thought that workers were already an important part of the party membership. Moreover, Trotsky argued that the party was not so torn by factional disputes that it was in need of rescue by a workers' congress. In actual fact, he reasoned, factional disputes were a perfectly natural part of a process that would culminate in the fusion of scientific socialism with the labouring masses. On the path to this goal it would be unsurprising if comrades differed over which slogans and tactics best met the tasks of the day and what the general line of development to the ultimate goal would be. For Trotsky, 'Bolsheviks' and 'Mensheviks' constituted equally important elements of the RSDLP. Stating that he belonged to neither faction, he was nevertheless equally proud and willing to co-operate with each as they, in turn, developed the right response to individual issues. Moreover, from his experience in the Soviet Trotsky knew that both factions could work together effectively when the revolution demanded it. When the ultimate battles of the revolution would be fought, Trotsky was confident that the differences 'formed under the influences of fleeting causes' would be wiped out. In the meantime, the way to prepare for this outcome was to call for unity, not splits; for raising party consciousness, not succumbing to the 'mildew' of factionalism.

Having spent so long in jail, Trotsky worried that, however wise his words, he had indeed come adrift from the life of the party. Before he could rejoin the political fray he would have to avoid the punishment of internal exile to Siberia given him for participation in the Soviet of Workers' Deputies. Fortunately for Trotsky, escapes were quite common, as adequate police surveillance could not be guaranteed in Siberia's open and inhospitable climate. Although Trotsky was not achieving anything too unusual in effecting an escape, he penned an effective and dramatic account of his adventure from captivity to life on the run in the essay 'There and Back'. Here Trotsky reveals his disgust with the drunkenness and Christianity of the wilds, regretting the fact that even if 'a Provisional government were formed in Petersburg today, the local policeman will still be king in Obdorsk for a long time'. Yearning for 'electric street lamps, the noise of trams and the best thing in the world

– the smell of fresh newsprint', Trotsky relied upon the skills of the local tribesmen to carry him to the nearest railroad, where the train would return him to civilisation, 'forward, forward, always forward'.[36]

2

THE FIGHT FOR UNITY, 1907–14

Isaac Deutscher has Trotsky spending the years between his escape from internal exile to the outbreak of World War One in 'the doldrums'. This may be true in the sense that no new revolutionary upsurge occurred on the scale of 1905. Furthermore, Trotsky did not see the achievement of unity in the RSDLP, a cause for which he expended considerable propagandistic efforts. Nevertheless, these were important years for Trotsky, in which he endeavoured to maintain an independent and critical stance on internal party matters, as well as developments in Russian and international affairs. There was also some personal happiness. In fleeing Siberia in 1902, Trotsky left a wife and two daughters behind. However, the marriage was at least in part one of revolutionary convenience. When in Paris in 1903 he met another attractive party member, Natalia Sedova, at an art exhibition he felt himself free to establish a new relationship, one that was to last until his death in 1940. The pair had returned to Russia in 1905, and in 1906 Natalia had given birth to their son Lev while Trotsky was in prison. Now the family could establish a more permanent home together in Vienna. Here Trotsky mingled with the luminaries of Austrian social democracy. He was also a regular contributor to the party press, whether Polish, German, Austrian or Russian, and to the non-party press. Most importantly, with financial backing from his wealthy friends A. Ioffe and M.I. Skobelev, he established his own newspaper, *Truth*. From the first issue of 1908 to the last of 1912, *Truth* acted as a forum for the promotion of party unity.

Trotsky also hoped that its popular style would attract a readership amongst working-class activists in Russia. His first port of call, however, was England, where in May 1907 several hundred delegates convened for the London (sometimes known as the 'Fifth') Congress of the RSDLP.

TROTSKY AND THE RSDLP, 1907–13

Much had happened in the party while Trotsky was otherwise engaged as a prisoner. Over the course of late 1905 and the first half of 1906 Bolsheviks and Mensheviks had gathered first separately and then together, most notably at a unification congress held in Stockholm. The May 1907 Congress was to be the largest such 'unified' gathering to date. Trotsky's position had changed considerably since the previous party event held in London, the infamous Second Congress of 1903. Then he had been a voting delegate; now he had an advisory voice only.

The debates of 1907, held at the Brotherhood Church, largely concerned the prospects for political action in Russia. On these issues the Bolsheviks, supported by the Polish and Latvian sections, won the day. There would be no co-operation between socialist and liberal deputies in the Duma, and the party's main emphasis would remain on the development of a centralised, underground organisation. Agitation for a workers' congress, seen by the Mensheviks as an integral part of the creation of an open West European type of party, was declared 'harmful'. Although the Congress resolutions reflected a Bolshevik spirit, the Mensheviks were not routed. The national organisations, the Poles and the Latvians, for example, deplored factional intrigue and they used their votes to ensure that neither Bolsheviks nor Mensheviks would have inbuilt majorities on the Central Committee or on the editorial board of the party publication, the *Social Democrat*.

Trotsky made only several, but lengthy, speeches at the Congress. Judging from these interventions he was more on the side of the Bolsheviks than the Mensheviks. He chided the Mensheviks, for example, for their 'revolutionary pessimism', evident in their invention of a Russian bourgeois democracy 'out of the rich fund of their own imagination'. Here Trotsky reiterated his view that it would be the workers, not the bourgeoisie, that would head a Russian revolution. In a subsequent aside Lenin admitted that, some differences over permanent revolution notwithstanding, there was solidarity with Trotsky on the critique of bourgeois parties in Russia. Both Trotsky and the Bolsheviks rejected the Menshevik view that co-operation with bourgeois parties was possible and in some instances desirable.

Despite some common ground with the Bolsheviks, however, Trotsky was keen to maintain a distance from both factions. At the conference's opening sessions he opposed Bolshevik proposals for lengthy discussions of theoretical problems. He then clashed with Lenin over the wording of a resolution on the social democrat faction in the Duma, preferring a less harsh condemnation than that demanded by the Bolsheviks. Elsewhere he corrected an impression given by Lenin that Trotsky also agreed with the Bolshevik view of peasant–worker collaboration in a forthcoming Russian revolution. He insisted that his difference with the Bolsheviks, i.e. Trotsky's denial that the peasants could play an independent political role, be noted. He also ridiculed part of a Bolshevik resolution condemning the notion of a workers' congress that sought to ban party members from discussing the very idea of it. How would such a level of thought control be monitored, he wondered? Finally, the Bolsheviks were angered by Trotsky's suggestion that the Central Committee should not be allowed to alter the membership of the party newspaper's editorial board without the prior approval of a party conference.

Although he sniped at Bolsheviks and Mensheviks, the role Trotsky actually cast for himself in London was that of peacemaker. On several instances he touched upon his understanding of unity in diversity. The fact that comrades differed over theoretical matters such as the future outcome of a Russian revolution should not, he reasoned, result in a formal split in the ranks. He, more than anyone else, appreciated the need for ideological struggle. In this process he, Trotsky, reserved for himself the right to his own opinions, which he would defend in intense debates. However, he called upon both factions to follow him in subordinating his theoretical convictions to the overriding demand of unity in political activity. The fact that in so thinking Trotsky found himself against his will in a minority labelled 'the centre' was, for him, a sign of the crisis facing the party. Only a 'raising of the level of party culture', a 'growth in the maturity of party members' and a 'greater sense of responsibility from party leaders' could, he argued, restore the party as a united body.[1] In advancing such arguments, Trotsky appealed to the national sections, the Poles, the Latvians and the Bund, as well as to socialist 'practicals', party workers in Russia, for whom the leading émigrés bore responsibility for needless factional intrigue. In a post-Congress report it was even suggested that Trotsky cultivated the central ground so as to assume leadership of the RSDLP.[2] If this was his intention, future events were to prove how impossible such a balancing act would be. At no point did Trotsky manage to establish a healthy working relationship with either of the factions, let alone to act as a bridge to bring the two together.

Trotsky's problems with Lenin were twofold. First, there were disputes over theoretical issues, principally the question of the moving forces and likely outcome of a revolution in Russia. For Lenin, Trotsky's chief sins were 'that he ignores the bourgeois character of the revolution and has no clear conception of the transition from this revolution to the socialist revolution'.[3] In particular, Lenin felt that Trotsky was confused over the exact meaning and significance of a union between the proletariat and the peasantry in a Russian revolution. No doubt disagreements over theoretical niceties did not aid Trotsky's relations with Lenin. The main bone of contention between the two, however, was the state of affairs in the RSDLP.

Trotsky refused to join Lenin's various campaigns to cleanse the ranks of several types of 'deviationist', from the ultra-radical to the neo-liberal wings of the RSDLP. Lenin railed against the former for insisting upon revolutionary tactics – above all the recall of the party's deputies in the Duma – in a period of reaction. He fulminated against the latter for wanting to liquidate the underground organisation and to concentrate on legal possibilities only, for example in the permitted trade unions. No doubt Trotsky was put off Lenin's inter-party policies because of their expulsionist demands and because, as several subsequent commentators have recognised,[4] Lenin tended to present his opponents' views in their most extreme form for strictly polemical purposes. In this process he invented straw men so as to have seemingly watertight grounds for demanding a recantation.

There is evidence to suggest that, initially, Lenin wanted Trotsky on his side. On two separate occasions he approached Trotsky with offers of co-operation. In 1908 Trotsky was invited to join the editorial board of the Bolshevik faction's newspaper *The Proletarian*.[5] In 1909 a meeting of the expanded editorial board of *The Proletarian*, impressed by the popular appeal of the Viennese *Truth*, agreed to consult with Trotsky over the possibility of some kind of merger.[6] These political manoeuvres are not the only signs of Lenin's regard for Trotsky's abilities. Also in 1909, Lenin approved the transfer of 100 roubles of party funds to help Trotsky out of some financial difficulties.[7] At the time the Bronsteins were living largely off credit in Vienna.[8] It was following a rejection of Bolshevik political overtures, however, that Lenin began to view Trotsky as part of the 'deviationist' tendencies. For Lenin, Trotsky failed to see that what lay behind the Bolshevik campaign against the 'liquidationists' and the 'recallists' was not intellectual arrogance or isolationism or, heaven forbid, personal animosities, but a genuine concern for the Marxist integrity of the RSDLP. By insisting on the false and contrived nature of factionalism, by making appeals for conciliation, Trotsky, according to Lenin, was in fact helping anti-party tendencies to take control of the movement. This is why Lenin called Trotsky a 'Judas', an 'empty phrasemonger', and demanded a struggle against Trotsky's 'splitting tactics and unprincipled adventurism'. From 1910 onwards Lenin was continuously frustrated by Trotsky's 'conciliationist' stances. In a letter of October 1910 Lenin admitted that he saw no grounds for a political alliance with Trotsky:

> In Copenhagen we spoke with Plekhanov about the publication of a popular newspaper. This is necessary. (It is clear that Trotsky has joined forces with the liquidationists ... and turned his face against a party bloc of Bolsheviks and Plekhanovists). We agree with Plekhanov that it is impossible to do anything with Trotsky.[9]

Given Lenin's refusal to be bound by agreements with 'deviationists', Trotsky was pushed into negotiations with the Menshevik faction of the RSDLP. The most famous of Trotsky's attempts to forge an alliance of anti-Lenin forces, if only because Lenin refused invitations to attend, took place in 1912. In the lead-up to the holding of a 'Unity Conference' in Vienna in August 1912 Trotsky seems always to be reacting to earlier provocations from Lenin.

In the previous year Trotsky was hoping that an all-party conference of the RSDLP could be convened. If all factions would attend, this could form the beginnings of a new coming together for the party. The events of 1911, however, did not bode well for Trotsky's intentions. In late May and early June Lenin arranged a Meeting of the Members of the Central Committee in Paris, one of whose decisions was to call for an all-party conference. For Trotsky, this was an attempt by Lenin to 'usurp the name of the Party'. In a counter-meeting held in Bern in August Trotsky and several other comrades established an 'Organisational Committee', also given the task of calling an all-party conference. As a consequence there emerged two separate groups, each seeking to hold an 'all-party conference', and neither recognising the legality of the other.[10]

Despite these worrying developments, Trotsky may have hoped that the balance of forces was on his side. After all, Lenin was isolated from the local organisations in Russia and it was unclear how strong the underground really was. Furthermore, Lenin faced strong opposition to his splitting tactics even within his own faction. Moreover, Trotsky could claim that he was the true representative of the 'unity' January 1910 Plenum of the Central Committee. This had been a defeat for Lenin. Its spirit might still have been sufficiently strong to give Trotsky the edge.

The race to hold an 'all-party' conference first was won by Lenin when in January 1912 some dozen or so of his supporters gathered in Prague. To the annoyance of Trotsky and other party members, Lenin claimed this as a genuine 'all-party conference', with full power to reconstitute the party. Following the first publication of the minutes of the Prague Conference in the late 1980s, it became clear that Lenin controlled the delegates in Prague only with extreme difficulty: even some so-called Leninists doubted Lenin's claims to legitimacy.[11] At the time Trotsky interpreted Lenin's machinations as a further attempt to assert his authority over the RSDLP and to destroy Trotsky's moves for unity. Trotsky responded by throwing the credentials of the Prague delegates into doubt, disputing whether they represented any existing local party bodies. He also set about completing his plans for a counter-conference.

It was Trotsky's hope that this conference would be the genuine 'all-Russian' gathering that he had desired, with representatives of all of the factions in attendance. Only a meeting of this type, he reasoned, could bring about the much-needed unity of the RSDLP. Not surprisingly, Lenin refused to attend. However, just as serious for Trotsky were sceptical voices amongst the Mensheviks. Adding to their personal mistrust of Trotsky's 'arrogance', key figures, including Martov and Akselrod, doubted whether Trotsky could conjure up unity out of the real differ-ences over organisational, theoretical and tactical questions that divided Bolshevik from Menshevik, as well as Bolshevik from Bolshevik and Menshevik from Menshevik! The leading Mensheviks did not offer Trotsky any help in organising the conference. When it actually met in Vienna in August they participated without any real enthusiasm. In this context Trotsky was frustrated by divisions with the Menshevik faction itself. Everywhere Trotsky turned he found an atomised RSDLP, with each section unwilling to answer his demands for unity. For Trotsky, even taking the chair during conference sessions was frustrating, as he tried to keep delegates to his preferred issues. Despite an eventual set of agreed resolutions, there is a consensus amongst historians of the so-called 'August Bloc' formed in Vienna that it was soon to disintegrate.[12]

Trotsky no doubt suspected that his efforts to hold a harmonious and effective unity conference would come to nought. Even before 1912 he had encountered opposition within Menshevik ranks to his conception of party unity. Writing in the Menshevik 'liquidationist' journal *Our Dawn* in late 1911, for example, Trotsky outlined how old and harmful factional mentalities could be overcome. In his proposed schema com-rades should unite around the programme of Russian social democracy as the advanced workers entered the movement. The ideal opportunity for this would soon present itself in the forthcoming elections to the Fourth Duma. While welcoming Trotsky's vision of a party united in action with the workers, *Our Dawn*'s editors doubted whether some of the movement's wings, most notably Lenin's, would be willing to aban-don their factional loyalties. Trotsky himself was also warned about holding common misconceptions about so-called 'liquidationism'. The editors pointed out that Trotsky wrote of 'liquidationism' as though it was a real political philosophy that rejected work in the underground, whereas in fact it was an invention of Lenin's polemical pen. Finally, *Our Dawn* worried that Trotsky was pursuing unity as a goal in itself devoid of real content. Unity was fine, but only, they reminded him, when grounds for unity actually existed.[13]

Faced with such evident hostility between the sections of the RSDLP one can appreciate how unlikely it was that Trotsky's calls for unity would succeed. In the midst of all the doubts and opposition in the run-up to the Vienna Conference he almost gave up the idea altogether. Post-conference events provided further examples of Trotsky's difficul-

ties in dealing with the Menshevik faction of the RSDLP. Trotsky was to
fall out, for example, with the editors of the Menshevik newspaper *Ray*.
This publication had been established to support the resolutions of the
August 'unity' conference of 1912, but Trotsky was soon to suspect that
one faction of the August Bloc was turning *Ray* into its exclusive organ.
These suspicions were not helped by delays in the publication of
Trotsky's articles. Over the winter of 1912–13 there raged a hostile correspondence between Trotsky and *Ray*'s editors, in which each accused
the other of factionalism. From this correspondence it became clear that
Trotsky could not share a platform with members of the Menshevik faction with whom he had political disagreements. For Trotsky the main
issue was unity; for *Ray*'s editorials the chief concern was the furtherance
of Menshevik political tactics. In self-defence *Ray*'s editors pointed out
that they had not rejected Trotsky's submissions; it was unfair of one
correspondent to demand that they abandon their views and submit to
his line. In making this demand was not Trotsky himself displaying a
'factional spirit'? In response Trotsky defended himself from the charge
of 'factionalism', stating that '[t]he heart of the matter lies not in factions, but in *Ray*'s editors not understanding what a workers' newspaper
is in the current epoch, with what language it should speak, what questions it should pose'.[14]

If the various factions of the RSDLP could not unite on terms agreed
amongst themselves, there was for Trotsky one further source of hope
that internal party affairs could be put on a more comradely footing. The
grandees of the Second International, especially its influential German
section, had as little patience with the squabbling in the Russian party
as Trotsky. The Second International took an interest in Russian developments and some of its leaders became very involved in Russian issues,
particularly after a committee of trustees was set up to manage disputed
funds. Trotsky was on excellent terms with some of the leading figures
in European social democracy and often acted as a source of information
on Russian matters. Lenin fought hard to correct Trotsky's frequent
'misrepresentations' in the German party press.[15]

Nevertheless, despite his good connections Trotsky was not able
to manoeuvre a position of dominance for himself as the sole
spokesman of Russian social democracy amongst the International; nor
was he able to apply pressure from gatherings of the International to
steer Russian affairs in a direction which he desired. Indeed, Trotsky's

displeasure at Lenin's 'organisational games' seems, if anything, to have upset some influential figures. After the debacle of 1911, in which a group of five, including Lenin, met in Paris and then a group of six, including Trotsky, gathered in Bern, each claiming to represent the RSDLP, Rosa Luxemburg, for one, saw Trotsky as part of a larger problem. In the summer of 1911 she sent a letter to Luise Kautsky, wife of Karl, which expressed more sympathy for the Bolsheviks than for Trotsky:

> The vigorous behaviour of the trustees has had a very good effect on Lenin & Co. They have complied, and have given up splitting the newly created institutions. In contrast, the Mensheviks have fallen into a veritable delirium. They are now on their own responsibility summoning as soon as possible – after saying for 18 months that it was impossible – a plenum session of the Central Committee or the party conference, which of course can only help a split, and are abusing the Bolsheviks, the Poles and the Unity Commission in the most incredible manner. The good Trotsky is more and more exposed as a rotten fellow. Even before the Technical Commission had got financial freedom from Lenin to enable it to give money to *Truth*, Trotsky blasted away in *Truth* against this commission and the whole Paris conference in an unheard of manner. He directly accuses the Bolsheviks and Poles of being 'party splitters', but says not a word against Martov's pamphlet against Lenin which excels everything else so far in baseness, and is obviously aimed at splitting the party. In one word it is a beauty.[16]

It was perhaps over similar worries that Trotsky was himself not an unbiased commentator that Karl Kautsky, however much he admired the editor of *Truth*, always maintained a certain distance and never allowed himself to view Russian events exclusively through 'Viennese' eyes. Several of his other advisers on Russian matters counselled Kautsky not to become overly absorbed in the hopeless situation ruling in the RSDLP. In any case, even if Karl Kautsky had fully shared Trotsky's analysis of the woes besetting the RSDLP, he was unable to broker an agreement that all factions could sign up to. Disillusioned by disappointments and setbacks, Kautsky worried lest he had wasted too much of his time over Russian problems.[17]

The failure of Trotsky's unity campaign in the RSDLP therefore mirrored that of all other attempts to bring the warring Russian factions together. Unable to convince internal and international socialist opinion of the viability of his views on internal party affairs, Trotsky's calls for unity ultimately fell on barren ground.

TROTSKY AND RUSSIA, 1907–12

If the spring of 1907 was to be the starting-point for Trotsky of a tortuous relationship with the RSDLP, for Russia it was to mark a return to reaction. This was emphasised above all by the government's decision to dissolve the Duma and issue a new electoral law on 3 June 1907. At a stroke whole areas of the empire were disenfranchised. The Duma itself was scaled down from 542 to 442 deputies. The regime intended to produce a Duma more 'Russian in spirit' and one more in harmony with the interests of the ruling elite. Trotsky, like numerous others on the left, reacted with horror. This was, they stated, nothing other than a *coup d'état*. By this Trotsky thought that a reactionary alliance of large capital (worried by worker activity opposed to its economic interests), the landed gentry (fearful for its privileges) and the bureaucracy (attractive to large capital and the landed gentry because it had the army at its disposal) was forged. In this arrangement the government would no doubt have preferred to do away with the Duma altogether. However, according to Trotsky there were two restraining factors that made the Duma necessary. First, tsarism would find it easier to raise loans on the international money markets if it possessed a veneer of democracy. Second, the Duma could operate as a regulatory mechanism, a point of contact, between the tsar, large capital and the landed gentry. If Nicholas II and his ministers thought that they had at last attained a stable political arrangement, Trotsky argued that they were seriously mistaken. He advanced several reasons why instability would remain a constant feature of Russian politics.

First, Trotsky saw no leaders of genuine calibre in the mainstream of Duma politics. A. Guchkov, head of the Octobrist Party, which held the majority in the Third Duma of 1907–12, for example, was dismissed by him as an 'unbridled bragging nonentity' with 'a complete absence of moral bravery'. One could hardly expect such a figure to mount an extensive legislative programme from the floor of the Duma.

Furthermore, according to Trotsky the leaders' personal failings were also a reflection of broader shortcomings in the parties. He claimed, for example, that the leader of the Constitutional Democrats, Milyukov, merely reflected the 'narrow-mindedness and egoism' of his party's social base. Little wonder then that the Constitutional Democrats proved themselves to be such poor defenders of a constitutional order, as was evident in their failure to guarantee even the minimal electoral rights enshrined in the First and Second Dumas. Caught between reaction and revolution, the Constitutional Democrats, Trotsky stated, were capable only of betraying the cause of progressive political change.

Most serious of all for the regime's stability, however, was the clash of interests that Trotsky perceived at the very heart of the 3 June bureaucracy–landowner–capitalist bloc. According to Trotsky, the landowners desired above all else the full restoration of absolutism. This regime would protect their estate interests and guarantee privileged access to state subsidies. For the capitalists, though, the landowners' plans, if realised, would place unbearable demands on the state budget and divert resources away from the internal market, which had to expand if future capitalist development was to occur. As the fear of proletarian uprisings that had brought forth the bloc of 1907 receded, so, Trotsky reasoned, the antagonistic interests of the June 1907 allies would come more and more to the fore. In this event, it would be up to the tsar and his ministers to bring unity to the various sections of the ruling elites. However, they were to prove as unsuccessful in this as Trotsky was in encouraging unity in the RSDLP. For Trotsky, the major policies of the tsarist regime – agrarian reform and an active foreign policy – failed.

Agrarian reform was associated with the prime minister, P.A. Stolypin. He developed a series of land reforms, most notably a land law of 9 November 1906, under which peasants were given the right to leave the commune – the traditional form of running peasant affairs, including land cultivation and its periodic redistributions – and set up as individual landholders. This major reform sought to strengthen the social supports of tsarism in several respects. The large landholders would hopefully be satisfied, as their estates were to be left intact. Furthermore, administrative opportunities to oversee land transfers from communes to individual farmers should come the large landholders' way. The peasant hostility to the regime typical of the 1905 Revolution would also die down. As peasants competed for ownership of the communes' holdings their grievances against the nobility would be put to one side. Moreover, the stronger and wealthier peasants, who would make most out of the land transfers, would look to the tsar to guarantee their newly found property rights. A Western notion of the rule of law would at last take hold in the countryside. Any losers in the land redistributions, those too poor to purchase land, for example, would form a fresh reservoir of cheap labour in town and countryside.

Trotsky was attracted to some elements of the Stolypin reforms. He considered the break-up of the commune, for example, to be inevitable and progressive. But, he pointed out, wherever this had occurred to date it had been a painful process. In eighteenth-century Britain, France and Saxony peasant upheavals and national revolutions had resulted. And, for Trotsky, Stolypin's agrarian programme would not escape similar unrest. The major flaw in Stolypin's reforms, he reasoned, was the absence of measures to provide an expansion of the economy alongside the disintegration of the commune. Here Trotsky had in mind the expropriation of the nobility's land to help alleviate land-hunger, and the rapid growth of industry to absorb dislodged labour and to support an expansion of agriculture. Of course Stolypin could not offer the reforms demanded by Trotsky. These were clearly impossible within the confines of the 3 June system. But it was precisely such restrictions that, for Trotsky, doomed Stolypin to failure. The outcome of Stolypin's reforms, according to Trotsky, would be to increase poverty in the countryside, a prerequisite for further social instability.

If the government could not generate economic growth and social harmony in its internal programme, there remained the international arena as a possible source of gain. Trotsky argued that it was precisely in this direction that tsarism was being forced, with the active support of a majority in the Third Duma. The landed interest hoped that land-hungry peasants could be resettled on the empty plains of the Far East. Capitalists expected a boost to their factories' order books from government investment in the army. Trotsky pointed out, however, that foreign adventures were a high-risk strategy. Could an underfunded state budget afford an expansionary foreign policy, for example? But, with an alliance with Britain and France in hand, and encouraged by the fact that the various sections of the ruling elite found it easier to unite around this than over any other issue, tsarism pressed ahead. In 1908 Trotsky warned the tsar that he was courting military defeats on the scale of 1904–5, with all the negative consequences for his regime's survival. Although nothing so drastic happened so early, several years later Trotsky was able to survey post-1907 Russian foreign policy as a series of successive disappointments:

> In Persia, considered our natural market, the influence of Britain and Germany has been strengthened. ... In the Balkans Bulgaria, betrayed by Russian diplomacy, hates [Russia]. The 'hereditary enemy', Austria, annexed Bosnia and Hercegovnia in 1908 and in the independent Albania acquired a strong buffer against Serbia. Germany strengthened its position in Constantinople and took the key of the Bosporus Straits into its hands. Finally, in the Far East, the Mongolian adventure, as well as turning this country away from us, made China our sworn enemy.[18]

Modern historians may wish to question or supplement Trotsky's reasons for his pessimistic evaluation of developments in Russia between 1907 and 1912. Regarding the Stolypin reforms, for example, several commentators stress peasant resistance to the prime minister's intentions because they clashed with peasant understandings of the rural economy and the vital role of the commune in it. The commune, and the network of peasant social relations around it, were therefore far more resilient than Stolypin or Trotsky expected.[19] Moreover, constitutional historians may wish to place more emphasis on the absence of an education in parliamentary procedures to explain the Duma's ineffectiveness than on the bankruptcy of the political forces as identified by Trotsky.[20] No doubt Trotsky's revolutionary outlook biased his Duma portraits somewhat. However, few historians would deny that Stolypin was not as successful as he had hoped. Even Nicholas II showed little regret when learning of his assassination. Furthermore, Trotsky's analysis of political instability in Russia has much to commend itself in broad outlines, even if one may be sceptical about some of the details. It also kept his revolutionary optimism alive when many abandoned the revolutionary movement altogether.

TROTSKY ON ART, 1907–12

Turn-of-the-century Vienna is, of course, famous as a centre of cultural developments in numerous spheres of the arts. Trotsky was able to take advantage of the cultural delights that lay on his doorstep to produce several essays surveying the art of his time. This was not only a reflection of Trotsky's enduring interest in cultural affairs. Using family connections, he also negotiated the publication of his essays in radical newspapers and journals in his native Southern Russia. In this way there started a lengthy partnership with the liberal daily *Kievan Thought*, whose commissions also provided Trotsky with a small source of income.

The style adopted by Trotsky for his cultural excursions varied. Sometimes he would have several characters – professors, doctors, critics – debating the representation of death and eros in the contemporary novel or discussing the nature of the impressionist school of painting in smoky Parisian or Viennese cafes. Elsewhere he would simply report his own musings when visiting an exhibition, such as successive holdings of the Vienna Secession. Whatever the format, however, as an art critic Trotsky was concerned to give an appreciation of what was on offer, as well as a hint of how art should develop. In an account of the Vienna Secession of 1913, for example, Trotsky singles out Otto Friedrich's 'Cycle of Rhythms' paintings as 'aesthetically convincing'. The subsequent evaluation is a good example of Trotsky's critical sensibilities:

> [Friedrich's] growing collection of nude figures on five canvasses: nebulous and touching children's bodies, supple adolescent bodies, nobly passionate women's bodies, and strong, intense men's bodies, despite the complexity of composition, speak in a language of clear and pure harmony. Whilst the images of the domestic temple (in which a commercial councillor will entrust his daughter to a colonel of the general staff) are external allegories, where courage is represented by a man in armour who wields a sword, and fidelity by a man who is bound to a post pierced by a javelin, the 'rhythms' of Friedrich are not replaced by conventional signs, but directly inspire the viewer with the inner rhythmicality of the depiction itself, the harmony of line and colour.[21]

Trotsky's praise of the finest exponents of modern art was also tinged with a dose of disappointment. His chief complaint was that modernism and impressionism had so far been unable to move beyond the subjectivity of an individualistic outlook. For Trotsky, the form of painting had been revolutionised as life itself had been transformed by the emergence of the mass city. But he bemoaned the fact that the art he surveyed did not communicate the enormity and power of these social and economic changes. Isolated from the struggles of the working class, the sculptor Constantine Meunier or the painters Karl Schulda and Olaf Lange, although they included the workers as subjects, were, according to Trotsky, unable to capture the labourers in their totality. Trotsky looked in vain for the embodiment in art of the political battles in the Balkans, the fight of the English suffragettes for the franchise or the rising strike movement of the masses. And, he pointed out, art would not progress beyond its current stage; it would flounder in a 'cul-de-sac', while it continued to 'repeat and turn over old motifs'. Before art could genuinely reach new heights, Trotsky stipulated that a social revolution would have to occur. Human creativity would take a qualitative leap in a post-capitalist order. In the meantime he urged art to 'enrich itself with the drama of the working and struggling man', in this way enriching 'labour and his struggle'.

TROTSKY AND THE BALKAN WARS, 1912–13

The bulk of Trotsky's journalism for *Kievan Thought* was composed not of art reviews but of political reports on Europe's tinderbox, the Balkans. Trotsky's interest in Balkan affairs was reflected in a series of articles printed in his own *Truth*, as well as in other Russian, German and Polish socialist publications, from 1908 onwards.[22] Trotsky's writings on the Balkans can be conveniently divided into those written before and after the first Balkan War that erupted in 1912. In the earlier pieces Trotsky identified several sources of instability in Balkan politics, cutting across internal, regional and international factors.

Inside the various Balkan states and semi-states Trotsky perceived a precarious social order. At the bottom of the social pyramid, for example, there was a large, part-enslaved, mostly illiterate and impoverished peasantry. At the apex of power stood parasitic reactionary-dynastic cliques, equally at war with their own populations and with their neighbours. Each sought to create support at home through aggrandisement and territorial conquest, as was evident in the slogans for a 'Greater Serbia', a 'Greater Greece' or a 'Greater Bulgaria'. As if this was not bad enough, these local and regional conflicts played themselves out against the imperialist rivalry of the Great Powers, between, for instance, Anglo–German–Russian hostility in the Balkans and Persia. The regional manoeuvres of the local elites were continually subject to the intervention of and arbitration by Europe's major states, with the real interests of the Balkan peoples as the lowest priority. Indeed, ordinary workers and peasants were made to pay, whether via excessive taxes and military drafts, for the ambitions of local and European rulers.

Trotsky's solution to the dilemmas faced by the Balkan peoples was simple enough, and it came straight out of the demands of the emerging indigenous socialist movements. Only a Balkan Federative Republic organised on a democratic basis and with full autonomy for all the region's nationalities would, he argued, provide a large and united internal market for economic progress, and respect for cultural rights and differences to ensure a flowering of education and art. Only under this arrangement would the region enjoy prosperity and political and cultural equality. Trotsky not only identified the solution to the problems besetting the Balkans, but also saw the means by which this end could be achieved. Although capitalism had shallow roots in the Balkans, all the signs were that it would develop, especially via railway construction. As in Russia, this would give birth to a class of workers who, when they became sufficiently large and powerful, would lead an assault on the existing unjust order. And, as Trotsky reported from several congresses, there already existed in the Balkans a lively social democratic movement, which, through publications and trade unions, was ready to educate the workers in socialism. Most important of all, for Trotsky, was the fact that the various branches of Balkan socialism put contact with each other above support for national governments. Thus, Serb, Bosnian, Bulgarian and other local organisations would enter the Second International as one Balkan force rather than as splintered and hostile groups.

In his first reports on Balkan affairs Trotsky identified grounds for hope as well as for despair. He was to gain greater familiarity with the Balkans when, in the autumn of 1912, *Kievan Thought* asked him to become its war reporter at the front on the eve of the first Balkan War.

Trotsky returned to the region on a regular basis over the next two years, as one war followed another. The articles he penned for the radical press of Southern Russia, as well as his submissions to party publications, are classics of anti-war journalism. Trotsky's chief aim was to expose the horrors, the hypocrisy and the ultimate futility of the conflict. As far as possible he tried to present events from the point of view of the ordinary person, whether at or behind the lines. Trotsky's description of the various motivations that encouraged people to sign up, from the personal to the political, from the idealistic to the banal, is positively Tolstoyan in tone. Similarly, Trotsky's account of individual acts of courage on the battlefield, undertaken without any sense of the broader picture or of their wider significance, brings to mind Tolstoy's portrayal of the importance of the 'little' heroics of warfare contained in his masterpiece *War and Peace*.

Of course, although Trotsky did aim for literary effect, he was not writing literature. In an age in which the arms race was a reality, Trotsky wanted to draw his readers' attention to the brutal reality of war. War, he declared, is a brutalising process, evident in the increasingly harsh regime imposed on soldiers, as well as in the rape, pillage and murder of the wounded undertaken by the soldiers. This was true for all combatants, of whatever nationality, and Trotsky raged against the Slavophile Russian press, who reported Turkish atrocities but ignored similar acts committed by the Bulgars. Trotsky appealed to simple humanitarianism as the only principle to which journalists should owe loyalty. It was their clear duty to publicise evil deeds of whatever origin in the hope that they would cease if condemned by European 'opinion'. He also recounted his troubles in overcoming a foolish military censorship. This sought to banish anything that might have shed poor light on 'its liberating mission', even if a journalist's article contained no military secrets. Fortunately, Trotsky seems to have won more battles with the censor than he lost, and he was able to say more or less what he wanted. His main message was that, however enthusiastic initial reactions to declarations of war might be, nations would soon be drained by the demands of contemporary warfare. An increased sense of grievance and poverty were inevitable results.

Apart from very moving pictures of the psychological and physical torment of the actual fighting, Trotsky's Balkan portraits offered some lasting political lessons. First, the relatively minor territorial gains achieved by some of the combatants were not worth the cost. For example, military budgets absorbed more than ten times the amount spent on education, and this in a region of high illiteracy. Social and economic dislocation had occurred instead of a much-needed expansion of interregional trade. Second, the wars had not brought the region closer to peace and stability. If anything, matters had been made much worse, both in a local and pan-European setting. Locally, inter-ethnic tensions had risen as Bulgar sought revenge on Romanian, Armenian on Turk, Turk on Bulgar and so on. For others, such as the Jews of Romania, conditions remained as bad after the battles as before. In the broader context of European imperialism, Trotsky worried that the machinations in the Balkans were bringing Europe closer to an all-out war. This he dreaded, not least because the damage to culture and the social and economic destruction that he had witnessed in the Balkans would be replicated on a much larger scale. Third, despite an abhorrence of war, Trotsky's forays in the Balkans did bring him face to face with its practicalities. He learned the importance of adequate supplies, of an officer caste keeping in contact with the foot soldiers, of maintaining high spirits at the front as well as at the rear, and of guarding against the corruption and embezzlement of war that can sap an army's morale. Finally, Trotsky saw grounds for some hope in the developing Balkan socialist movements and an emerging regional proletariat. He became better acquainted with some of the leading lights of the local socialist parties. He wrote lengthy and flattering portraits, for instance, of the Romanian socialists Konstantin Dobrugeanu-Gherea and Christian Rakovsky, and the latter was to remain a friend for many years to come.

1914

Trotsky ended his stint as a war correspondent in the Balkans enriched in personal experience. His thoughts were not to stray for too long, however, from how to rectify the factious situation in Russian social democracy. In 1914 he was to make one further attempt to conjure up unity through the publication of a workers' journal, *Struggle*. This was to differ from his Viennese *Truth* in several respects. It was to be published directly in St Petersburg. Furthermore, it was not to be a broadsheet of several sides, but a thick journal of several hundred pages.

Trotsky resolved to found a new journal for several reasons. First, he was isolated from all the existing publications, from the Bolshevik *Truth* to the Menshevik *Ray*. Second, at a time when the workers' movement in Russia was returning to life, he may have felt an urgent need to overcome what were, for him, the baneful effects of 'factionalism'. Certainly *Struggle*'s main goal was to engender unity amongst Russian social democrats as an essential precondition for the advanced workers' education in Marxism, crucial if the workers were to be effective at a time when they were assuming leadership of the struggle for socialism.

To get his project off the ground Trotsky needed money, fellow editors and contributors, and a team of printers and distributors in St Petersburg. There were several possible means of obtaining money, from individual backers and donations from sympathetic organisations (German and Latvian socialists, for example) to Trotsky's earnings as a journalist. Although the exact sources of revenue have never been clearly identified, evidently Trotsky did manage to raise sufficient funds. He was less successful in attracting a broad editorial team. There was evident hostility to Trotsky's new project from within the existing factions. Even a former close ally of Trotsky, Semkovskii, refused an invitation to become a founder member because he saw *Struggle* as nothing less than an attempt to form a 'third non-factional' faction. Similarly, sections of the social democratic movement in St Petersburg, from the influential Organisational Committee to the 'Inter-Districters', held aloof. In the end Trotsky was unable to build a wider support network. His project was to be beset by delays, and the lack of sufficient activists meant that plans to market the journal in the Russian provinces would come to nothing.

Although Trotsky did not achieve the level of support he desired for *Struggle*, affairs were managed well enough for the journal to appear. Trotsky's own writings for it covered a range of topics – a survey of recent Russian history, a condemnation of the finances of the Russian state for its heavy reliance on the government monopoly on the sale of vodka, the place of parliamentarianism and the strike weapon in the workers' struggle. Apart from his own articles, Trotsky attracted a glittering array of contemporary Marxists to write for *Struggle*. Their contributions ranged from the abstract to the particular, from aspects of Marxist theory to the current situation in the workers' movement. Prominent amongst these are M.N. Pokrovsky's study of the development of social classes in Russia; A. Lunacharsky's discussion of the meaning and significance of proletarian literature; N. Zhordanaya's examination of the national question; and K. Radek's insights into the nature of current imperialism. Today's reader cannot but be impressed by this content and Trotsky's ability to organise this venture. It was a success to the extent that it was the outbreak of World War One, not commercial or internal disputes, that closed it. While Trotsky may have appreciated this retrospective praise, he could have been less pleased with its contemporary reception.

To begin with, its impact was limited by police repression. Several issues were confiscated outright, obviously cutting the journal off from its intended readership. Second, both Mensheviks and Bolsheviks were highly critical of *Struggle*'s campaign for unity. Writing in the Menshevik journal *Our Dawn*, for example, K. Oranskii, while welcoming Trotsky's programme of unity and his educational-propagandistic aims, argued that his publication was fundamentally misconceived. It could not work because it refused to accept that the main obstacle to unity was not sheer 'factional prejudice' but real policy differences. Furthermore, the very foundation of *Struggle* merely added to and complicated the 'factional' maze, defeating the project's intended goals. The most vehement of *Struggle*'s opponents was Lenin, however. For him, Trotsky had no understanding of the real state of affairs in Russian social democracy. Here the main issue was not factionalism, but a battle between two irreconcilable parties that had taken shape in 1912. One, headed by Lenin had remained true to Marxism; the other, under the control of the 'liquidationists', had gone over to liberalism. The battle of these two parties for control over the masses was not 'chaos' or 'factionalism', as Trotsky contended, but a normal part of the political struggle, and one, Lenin was happy to report, that the Marxists were winning. It was the growth in Bolshevik influence that, according to Lenin, lay behind Trotsky's chagrin. It was typical of Trotsky's arrogance that, unhappy that the workers were following Lenin, Trotsky declared them 'politically confused' and the 'unknowing agents' of the splitters. For Lenin, however, it was precisely Trotsky who was 'attempting to disorganise the movement and bring about a split'.

Even though *Struggle* was for the most part rejected by Trotsky's socialist contemporaries, and even given the lack of any firm evidence that it exerted an influence over the workers, one historian of the early

RSDLP, Geoffrey Swain, has cautioned against writing Trotsky's project of 1914 off as a complete disaster.[23] He has argued that the chances for realising unity in the RSDLP were in fact quite high. In 1912, for example, the movement's deputies to the Duma were elected on a unity ticket, while workers and influential trade unions like the Metal Workers' Union demanded unity in the party. For Swain, although *Struggle* 'never really got off the ground before the First World War began, it is clear that there was a market'. Indeed, because of his emphasis on conscious workers, who rather than factious intellectuals should guide socialist politics, Trotsky is 'the hero' of Swain's study, according to which 'the party of 1914 was far more [Trotsky's] creation than Lenin's'. Swain states that it was Lenin's obsession with 'control', engineering a split in the Duma group for example, that scuppered Trotsky's hopes for unity. However, Swain also makes the bold claim that unity could still have been achieved if the International Socialist Bureau had intervened. Had it done so, 'Trotsky, with his close contacts with German social democrats, would inevitably have emerged as the chief party spokesman'. If Trotsky shared this evaluation of the balance of forces in Russia and abroad, one further reason emerges for founding *Struggle*. It was no less than an attempt to take control of the party in Russia, both by appealing to a natural market among the Russian workers and by impressing upon the international socialist movement the identity of the true unifier. Rather than an obscure and largely unknown episode in Trotsky's biography, setting up *Struggle* could be a key moment in his pre-revolutionary political activity.

If there was a grand political plan motivating Trotsky at this time, there are several reasons to doubt whether he could have succeeded. As reactions such as Semkovskii's illustrate, there was a broad antipathy to Trotsky and his project. It is unlikely that any of the leading Russian social democrats – from Plekhanov to Martov and Lenin – would have accepted Trotsky's leadership, especially if this was going to be imposed under external pressure. Second, Swain calls the 'Inter-Districters' the 'biggest underground group' in St Petersburg, and its historian has made it clear that in 1914 it did not support Trotsky. Even those who did follow Trotsky claimed that he overestimated his influence in Russia. Third, Trotsky did not advance a detailed programme to overcome the very real differences which separated Russian social democrats over problems of social insurance or the role of the strike movement –

differences which Swain himself outlines. Here, perhaps, Lenin and Oranskii were correct: the RSDLP had divided into separate and competing parties that could not be united easily, if at all. Finally, if unity had been achieved in the summer of 1914 it would have been short-lived. Not only did Russian social democrats disagree on how to respond to the war, but the reaction of German comrades who backed their government led to a collapse in the prestige and authority of the very people and institutions which Swain identifies as guaranteeing Trotsky's position as head of an imagined united party.

3

WAR AND REVOLUTION, 1914–17

When the heir-apparent to the Austro-Hungarian crown was assassinated on 28 June 1914 during a visit to Bosnia-Herzegovina, it was
possible to dismiss the murder as one more tragic episode in a turbulent
but insignificant region. Yet this proved to be the starting-point for a
chain of events that led to a general European conflict by early August.
When the war concluded some four years later, the Austro-Hungarian,
German and Russian empires stood in ruins, their emperors overthrown.
It was an outcome that cautious voices at the imperial courts of 1914
feared and predicted, but the major powers of Europe 'slithered over the
brink' of war without a clear conception of what they were letting
themselves in for. Each nation mobilised its armies without knowing for
certain the positions of the other likely belligerents. As a recent authority points out, 'the speed of events outstripped the speed of communications. Insufficient time elapsed for reflection and calculation'.[1] Once
war was declared, however, civilians rallied to the national cause; in the
major European capitals gleeful crowds gathered to greet the declaration
of hostilities.

The actual outbreak of World War One took Trotsky somewhat by
surprise. He rushed to the offices of the political police in Vienna, asking what a Russian émigré should do, now that his homeland was at war
with Austria-Hungary. He took the advice to leave at once; he and his
family were on a train bound for neutral Switzerland that very day. The
'war to end all wars' was to be a significant turning-point in Europe's

history. It was also to be another fascinating period in Trotsky's political battles. He lived variously in Switzerland, France, Spain and America, before finally returning to Russia after the February Revolution of 1917. For the most part he continued his work as a revolutionary journalist, writing anti-war articles in a series of newspapers, including the Parisian *Our Word*, the American *New World* and, of course, the Southern Russian *Kievan Thought*. It was in the capacity of the latter's war correspondent that Trotsky was able to spend a large part of the war in belligerent France.

In articles published in Paris and in Kiev Trotsky enjoyed a remarkable amount of freedom of expression. Yes, the French and Russian censors tended to object to some of his more direct remarks. But he always managed to print most of what he wanted to say, if not always in the language he wanted to employ. Apart from charting the nature and impact of warfare, Trotsky was as ever in the midst of socialist politics. He never became the leader of an actual and mass anti-war movement, but he maintained what contact he could with the anti-war left. As for Russian social democrats, the war did nothing to heal their factious differences. If anything they were to be magnified against the background of the carnage taking place around them.[2]

TROTSKY ON THE WAR: ORIGINS, NATURE, OUTCOMES

Although the military propaganda machines of the various warring powers presented the war as one of defence and liberation, Trotsky saw a profound change in the world economy as having produced the current conflict. As a Marxist Trotsky accepted that capitalism was increasingly reproducing itself on a world scale. By 1914, he thought, European capitalism had clearly outgrown the confines of the nation-state. To develop further it needed to be governed on a pan-European basis. In classic Marxist-speak the formula was 'the productive forces have outgrown the narrow confines of the national boundaries'. In seeking to assert its hegemony over the continent of Europe, the French, German, Russian and British bourgeoisie was trying to resolve a progressive historical task. The problem with the capitalist solution was that it took an imperialist form: aggressive, violent and ultimately destructive.

For Trotsky, only the proletariat, staging a revolution across Europe, could create the necessary democratic, transnational governmental frameworks to meet the requirements of genuine economic and social progress. If the proletariat could create a socialist United States of Europe and a Balkan Federative Republic, Trotsky predicted that the continent's economy would attain previously unimagined affluence. Furthermore, nationalism as a reactionary phenomenon would be overcome. With each nation enjoying the right to free cultural expression and autonomy, nationalism would be neutralised politically and economically. Such would be the advantages of continent-wide socialist rule that the United States of Europe and the Balkan Federative Republic would be but the first steps on the path to a socialist republic of the world.

For Trotsky's programme to be realised the proletariat of Europe and the Balkans would, first of all, have to abandon their national armies. Indeed, his immediate political demand was one of 'peace'. Initially, however, he could do little but note the enthusiasm with which the crowds had greeted the conflict. Even the erstwhile socialist parties of the Second International, a body that had long debated how to overcome militarism, had succumbed to nationalism and voted for the military budgets in parliamentary sessions. Previously respected socialists, from Kautsky to Plekhanov, had to be rejected as they came out in support of the war. Trotsky, however, did not lose his revolutionary optimism. From the outset of the hostilities he was convinced that one day soldiers and workers would turn against the conflict.

First of all, Trotsky doubted whether the fiscal and human demands of World War One could be sustained indefinitely. This was true, above all, of his native Russia, with its weaker economy and ineffective fighting machine. Surely discontent would become frequent and widespread as the hardships of war hit home. Second, Trotsky did not see any real prospect of one nation emerging as a clear victor. In a series of articles he examined the nature of trench warfare, and concluded that the war was developing into one of bloody attrition and a hopeless stalemate. Third, Trotsky perceived a psychological change in the fighting nations. The war witnessed the mass movement of peoples across Europe on a previously unheard-of scale. In this process Trotsky argued that not only was dull parochialism being knocked out of peasants, but they were increasingly adopting a revolutionary psychology. They were being made aware, for example, of the power of modern technology, and would come to see how it should be used to the advantage of the people rather than of the propertied ruling classes. Finally, as national governments seized control of their economies to prioritise war needs, the advantages of socialist planning would increasingly reveal themselves. In these senses the war was providing the preconditions for socialist revolt and construction.

The movement from war to revolution, though, was not to be a mechanical and automatic process. Trotsky knew that an end to the fighting on his terms would have to be fought for. There had to a battle for the hearts and minds of the people. This meant, first of all, building a vibrant socialist movement with its own press and membership, so that the machinations of the Great Powers and the lies of the war machines could be exposed, and so that a genuine alternative could be offered. This was a huge task. How could the resources of a few socialists, isolated by national boundaries and with communication more difficult in the conditions of war, overcome the might of the warring powers?

With the odds against him Trotsky nevertheless carried out his duty as he saw it. Above all, he wrote polemical articles damning the traitors to the cause, the so-called social-patriots that were for the war. Having the authority of socialism behind them, Trotsky saw the social-patriots as his main enemy. They, more than anything else, were the butt of his anger. He raged against the Russian social-patriots in Paris and in Russia, as well as in the French, German, Austrian, Balkan and British socialist movements. Although Trotsky's propagandistic battles against Plekhanov's, Aleksinskii's, Kautsky's and other pro-war socialists' output contain no great insights or original thought, Trotsky was right to devote so much of his time to unmasking his social-patriotic enemies. After all, it was precisely the authority of the pro-war socialists, Trotsky argued, that helped the bourgeois governments to ensure that workers went off to battle. The social-patriotic lies had therefore to be exposed at each and every instance if the workers were to have any chance of understanding what their real reaction to the war should be. When war-industries committees were established in Russia in late 1915 with the intention of better organising the nation's resources for war, Trotsky urged socialists to use the election of worker representatives to agitate amongst the masses for a revolutionary response. Viewing the Duma as an important forum for the expression of anti-war views, Trotsky was bitterly disappointed when the party's Duma representatives did not speak with a sufficiently revolutionary fervour.

The reverse side of Trotsky's campaign against the social-patriots was to highlight and praise the activities of anti-war socialists whenever and wherever they appeared: John MacLean in Britain, Z. Hoglund in Sweden, and Karl Liebknecht in Germany. Trotsky also tried to encourage the anti-war left to pool its resources to found a new, revolutionary Third International. To this end he attended a small gathering of anti-war socialists in Zimmerwald, Switzerland, in September 1915, at which he helped to draw up the conference's Manifesto. Just how difficult it was to unite the anti-war left, however, is clear from an examination of Trotsky's relations with the main anti-war factions of the RSDLP, the Bolshevik and the Menshevik internationalists.

TROTSKY AND RUSSIAN SOCIAL DEMOCRACY

There were some early hopes that the anti-war Russian socialists would be able to agree a common programme on the war. For example. Lenin noted Martov's anti-war articles in the Parisian newspaper *Voice*, the precursor to *Our Word*, with guarded approval. Indeed, when the Belgium social-patriot Emile Vandervelde decided to call a conference of socialist parties of the Entente countries only, to be held in London in February 1915, Trotsky, Martov and Lenin entered into negotiations for a joint response. However, this attempt, like all others to unify the Russian 'internationalists' during World War One, broke down. There are several reasons why.

Most importantly, the existence of perhaps seemingly minor but in fact very serious differences in outlook in the internationalist camp hampered the formation of broader co-operation and the establishment of truly comradely relations. For example, Lenin refused to give priority to the slogan of 'peace', even to Trotsky's revolutionary understanding of this phrase. For Lenin the key slogan that internationalists should advance was to call for the defeat of one's own government in the war. From a conflict between nations the war should be turned into a civil war in which each national working class would attack its bourgeoisie.

Trotsky objected to Lenin's priorities because, he argued, in taking each country separately Lenin's model for political action was sharing the same outlook as social-patriotism. Furthermore, the defeat of one's own country was not the best circumstances in which to begin a revolution. Did Lenin not know that a defeated country presupposed one physically ravaged and psychologically depressed? What sort of base was this, asked Trotsky, to begin the construction of socialism? Lenin responded by defending a concept of national revolution, claiming that the 'uneven development of capitalism' meant that a socialist revolution would occur first in one or several states taken separately, but certainly not on a Europe-wide scale. In turn, Trotsky defended his conception of the forthcoming revolution as one that would realise itself in the form of a United States of Europe. Trotsky accepted uneven development under capitalism which 'it is useful and necessary to repeat'. Nevertheless, he argued that 'in comparison with Africa and Asia, all of these countries are a capitalist "Europe" ripe for socialist revolution'.

The nature of Trotsky's relations with Lenin and the Bolsheviks during World War One was a fairly stable picture of opposition and occasional acrimonious outbursts. At their lowest points Trotsky described Lenin as a 'terribly egocentric person ... seeing in himself, in the last analysis, the axis of world history'. From within the Bolshevik camp Trotsky's thought was labelled the most 'vacuous and unprincipled ever to have existed in Russian Social Democracy'. It was disagreements of this sort that prevented Trotsky from co-operating with Lenin and the Bolsheviks. In 1915, for example, the Bolshevik faction, once again impressed with Trotsky's ability to help run the production of the popular and important daily newspaper *Our Word*, sent him a letter of invitation to join the editorial board of a proposed journal, *Communist*. Trotsky reacted angrily to the offer, listing his many disagreements with the Bolsheviks in an 'Open Letter'.

Leaving personal invective to one side, however, Lenin was not alone in finding Trotsky's notion of the United States of Europe problematic. Several members of the Menshevik faction thought that Trotsky was being far too optimistic about the prospects for socialism opened up by the war. Although they may have agreed with the construction of the United States of Europe as a long-term goal, they rejected Trotsky's proposition that its creation was a near possibility. Surely, they objected, the necessary preconditions for a United States of Europe, i.e. overcoming nationalism, capitalist ideology and traditions, could only be achieved over the course of several decades of the post-war era. For the

Menshevik internationalists Trotsky was ignoring the complexities involved in guaranteeing the subjective aspects of his programme. He was therefore left with unrealisable expectations. The best one could hope for from the war was a 'peace without annexations' and 'neither victory nor defeat' for any side. Trotsky and the Mensheviks clearly understood the significance of the slogan 'struggle for peace' in very different ways. This also had implications for their views on how to re-establish ties between the parties of the Second International. For Trotsky, this body was finished. The masses would be mobilised for the immediate conquest of state power under the leadership of a new, Third International. For the Mensheviks the solidarity of the international working class would resume under the auspices of a reunited Second International.

With these programmatic disagreements in place, a second reason why the Russian internationalists could not coalesce into one force is that each accused the other of 'factionalism' by placing their own responses to the war above the need for unity. Thus, for example, although the Zimmerwald Conference did conclude with a single Manifesto, Trotsky, Lenin and Martov left Switzerland with competing evaluations of what had occurred and what was the significance of what had taken place. According to Lenin's publication, at Zimmerwald Trotsky had 'struggled with all his might against a revolutionary Marxist appraisal'. For Trotsky, the Leninists at the international gathering were the most sectional and the most hostile to compromise. Nevertheless, under the weight of arguments they had been forced to accept Trotsky's call for a struggle for peace as a 'slogan of mass proletarian struggle'. Martov claimed, meanwhile, that it was the Menshevik-internationalists that had saved Zimmerwald from disbanding without agreement. It was a Menshevik understanding of the struggle for peace as a first step in a lengthy period of class struggle that had won the day. According to Martov, Trotsky had made no special contribution at Zimmerwald, at which a Trotskyist tendency was simply absent.

Trotsky, as before, was thus under attack from the Bolshevik and Menshevik sections of the RSDLP. According to the former, Trotsky was not decisive enough; for the latter he was too hasty and too radical. The one thing that Bolsheviks and Mensheviks agreed on was that Trotsky was engaging in 'non-factional factionalism'. Despite numerous articles on the theme of unity, this remained as elusive a goal as ever for Trotsky.

Although Trotsky was not able to unify Russian social democrats, and even if his political and journalistic activities had little impact on the course of events unfolding around him, there is much significance in Trotsky's stay in Paris for his political life. He remained committed to the concept of permanent revolution. Indeed, the fact that he saw the war as opening up a revolutionary epoch made him even more convinced of its correctness. This, coupled with Trotsky's engagement in the politics of the socialist movements in each of the warring countries, made of him the most bold and wide-reaching Marxist commentator. He felt well qualified to pronounce upon developments in any of the major and minor European and Balkan countries.

It was not for these reasons, though, that in the autumn of 1916 Trotsky was asked to leave France. In many ways this was a bizarre expulsion. After all, what real harm was Trotsky causing, writing articles for a minority newspaper published in a foreign language? Perhaps Trotsky was right, however, when he claimed that the tsarist secret police was sensitive to his presence in France after a rebellion of Russian sailors at Marseilles. The French authorities may well have been fulfilling an ally's request. No doubt the truth of this version can be tested in the relevant Russian and French police archives. For Trotsky the expulsion order began a new period of uncertainty and impatience as he was removed first of all from the capital of France to the backwaters of Spain.

FROM THE OLD WORLD TO THE NEW: SPAIN AND AMERICA

Trotsky and his family were to spend only several months in Spain. They were not able to establish themselves in one place, but had to move from San Sebastian to Madrid, where Trotsky underwent a brief arrest before being transferred to Cadiz. Finally the Bronsteins were allowed to go to Barcelona, where they were to board a boat to take them to America.

Trotsky's 'Spanish interlude' was neither the most comfortable nor the most exciting of his life. He could not speak or read Spanish, and several times complained that a Spaniard's knowledge of foreign languages did not extend beyond his *'Parlez-vous francais?'* He found the pace of life in Madrid 'lazy', the city 'provincial', the people devoid of 'entrepreneurship'. His main enjoyment was derived from visits to Madrid's museums, 'temples of art', but in the copy work of the young Spanish artists who also frequented the museums he saw no evidence of any contemporary Spanish artistic talent. It was only in the corruption of the prison regime in Madrid that Trotsky at last saw some sense in Spanish customs. The practice of arranging better conditions for prisoners who could pay was merely a reflection of the broader inequality in society. It also helped raise money for an impoverished state budget. When he reached Cadiz he described it as even more backward than Spain in general. In the local library Trotsky came across one German and two dozen French books, all of which had been attacked by bookworms. He was able to take some notes on Spanish history from early nineteenth-century French books, regretting that the masses were prevented by poor education from learning of the crimes of the forefathers of the current ruling elites. Indeed, after emerging from an empty museum and being struck by the behaviour of the 'democratic public' on a pier, he commented that 'gigantic efforts will be needed to raise the culture of the mass'.

Although Trotsky was able to maintain some correspondence with his friends in Paris while in Spain, it must have been with a sense of relief that he was given permission to set sail for America. After all, New York had a substantial émigré Russian community, including a large section sympathetic to socialism. A revolutionary newspaper, the *New World*, edited in part by Nikolai Bukharin and Alexander Kollantai, was already in existence. Trotsky established connections with it before leaving for America. When he arrived he was met by an international meeting of greeting. Trotsky was soon making speeches and submitting articles to the *New World*.

His first contributions revealed the horrors of life in the trenches and how war was far from a liberating experience for a society. Repression and censorship increased, as did physical and material poverty. Tensions were rising to such a point, Trotsky declared, that revolution in Europe could not be delayed for much longer. These pieces could not have brought much comfort either to a government considering declaring war or to those who would have to answer a military draft. However, at the time of Trotsky's stay in New York it was becoming increasingly likely that America would enter the conflict. At the end of January 1917 the German government, hoping that it could starve Britain into submission, announced that it was going to engage in unrestricted submarine warfare. This meant breaking the terms of American neutrality. Interventionists immediately called upon President Wilson to declare war on Germany. For Trotsky, the clamour for war now underway in America was all too familiar.

In the aptly named article 'A Repetition of Things Past', for example, he claimed that America, a country without its own traditions and ideology, had many times provided a home for ideas that had exhausted themselves in Europe. Previously this had been true of political and religious ideas; now it was the turn of the legend of a 'war of liberation'. Trotsky advised Americans to scan the European newspapers of late July and early August 1914, from which they would gain an understanding of the patriotic campaign underway in the American press. The people had to be convinced of the government's concern for 'freedom' and 'justice', and how it was a victim of aggression. Above all, the real reasons for intervention, concerns about profits and markets, had to be hidden:

> What about the war deliveries that the German submarines threaten? What of the billions of profit falling with a Europe bleeding to death? ... Who can speak of this at a time of great national enthusiasm! If the New York stock market is prepared to make great sacrifices (the people will bear them) then, of course, this is not for the sake of contemptible money, but for a great truth ... how to call it? – morals. It is not the stock market's fault if, in serving eternal justice, it receives 100% and more in profit![3]

As well as laying bare the profit motives that he considered brought forth war, Trotsky also argued that the real winner from American intervention would not be the capitalist bosses, but revolution. When he summarised his New York experiences in his autobiography Trotsky mentioned the conveniences in his flat (including electric lights, a bath and a telephone) that Europeans were unused to. In one of his comments on daily life in New York at the time, however, he wrote a moving description of the effects of the drudgery suffered by ordinary people. He noted, during a rush-hour ride on the subway, a humble and depressed crowd whose only solace lay in chewing gum. The war, he predicted elsewhere, would show the proletariat that only they, through social revolution, could resolve the problems that beset capitalism, problems that had pushed America to war. He advised his American comrades to 'prepare the soldiers for revolution!'

Above all, Trotsky advised the American Socialist Party to have no truck with social-patriotism. The disease that he fought so hard to combat in Europe had also to be unmasked in America. In this context Trotsky entered into fiery and polemical exchanges with the pro-war newspapers, including the powerful Jewish daily *Forward*, and the broadsheets of the local Russian community, *Russian Word* and *Russian Voice*. He urged the Socialist Party to avoid common platforms with pacifist organisations such as 'The Friends of Peace'. He warned the workers to beware institutional social-patriotism, for example Samuel Gomper's Labour Committee, formed to guarantee uninterrupted work for war at the nation's war industries. Before revolution could occur, Trotsky argued that socialists had to raise the 'mighty melody of the International' as powerfully and as purely as possible.

After Nicholas II's abdication of the Russian throne in March 1917 against a background of civil strife and protest at deteriorating economic conditions on the home front, anyone seeking confirmation of the link Trotsky constructed between war and revolution had a ready and current example to hand. Events in Russia continued to occupy Trotsky while he was in New York both before and, especially, after the collapse of the monarchy. Three points had long been part of Trotsky's analysis of the pattern a revolutionary upheaval in Russia would take. The proletariat would be its leader, it would be socialist and it would call forth, either by inspiration or by force of arms, a spate of revolutions across the whole of Europe. During World War One Trotsky modified his analysis somewhat, adding that the United States of Europe would be the state form through which the European revolution would realise itself and that revolution would occur first of all in Germany. News of the fall of tsarism obviously confounded Trotsky's last prediction, but for the most part he was able to retain his prognoses for interpreting the events taking place in his homeland.

According to Trotsky, it was street demonstrations by the workers, eventually backed by the army, that had brought about the tsar's abdication. The bourgeoisie, led by his old antagonist Professor Milyukov, had not wanted the monarchy's collapse. On the contrary, Trotsky claimed, the liberals looked to the tsar as the most trusted defender of property against the proletariat, and to the institution of monarchy as the form of government best suited to conduct an imperialist foreign policy. For Trotsky, the liberals had been *forced* to form a Provisional Government by two pressures, one external and the other internal. First, the British, French and American money markets had told the Russian bourgeoisie to assume power lest Nicholas II conclude a separate peace with Germany. Second, the liberals had to forestall a workers' seizure of power, for a workers' government would end the war and hold the liberals to account.

Thus far Trotsky may have been a little harsh on the liberal opposition. It would be foolish to deny the impact of the street demonstrations and the army's defection in bringing down tsarism. However, the liberals do seem to have been plotting the composition of a Provisional Government many months prior to February 1917.[4] They thus played a far larger role in the monarchy's collapse than that assigned to them by Trotsky. Although Trotsky may have overlooked some aspects of how Nicholas II was removed, he quickly grasped the problems a Provisional Government would face in ruling Russia.

Trotsky argued that the Russian bourgeoisie could not stay in power for long. The fall of the Provisional Government was guaranteed because it could not satisfy the people's demands for peace, bread and land. He noted that a workers' committee, the Soviet, had already been formed to 'protest against liberal attempts to misappropriate the revolution and betray the people'. He called upon the Soviet to wrest power to take Russia out of the war and to resolve the agrarian question. Any other outcome would mean the revolution's failure, since only a 'Revolutionary Workers' Government ... will be able to secure the fate of the revolution and of the working class'. Furthermore, he argued that the establishment of a revolutionary workers' government in Russia would set an example for the German proletariat to follow. Trotsky was so convinced that the whole of Europe was simmering with discontent, that 'the war has turned the whole of Europe into a powder-keg of social revolution', that he thought the prospect of revolution leaping from Russia to Germany real and realisable.

It was in a buoyant mood, therefore, that Trotsky and his family set sail from New York to Russia on 27 March 1917. He could look back on his time in America with a certain amount of satisfaction. He had argued for a revolutionary socialist analysis of contemporary events in print and at a host of meetings. His campaign against social-patriotism had not prevented America entering the war, but Trotsky no doubt realised that his journalism could not do this. He could also look forward to some exciting battles. Leaving New York he anticipated no delays in his passage to Russia. After all, he had in his possession the necessary transit visas from the Russian and British embassies. It was when his boat was awaiting permission to travel beyond Canada, however, that Trotsky and some of his compatriots were removed and taken into detention. British intelligence had sent warnings that Trotsky and his friends were dangerous revolutionaries, funded by German sources. When this information was revealed to be false Trotsky and his family were allowed to continue with their journey. Even had the British wanted to detain Trotsky further, however, it is unclear for how long they could have done so. The Provisional Government was for his release, arguing that it had much worse revolutionaries to deal with at home already. The Canadian officials were also happy to see Trotsky go. They worried about the legality of his detention and in any case Trotsky was proving himself to be something of a troublemaker amongst his fellow inmates, from whom revolutionary proclamations were beginning to be heard.[5]

FROM FEBRUARY TO OCTOBER

Trotsky reached Petrograd in early May 1917, several months after the formation of the so-called Committee of the State Duma or Provisional Government and the simultaneous rebirth of the Soviet of Workers' Deputies, and one month after Lenin had returned in a sealed train provided by the German General Staff. The exact nature of the post-tsarist political order was to be decided by promised nationwide elections to a Constituent Assembly. While preparations for this were being put in place, power was to reside with the Provisional Government supported by the Soviet. These arrangements did not bring any real order to the Russian political scene. Not only were the Provisional Government and the Soviet unable to establish and maintain a harmonious working relationship, both suffered from defects and setbacks. The political situation in the capital thus remained confused. It was in a constant state of flux throughout the coming months. The Provisional Government was to flounder from crisis to crisis, as one set of ministers replaced another. The Petrograd Soviet was racked with debates and disagreements over how far it should back the Provisional Government and whether it should not take a more active role in the governance of the country. And all the while the composition of the Soviet was under constant revision as a consequence of ongoing elections in the factories and in the barracks. The paralysis, or semi-paralysis, of government did nothing to further a resolution of Russia's pressing military, economic and social troubles. Political uncertainty was matched only by social instability.

This period was also to see significant twists in Trotsky's political fortunes. He found an initial political home in a group called the united social-democratic internationalists (or 'Inter-Districters'). It was as a representative of this faction that Trotsky entered the Soviet. As early as July, however, the Inter-Districters joined forces with Bolsheviks. In this way Trotsky became a member of the Bolshevik faction of the RSDLP, a faction with whom he had long had serious disagreements. He was to spend some six weeks, from the end of July to the beginning of September, in prison – arrested during a crackdown on extremists following outbursts of popular discontent against the Provisional Government in the capital in early July. Then, after his release, he played a significant role in the events that led to the Bolshevik faction's overthrow of the Provisional Government and the proclamation of Soviet Power in October 1917.

Trotsky gave his prognoses of the situation in Russia and regarding the war in a series of speeches delivered at sessions of the Soviet, in articles published in the weekly journal of the Inter-District faction *Forward*, whose editorial board Trotsky also joined, and in several pamphlets. There were also frequent reports of Trotsky's activities in the broader socialist press, including Maxim Gorky's *New Life* and the Soviet's bulletin *News*. In his various roles Trotsky had several clear messages to convey.

First, the revolution had changed little if one examined the Provisional Government. This had continued the practice of using the awards and titles of the old order, evident in the fact that the office of prime minister was held by Prince Lvov. Its refusal to radically reform the police and local government was further evidence, for Trotsky, that the Provisional Government was not committed to making Russia a republic. Indeed, the policies pursued by the Provisional Government, from continuing the war to a successful conclusion to protecting the rights of factory and landowners, showed that it was a full member of the capitalist-imperialist club. The ultimate aim of the Provisional Government, according to Trotsky, was to unite the ruling classes to stage a counter-revolutionary coup and restore the monarchy. After all, in February the leaders of the Provisional Government had been reluctant revolutionaries, forced to take power from the tsar under pressure from below. It was therefore a huge mistake for socialists to become ministers in the Provisional Government. Not only would their hands be tied by the capitalist interests dominating the government, making implementation of any measures that smacked of socialism impossible, but they would also be fooling the masses into placing their hopes in the class enemy. Given Trotsky's belief that only a socialist government could solve Russia's international and domestic needs, he condemned the Provisional Government as impotent.

There was one institution that Trotsky perceived as holding out a promise of a new socialist Russia, namely the Soviet of Workers', Soldiers' and Peasants' Deputies. He argued that the Soviet, as the class body of the advanced workers, represented the real moving forces of the Russian Revolution. The revolution could progress only if all power was transferred to the Soviets. The programme of a revolutionary Soviet regime would, he pointed out, be broad and far-reaching. In bare outline it would feature the restructuring of central and local state bodies along democratic Soviet lines; complete democratisation of the army, including the abolition of the death penalty; the arming of a Red Guard; the abolition of private property in land and its redistribution via peasant committees; the nationalisation of all industry and the expropriation of profits to be used in the national interest; a universal obligation to work an eight-hour working day; the establishment of workers' control over all branches of industry; and the publication of secret treaties and a demand for a just peace, including the right of each nation to full self-determination. If a government of this type could be established, Trotsky thought that the Russian people would become self-disciplined and active. He contrasted the failure of the Provisional Government to make the army effective – which had resulted in the failure of the June offensive – with what the army would become once the rank and file had a regime in which it could believe:

> The main reason for the catastrophe at the front is the contradiction between the imperialist policy of the Provisional Government and the

desires of the masses for a rapid and just peace. A new discipline and a genuine enthusiasm in the army can develop only out of the revolution itself, from the heroic resolution of its internal tasks and from its encounters with external obstacles. The people and the army, convinced that the revolution is their revolution, that the government is their government (i.e., a government that will not stop before anything to defend their interests against the exploiters, a government that will not pursue a rapacious foreign policy ...) ... will be enraptured with an indissoluble unity.[6]

In the summer of 1917 Trotsky thus saw two possible futures for Russia. One, represented by the Provisional Government, promised a return to reaction and would condemn Russia to being a colony of the European and American stock exchanges. The alternative, rule by the Soviets, would guarantee a proud and independent socialism. The outcome of this battle would, he pointed out, be determined by the strength and resolution of the socialist-internationalists in Russia, and by the course and tempo of a European-wide revolution. Convinced that the war had turned the continent of Europe into a simmering pot of social upheaval, Trotsky saw an unbreakable connection between the national and international revolution. He painted various scenarios in which a Soviet regime in Russia would be threatened by international capital but saved by the international proletariat. In the event of a delay in the international revolution Trotsky imagined the Soviet regime helping it along through the use of Soviet power, including military force. Whether the revolution developed first in Russia or elsewhere, however, was an open question for Trotsky. It was clear to him, though, that Europe faced a stark choice, 'permanent revolution or permanent war'.

In the midst of a class war for the future fate of Europe, Trotsky thought that his first duty as a Russian internationalist was to convince the Soviet to assume power. The main difficulty here was that when he first entered the Soviet its leadership was content to act as a revolutionary opposition, and occasional support, to the Provisional Government. Finding himself in a minority, Trotsky realised that it might take some time to win a majority of Soviet deputies round to his outlook. Too early an onslaught on power would, he cautioned, only play into the hands of the revolution's enemies. Trotsky was not prepared to countenance forcing the majority in the Soviet to act against its will. The revolution could not be achieved against the Soviet, he argued, but only with its consent. It was an important point of principle for Trotsky that democracy be upheld within the Soviet, and that the minority as well as the majority should not seek to silence its opponents.

His first task was not only to propagate the views of the Inter-District faction to which he belonged, but to broaden its base of support. As a long-time advocate of the unification of internationalist forces, it was quite natural for Trotsky to seek out fellow allies. Having spent several years polemicising against Bolshevik and Menshevik internationalists over a proper response to the war, could common ground be found on the issues facing the Russian Revolution? The outlook for co-operation with the Menshevik-internationalists was bleak. Successive meetings of the Mensheviks, such as the Organisational Committee in March and an All-Russian Conference of Menshevik and United Organisations of the RSDLP in May, had resolved that governmental power should reside with the Provisional Government. The 'objective conditions' for rule by the Soviets were missing, the Mensheviks argued. They also warned that an exclusively Soviet-based government would quickly isolate itself from important social classes, most notably the bourgeois democrats and the peasantry. For Trotsky, in holding such clearly petty-bourgeois prejudices the Mensheviks were ruling themselves out of the unification of internationalists.

There were, however, grounds for optimism for building a fresh alliance with the Bolsheviks. Following the February Revolution the Bolsheviks had been divided between those who thought the revolution had achieved its immediate tasks and those who saw it as but a first step on the path to a socialist upheaval. When Lenin entered the fray in April 1917 he threw his weight behind the more radical Bolsheviks. In documents such as his now famous April Theses Lenin argued that there should be no support for the Provisional Government, that all power should go to the Soviets, and that the Soviets should use this power to end the war and pursue socialist measures, if not as yet full socialism. This was the agenda that the Bolsheviks accepted as the faction's policy at their April Conference.

For Trotsky, the political differences that had once separated him from the Bolsheviks had now lost all significance. Certainly, Trotsky and the Bolsheviks held similar visions of how the Russian Revolution should unfold. Both were determined that the revolution should not sell out to the imperialists. Both emphasised the resolution of state power in the Soviets' favour as being the key task of the moment. Both had to face accusations of being German agents for holding such treacherous views. Even before Trotsky's return to Russia in May 1917 there was sufficient similarity of prognoses between the Inter-Districters and the Bolsheviks for calls for the unification of the two to be welcomed by a March meeting of the Russian Bureau of the (Bolshevik) Central Committee. Trotsky was happy to lend his backing to this unity spirit. The proletariat would also find it easier to reach an internationalist consciousness, he reasoned, if the internationalists spoke from one united organisational home.

There were, however, some obstacles to be overcome before a merger of the Inter-Districters and the Bolsheviks could take place. In particular, Trotsky pointed out, the Bolsheviks had to learn to overcome the 'circle mentality' that had for so long dominated the faction. In Trotsky's view previous factional mentalities could best be healed within a newly founded, open party of internationalists, one that would enjoy freedom of debate and discussion. Although Trotsky did not elaborate on this in great detail, one would imagine that this would entail each side abandoning previous loyalties and transferring them to a separately branded and constituted organisation. This could even have tied in with Lenin's suggestion that the RSDLP should be replaced by a Communist Party. Whatever the organisational form, however, unity negotiations are by their very nature complicated. Unfortunately, the Russia of 1917 provided both sides with neither the time nor the opportunity to engage seriously with the implications of a merger. In the event Trotsky joined the Bolsheviks in a far from satisfactory manner.

The merger took place during the Bolshevik faction's Sixth Party Congress of July–August 1917. This was held in conspiratorial circumstances, and delegates spent much of the time debating issues such as the party's tactics in the forthcoming elections to the Constituent Assembly. The resolution on unity noted that this was impossible with the Menshevik-defencists, but said nothing about the fruits of unity with the Inter-Districters, who had, after all, just joined the faction. There was no recognition of what the merger meant in terms of past, present and future political loyalties. Trotsky was in prison during the

Congress, and exerted no influence over its proceedings. We are therefore denied a possible grand political scene, in which Trotsky would
have explained the significance of his joining Bolshevik ranks. Trotsky
no doubt welcomed the merger and his own election to the Bolshevik
Central Committee. He had, after all, expressed regret about the delays
in bringing the Inter-Districters and the Bolsheviks together. He was
nevertheless very much co-opted into the Bolshevik faction rather than
into a union of equals. The implications of this, however, would become
clear only in the future.

Apart from the frustration he must have felt at being isolated from
the dramas of the capital's politics, Trotsky's period of several months
behind bars was not a pleasant experience. In press reports he exposed a
prison regime far worse than that managed by the tsars. Prisoners were
being held without charge and were denied such basic amenities as the
right to proper daily exercise. The food was appalling. Several of the
inmates had declared hunger strikes in protest. How right Lenin had
been, Trotsky subsequently felt, to have avoided arrest by going into
hiding. Trotsky was freed from the torments of gaol by some of the
more bizarre episodes of the Russian Revolution.

The turmoil of early July had resulted in yet another reshuffle in the
leadership of the Provisional Government and of the General Staff. The
moderate socialist Alexander Kerensky became prime minister. He was
determined to establish a sense of purpose in the government and in
the army. In civilian affairs he could depend upon himself. For the
army he hit upon General Lavr Kornilov, whose military exploits,
charismatic personality and strong views on discipline and duty had
made of him the darling of the right. The Kerensky–Kornilov partnership was, however, to explode in the so-called Kornilov Affair of late
August 1917.

Throughout the first half of August, Kornilov was courted by the
right as Russia's potential saviour. A vain man, Kornilov's ears were
more than receptive to these voices. He believed that the capital and the
war effort were being ruined by revolutionaries from below and trea-
sonous politicians at the top. When Kerensky became convinced, partly
because of mixed lines of communication, that Kornilov was in fact
preparing a coup, he sacked Kornilov as commander-in-chief. Kornilov
responded by ordering loyal troops to take Petrograd. Kornilov's men
were stopped in their tracks by a combination of factors. Workers and

soldiers rallied to the Red Guards to save the revolution. Railwaymen hampered the movement of Kornilov's forces. Finally, when Kornilov's soldiers were told by agitators sent from the capital that they were being used for counter-revolutionary purposes they disobeyed their orders. Kornilov's failure signalled a routing of the right. The groups that had looked to Kornilov to unite them and provide a national saviour were disgraced. The moderate socialists such as Kerensky were hopelessly compromised. Meanwhile the radical left was jubilant. Their success in repulsing Kornilov gave them a tremendous boost.

Even during the months of reaction, July and August, the more radical socialists had been increasingly successful in elections to the Soviet and its district committees. Bolshevik candidates were not the only beneficiaries of these trends. The left wings of other political groupings, including the peasant-based Socialist Revolutionaries and the Mensheviks, gained ground. After the surge in their popularity following the Kornilov events the radicals managed to capture majorities in the Petrograd and Moscow Soviets, as well as in some of the more important regional Soviets. The shift leftwards in the political mood was a reflection of how far Bolshevik and other radical propaganda was meeting popular aspirations. It was against this more congenial background that Trotsky was able to leave prison, freed along with several other comrades on Kerensky's orders as the prime minister sought to pacify the left.

Trotsky's political fortunes soon progressed by leaps and bounds. In May he had been a minority voice in the Soviet, a member of the small Inter-District faction, often struggling to make himself heard. In September he had a majority of delegates behind him and was part of the leading nucleus of the ever more important Bolshevik faction. The task of being the public face of Bolshevism fell to Trotsky. He was the main representative of the faction's viewpoint at events such as the Democratic Conference convoked by the Soviet's Executive Committee on 14 September to debate the issue of state power post-Kornilov. On behalf of the Bolsheviks Trotsky argued against further experiments in coalition government with the old order. Power, he reiterated, should fall solely to the Soviet. With Lenin still in hiding, Trotsky was to all appearances the unofficial head, or at least chief spokesman, of Bolshevism. More importantly, when the Executive Committee of the Petrograd Soviet was reconstituted on 23 September the now Bolshevik-dominated body elected Trotsky as chairman, allowing him to reoccupy the post after an absence of some twelve years.

With the right in disarray and Bolshevik popularity in the Petrograd and regional Soviets, trade unions, factory committees and other social organisations reaching new heights, a debate began in the faction's Central Committee over whether conditions had now matured for the overthrow of the Provisional Government and a declaration of Soviet power to be made. From mid-September onwards, Lenin, who was still in hiding, bombarded his comrades with a series of letters that insisted on an immediate seizure of power. Lenin thought any delay would present Kerensky with an opportunity to abandon Petrograd to the Germans. By this single blow, Lenin warned, the revolution and any hope that the Constituent Assembly would be elected might be wiped out.

Lenin's tactics met with some resistance. Kamenev and Zinoviev rejected them as too risky and based upon false assumptions. Lenin seemed to assume that support for the Bolsheviks had peaked. Any delay would risk sapping this popularity. Kamenev and Zinoviev countered with the view that the movement of the people to Bolshevik banners was only in its first stages. They also found it hard to accept that the momentum for elections to the Constituent Assembly could now be halted. A far surer way for the revolution to advance, according to Kamenev and Zinoviev, was to see the Bolsheviks as powerful members of a broadly based socialist government, one that would be formed after the Constituent Assembly had been elected. Such a government, they argued, would be far better placed to tackle Russia's pressing domestic and international problems. For them, Lenin's path promised a weak and isolated regime, one that would soon be defeated by internal and international foes. Its fall would also signify the collapse of the revolution.

Trotsky's preference was to remain true to the popular slogan of the Russian Revolution – all power to the Soviets. A Second All-Russian Congress of Soviets was scheduled to meet in Petrograd towards the end of October. In Trotsky's view this provided an ideal opportunity for this gathering to approve a transfer of power from the Provisional Government to the Soviets. The main task of the Petrograd and regional Bolsheviks was to ensure that nothing, in particular a counter-revolutionary coup, should be allowed to derail the convocation of the

Second Congress, and that its delegates should as far as possible be Bolshevik in outlook. Trotsky's strategy had several possible advantages. It was rooted in institutions that had popular appeal. Its defensive nature was also likely to appeal to ordinary soldiers and sailors. It also held out a prospect of a more peaceful and gradual accession to power. Lenin's sudden armed siege might, after all, bring bloodshed and failure.

A majority of the key Bolsheviks seem to have been happy to lend their support to Trotsky's policy, and it was according to Trotsky's expectations that the October Revolution actually took place. A key event in the realisation of Trotsky's strategy was the until very recently overlooked Congress of the Soviets of the Northern Region (CSNR), held in Petrograd from 11 to 13 October.[7] If there were to be a genuine threat to Petrograd in the lead-up to the Second Congress, it would most likely come from two sources. Either Kerensky would move troops to the capital or he would abandon it to the Germans. In either event the approaches to the capital would have to be safeguarded. This was one of the main aims of the CSNR. The powerful soviets of the Northern Region, several of which already controlled the administration, including the army, in the areas under their jurisdiction, agreed to form an executive committee. It was Lenin's hope, expressed in letters to Congress participants, that the CSNR would launch an offensive on Petrograd, that it would in fact stage a Bolshevik insurrection. Trotsky ensured that the CSNR evolved according to his policy. Several members of the CSNR's executive committee joined the Petrograd Military-Revolutionary Committee (MRC) that had been established by Trotsky and his associates on 9 October as an armed section of the Petrograd Soviet. In turn, the tactics pursued by the MRC were very much in line with how soviets elsewhere had arranged executive authority, especially over the troops, to fall into their hands.

The key task was to ensure that the capital's troop garrisons should not obey orders unless they carried a seal of approval given by the local soviet's MRC. There are some notable incidents of how this occurred in Petrograd. On 23 October, for example, Trotsky was one of the speakers who convinced the strategically important garrison housed at the capital's Peter and Paul fortress to recognise the authority of the MRC. It was for this act of service that Trotsky was to receive special praise from Stalin on the first anniversary of the October Revolution.[8] This event reveals how the revolution was occurring as Trotsky desired, via a gradual build-up of Soviet authority over key elements in the city's defences. The takeover of the city by the Soviet received an additional impetus from Kerensky's desperate attempt to regain control of events. On 24 October he sanctioned the closure of the Bolshevik printing presses and sent word to military units in Reval (Estonia) to march on the capital. Kerensky was, however, defeated by the very network that Trotsky had helped put in place at the CSNR. The commissars of the MRC began to capture control of Petrograd's main centres of communication, including roads, bridges, the Post Office and so on. Meanwhile the Estonian soviets fulfilled the role assigned to them by the CSNR and ensured that the soldiers remained in their barracks. By the time Lenin reached Bolshevik headquarters around midnight on the evening of 24 October he found that his preferred armed insurrection had been bypassed. The only real, if minor, fighting was to take place over the course of 25 October, as the Provisional Government was arrested following skirmishes around the Winter Palace.

On 25 October Trotsky told first a meeting of the Petrograd Soviet and then the opening session of the Second Congress of Soviets that the Provisional Government had been overthrown. Moderate socialists, fearful of this Bolshevik-inspired move, walked out of the proceedings. Ever the accomplished orator, Trotsky flung a harsh address at the departing delegates, consigning them to the 'dustbin of history'. He thus coined a phrase as memorable, in the context of the Russian Revolution, as Neil Armstrong's 'one small step for a man, one giant leap for mankind' in the first landing on the moon. The immediate impact of the walkout was to hand the Bolsheviks an absolute majority in the Congress of Soviets. The first decrees passed – promising peace and a radical redistribution of land – guaranteed the regime a warm welcome from the people. The Congress then approved the formation of a 'workers' and peasants' government to be called the Council of People's Commissars to rule the country until the convocation of the Constituent Assembly'. Lenin was confirmed as chairman of the Council; Trotsky received the portfolio of foreign affairs. Russia thus had a new Provisional Government, but for how long and with what success were open questions.

4

DEFENDING THE REVOLUTION, 1917–21

On the afternoon of 25 October 1917 Trotsky promised an extraordinary session of the Petrograd Soviet that the government of the Soviet of Soldiers', Workers' and Peasants' Deputies would 'undertake an experiment unique in history'. From 1917 to 1921 the policies of the Council of People's Commissars were indeed bold. They attempted, amidst all the chaos, bloodshed, shortages and confusion of the Russian Civil War (1918–20) to build society anew, on socialist foundations. Every aspect of life was under review. The economy was to be purged of private enterprise, money was to lose all its functions and there were serious debates about how to run a moneyless economy. Religious belief, understood to be a sign of backwardness and oppression, was to be discouraged. Soviet socialism was strictly secular and scientific. It was also to champion the working class. The extension of the franchise in bourgeois societies had normally been restricted by property qualifications. In Soviet Russia, in contrast, the propertied were to be disenfranchised. The workers were to be first in line in the distribution of political, social and economic power. And all of this was to serve as a model for others to emulate. The workers of the world, the Bolsheviks were convinced, would want to duplicate the Soviet experiment in their own countries. Before conquering the world, however, the Bolsheviks were besieged by pressing practical tasks at home, not least cementing the new constitution and overseeing Russia's exit from the war. Trotsky was at the centre of these dramatic events.

THE FIRST MONTHS OF POWER: WAR AND PEACE

In declaring Soviet power the Bolsheviks did not immediately close off other alternatives for Russian political development. Most notably, a long-held promise that free elections to a Constituent Assembly should be the first priority of a post-tsarist administration was kept. Given that Lenin and the Bolsheviks are often portrayed as power-hungry zealots, the election of a competing institution for power may appear strange. Of course, the regime may not have had the option of cancelling the elections. It did not, for example, have complete authority in all regions and districts. Even if a cancellation order would have been obeyed on the ground, however, it is likely that it would have caused a crisis in the party. Certainly, several prominent leaders would have been vehemently opposed. Amongst others, Kamenev and Zinoviev still harboured hopes of a broad coalition government. Annulling the elections would also have thrown the democratic credentials of the recently formed administration immediately into doubt. It may also have galvanised opposition at a time when Soviet power was not secure. Finally, there is little evidence to suggest that the Bolsheviks had a coherent, thought-out vision of the relationship between the Soviets and a Constituent Assembly.

Trotsky was as confused on this issue as any other Bolshevik. In the lead-up to the October Revolution, for example, he extolled the cause of a single source of vested authority. He also simultaneously championed Soviet power as the only guarantee for a Constituent Assembly, without outlining the functions each would fulfil. In a letter of 11 October 1917 to the Bolshevik Central Committee, Kamenev and Zinoviev spoke briefly about a power-sharing arrangement between the Soviets and the Constituent Assembly as the 'mixed type of state institution' the revolution was heading towards.[1] But this amounted to no more than a passing reference. The detail of how this would work in practice was missing. Whatever combination of factors permitted the elections to go ahead, they are a remarkable episode in the early history of the Bolshevik regime.

From a strictly formal point of view the elections, held in November 1917, were a clear success. In the midst of ongoing concerns about war, shortages and land redistribution, interest in the elections was high and turnout good: 70 per cent in the major cities and 80–97 per cent in the villages. More than thirty parties competed for the 44 million votes cast by men and women aged 20 years and over. Most electoral observers agreed that the elections were fair and proper. The Russian people had shown themselves more than capable of organising and conducting democratic elections. From the perspective of a Bolshevik-dominated Council of People's Commissars, the results were slightly problematic.

The general outcome was good for socialism. The vast majority had voted for left parties. The Socialist Revolutionaries topped the polls (40 per cent), followed by the Bolsheviks (23.9 per cent). The party of the liberal propertied classes, the Cadets, received less than 5 per cent. There can be no doubt that the Constituent Assembly would favour measures similar to those advocated by the Bolshevik-dominated Council of People's Commissars. When the Constituent Assembly met in Petrograd in early 1918, for example, its first act was to approve a radical land law indistinguishable from the earlier Soviet land decree. Even before it convened, however, Lenin and his associates decided that they had to rid themselves of the Constituent Assembly. It was dispersed by force on the first day of its opening session.

The official justification for the dispersal order was that in refusing to acknowledge the primacy of Soviet power the Constituent Assembly had revealed itself to be a bourgeois institution. As such it was a lower form of democracy. It was also imperfect in that it was an unreliable barometer of the country's political mood. In particular, the electoral lists used in the elections had not reflected unfolding splits in several of the parties, including the Socialist Revolutionaries and the Mensheviks. Trotsky agreed fully. Although a long-time advocate of a Constituent Assembly, and despite being nominated as a Bolshevik candidate to the Assembly by the Sixth Party Congress of August 1917, Trotsky took no active part in the electoral campaign. Indeed, he warned the Constituent Assembly in advance that it would be effective only insofar as it relied 'on the organised and armed masses'.[2] Under no circumstances would Soviet power permit it to become a tool in the political aspirations of the bourgeoisie. When the Constituent Assembly was elected with a non-Bolshevik majority it was little surprise that he was a fervent advocate of its dispersal.[3] Only the Soviets, he reasoned, could safeguard the revolution, and for Trotsky this took precedence over the niceties of formal democracy.

Some far-reaching consequences have been drawn from the Constituent Assembly's closure. A recent dictionary on the Russian

Revolution claims that it marked 'the one-party monopoly of power, the total state control of all social life and Russia's self-isolation from the rest of the world'.[4] On this view, Trotsky should be condemned for condoning the establishment of a dictatorship. It is best to keep in mind, though, that these drastic consequences were not evident at the time. Expectations that the revolution would spread across Europe were still current and democracy was still alive in the soviets, not yet one-party institutions. It is true, however, that the dispersal order did help to polarise political opinion, contributing to the eventual outbreak of the Russian Civil War (of which more below; see pp. 99–104).

In the period immediately following the successful removal of the Constituent Assembly the Bolsheviks were absorbed above all by the question of peace. Their decree on peace of October 1917, calling for an immediate halt to hostilities and general negotiations for a just peace, had met with a stony response. Trotsky's first act as People's Commissar for Foreign Affairs, the publication of secret treaties, had also had a minimal impact on the conduct of traditional diplomacy. In November 1917 the Bolsheviks communicated their readiness to begin armistice talks with the Central Powers.

The Bolsheviks divided from top to bottom over whether to conclude a separate peace with Germany. There was tremendous openness in debate, which was certainly not confined to the party's Central Committee. Regional, local and district organisations passed conflicting resolutions. Three main points of view fought for supremacy. Lenin, more or less in a minority throughout, was insistent about doing a deal with German imperialism. This was, he argued, the best way to guarantee a breathing space in which the Bolsheviks could consolidate their grip on power. The Left Communists, headed by Nikolai Bukharin, wanted to pursue a revolutionary war as consistent with internationalist principles. They attracted a wide range of support and enjoyed the backing of influential party committees in Moscow, in Petrograd and in other important regions.

Trotsky stood between the two alternatives of 'war' or 'peace'. He doubted whether the regime could muster the forces for the Left Communist policy of a revolutionary war. At the same time, however, he rejected a humble submission to German imperialism. For Trotsky, combining a rejection of war (demobilisation) with a refusal to sign a rapacious peace would offer several advantages. It would satisfy the demands of an honourable internationalist foreign policy. After all, throughout 1917 the Bolsheviks had promised not to conclude separate agreements with imperialists, but to concentrate their efforts on spreading the revolution. Furthermore, in rejecting Germany's harsh terms the Bolsheviks would be exposing the predatory nature of German imperialism. With the facade of the 'war of defence' torn to shreds, the German proletariat might be encouraged to overthrow the German power elite. Finally, it was also unclear how far the German army could advance into Russia's vast expanses. Even if Russia had to concede territory, would not the Bolsheviks become firmer and stronger the more the Germans overextended themselves?

The strengths of Trotsky's option were sufficient to win over a majority of the Central Committee. When, in December 1917, the negotiations opened at Brest-Litovsk, the German army's headquarters on the Eastern Front, the Bolshevik's first aim was to buy time. Talks with the Entente were ongoing. An alliance with Britain and France was still an option, and one that Trotsky pursued very keenly. He had no qualms about utilising inter-imperialist rivalries if the revolution's interests were served. There were to be several rounds of Russo-German negotiations. Trotsky led the Soviet delegation at the key second round of discussions, held through January and February 1918. It was during these sessions that the Bolshevik Central Committee agreed that if a deal with the Entente could not be reached and the Germans insisted on a final answer to their terms, Trotsky had the authority to respond with a declaration of 'no war, no peace'.

There are some picturesque, if unreliable, accounts of Trotsky's duels with the German General Staff over the negotiating tables. Indeed, a battle of wits between the Russian revolutionary and reactionary Hohenzollern statesmen is promising material for any playwright. But Trotsky's energies were not completely taken up with diplomacy. There were sufficient moments of solitude and quiet at Brest-Litovsk for him to pen one of the first histories of the October Revolution. This pamphlet is worth making reference to here, for it is an early example of how the Bolsheviks used history writing for political ends. It was important for the regime to have a concise and popular rebuff to current accusations, particularly from leading German comrades, that theirs was an illegitimate government, a product of an illegal *coup d'état*. In *The History of the Russian Revolution to Brest-Litovsk* Trotsky showed the

Bolshevik assumption of power to have been a purely defensive act, intended to protect the desires of the majority of Russians for rule by the Soviets. Furthermore, the Bolsheviks had not wanted to rule alone, but had been forced to do so by Menshevik and Socialist Revolutionary intransigence in power-sharing negotiations. Lenin was delighted with Trotsky's history, for it served propaganda needs perfectly. Trotsky's pamphlet was quickly translated into all the major European languages.[5] Yet, while Trotsky displayed his considerable talents as historian and publicist, he was less successful in drawing out the peace negotiations. He duly announced 'no war, no peace' to a German team now demanding a final response to their terms. The Germans, in turn, declared their intention to resume hostilities.

When the Germans restarted their offensive on Russia Trotsky's 'no war, no peace' strategy was not given the opportunity to prove itself. At the first signs of rapid German advances Trotsky lost his nerve. He swung his vote behind Lenin's demands for an immediate capitulation to the now harsher German terms. Even though Trotsky felt that it was wrong to give in to German imperialism, he admitted that he could not pursue a policy that Lenin and half of the Central Committee opposed. He was clearly incapable of claiming for himself the mantle of leader of the Bolsheviks, especially if he was challenging Lenin.

Historians have generally agreed that Trotsky suffered a tremendous defeat when a separate peace with Germany was signed in early March 1918. It is true that Trotsky's resignation from the Foreign Commissariat was not tendered in the best of circumstances. However, the harsh assessment of his performance in the dramas surrounding Brest-Litovsk relies far too much on the power of hindsight. It overlooks, for instance, how fraught matters really were and the difficulty of trying to respond to so many conflicting pressures. There was strong discontent with the peace. If Lenin is often presented as the master of *Realpolitik* during the conflict over Brest-Litovsk, this was not so obvious at the time.

The German communist Rosa Luxemburg, for example, was a particularly vehement critic of the peace. The German revolution that the Bolsheviks wanted so much was henceforth, she argued, much less likely following the triumph of the German bourgeoisie at Brest-Litovsk. Furthermore, she pointed out that the counter-revolution had gained strength in Russia following the establishment of puppet anti-Bolshevik regimes in the Ukraine and elsewhere. The Bolsheviks' sole allies, the Left Socialist Revolutionaries, were so opposed to the treaty that they resigned from the government in protest, and they began a terror campaign that resulted in the assassination of the German ambassador in Moscow and a near-successful attempt on Lenin's life. The final folly of Brest-Litovsk identified by Luxemburg is that the Entente would not watch idly from the sidelines while Germany overran Russia. Rather than gaining for the revolution a respite à la Lenin, for Luxemburg the peace treaty had dragged Russia further into conflict and exposed the revolution to greater danger.[6]

The treaty's opponents within Russia shared much of Luxemburg's analysis. For the Left Communists, for instance, Brest-Litovsk was the ultimate betrayal of the sacred principle of internationalism. There was also a widely held belief that the peace would not hold; that Germany, for example, was planning future blows. The determination to resist a German invasion is evident from an upsurge in support for pro-war Menshevik and Socialist-Revolutionary candidates in Soviet elections over the spring and early summer of 1918. With many newly elected deputies committed to replacing the current administration, the Bolsheviks' hold on power was looking increasingly tenuous.

Whatever the rights and wrongs of the positions adopted during the debates over Brest-Litovsk within the Bolshevik camp, the mounting uncertainties and dangers that followed its stormy reception in Russia brought the issue of the Bolsheviks' military capabilities (or lack of them) to the forefront of the party's attention. It is a sign of the esteem in which Trotsky continued to be held that the task of organising the armed defence of the revolution fell to him.

TROTSKY IN THE RUSSIAN CIVIL WAR

The battle lines of the Civil War were fought between three main forces. The Red Army sought to maintain Lenin's government in power and promised to defend the revolution's radical social programme. The Whites, led by the officers of the former tsarist army, wanted to uphold the rights formerly enjoyed by the land- and factory owners, largely by establishing military dictatorships. Finally, there were several brands of non-Bolshevik socialist participants, from Mensheviks to Anarchists and Socialist Revolutionaries, that demanded a more democratic, pluralistic form of socialism, albeit one that would support the gains made by workers and peasants following the February Revolution. These groups were often fragmented and did not fight each other simultaneously. There were divided loyalties. For a 'democratic socialist', for example, it may have been better on occasion to support Red against White. The White cause, which was hostile to all variants of socialism, could appear to be the greater evil. Indeed, a recent history of the Civil War has claimed that when the White armies entered the fray, from the autumn of 1918 onwards, the non-Bolshevik socialists (or 'Greens' in its terminology) largely threw their weight behind the Reds.[7] The exact course of the battles of the Civil War, with the various twists in fate and fortune, are too complicated to go into in any detail. There are several excellent studies for those interested in the military history of this period.[8] It is sufficient here to note that by 1920 it was clear that the Reds had won. The Whites were in disarray, and the country too exhausted to contemplate an all-out democratic socialist assault on the Reds.

It is Trotsky's exploits as Commissar of War in the Russian Civil War that define his image as a hero of the revolution. An army had to be organised, supplied and led effectively. Trotsky has received praise for excelling in each of these roles. It is not unusual for the Red victory to be put down to Trotsky's talents.[9] As the conflict unfolded, however, it was not always evident to his contemporaries that Trotsky was an impeccable military tactician. There has also been a re-evaluation of Trotsky's role in the Civil War, as part of a broader rethinking of the period.

Trotsky spent most of the Civil War on board a special train. Staffed by an incredibly dedicated crew, the train grew in size as it faced new tasks and challenges.[10] All told, it traversed as much as 100,000 miles from its first journey in August 1918 to the last battles of the Civil War. As the train rushed from front to front it served several functions. It printed and distributed propaganda and educational literature. It carried supplies, including a selection of items to be used as awards for outstanding behaviour at the front. Most of all, however, it carried Trotsky. As Commissar for War his main function was to be the public face of the Red Army, to provide it with an inspiring figurehead. It was to Trotsky that the Red soldiers swore their oath of loyalty. As a leader Trotsky displayed a willingness to appear personally on the front line –

exposing himself to several risks – that is rare for a man of his stature. He made speeches to the troops, rallying and encouraging, rewarding and scolding. He was constantly writing articles about the importance of ongoing battles through a newspaper written and printed en route. Finally, Trotsky was always prepared to take control of the conduct of the war and to do battle. There is much testimony to his and his crew's commitment to the Red cause, and much evidence of personal bravery to be admired. As a tactician and war commander, he showed a daring that often made a crucial difference. In the fight for Petrograd of late 1919, for example, it was his inspired counterattack that drove the White general Yudenich back into Estonia.[11]

As well as his daring and effective work as a morale booster and combatant, Trotsky must also be given credit for the way in which he organised the Red Army as a fighting force. Against much resistance within the party, he insisted that the Red Army use a centralised command structure, and that it draw upon existing expertise through the appointment of officers who had previously served in the tsarist army. Of course Trotsky was not alone in promoting the shake-up of the Red Army along these lines. It has been pointed out, for example, that a trusted tsarist officer, General M.D. Bonch-Bruevich, actually oversaw the details of the reorganisation of the Red Army and was personally responsible for winning over some of his colleagues to the Red cause. For these services 'Bonch was even more important than Trotsky in laying the foundations of the Red Army'.[12] However, Bonch may not have been as effective had he not had a powerful political ally in Trotsky.

An aspect of Trotsky's Civil War activities that has generated particular interest is the extent to which he advocated terror as an instrument of war. There can be no doubt that Trotsky favoured repressive measures if he thought the situation merited them. Well before the proclamation of Soviet power, he had the honesty to write that the revolution's victory would depend upon a willingness to shed blood. In the actual circumstances of the Russian Civil War there was no shortage of the necessary justification. Despite Trotsky's efforts to create a disciplined, well-supplied and effective fighting force, the Red Army suffered from high rates of desertion and a constant shortage of arms and munitions. The troops it was able to deploy in battle were always a tiny fraction of what grew into a very large army of several millions by 1920. With the pressure to keep every soldier in battle exceptionally high, it is understandable that Trotsky ordered the shooting of every tenth man of units refusing to fight.[13] The harsh measures adopted by Trotsky and the Red leadership (against civilian as well as military foes) may have been condemned by Western democracies, but on balance repression helped maintain Soviet power. German comrades, from Karl Kautsky to Rosa Luxemburg, were horrified and protested against the Bolsheviks' disregard for 'humanity and democracy'. Trotsky penned a robust defence of terror in his classic work of 1920, *Terrorism and Communism*. 'A revolution', he wrote, 'is not decided by votes ... repression [is] the necessary means of breaking the will of the opposing side'.[14] In this context it is worth pointing out, however, that Trotsky was also capable of leniency. For instance, he urged that ordinary White deserters be treated with understanding.

It is perfectly fair, then, that Trotsky was hailed as one of the Red heroes of the Civil War. In the party literature of the time it was he, above all, who epitomised the fighting spirit of Russian communism. A review of the (1922) re-publication of Trotsky's book *1905*, for example, highlighted the younger Trotsky's understanding of class warfare, which subsequently made him 'such an amazing organiser of the Red Army, recognised even by our enemies'.[15] Such praise does not, however, justify turning Trotsky into the main actor of the Civil War era. There were instances in which his forecasts were mistaken and his strategic advice misplaced. In the spring of 1919, for instance, Trotsky underestimated the threat the White forces led by Denikin posed in the south.[16] Nor was Trotsky always the chief tactician. Given that he was often en route, much depended on the local commanders, several of whom were exceptionally able. Perhaps military men like Antonov-Ovsenko, Kamenev, Tukhachevsky and Vatsetis should be praised as the real conquerors, rather than the 'politicals' such as Trotsky, Lenin or Stalin.

Whatever the quality of Trotsky's leadership, one can throw doubt on its significance by arguing that the fundamental causes of the Red victory lay elsewhere. Geoffrey Swain, for example, has claimed recently that from the very outset of their campaigns the Whites 'had no chance of success'.[17] Indeed, the weaknesses suffered by the Whites were many, including political divisions, uncoordinated offensives, irregular external backing and social policies that did not attract popular support. When one takes into account the strengths of the area controlled by the Reds (population, the supplies inherited from the tsarist regime, communication networks, etc.) and the anti-White intervention at critical moments from the Green armies, it would perhaps have been a miracle had the Reds lost. In this context Trotsky's war role may not have been so decisive, however heroic the propaganda of the time may have portrayed it as being. Certainly an eminent historian of the Civil War considers White failings to have been just as significant as Trotsky's military prowess in the (aforementioned) successful defence of Petrograd from Yudenich's attack.[18] The Harvard historian Richard Pipes goes even further in dismissing Trotsky's significance. His summary account of why the Reds won the Civil War, perhaps unfairly, mentions Trotsky not once.[19]

It is also important to note the damage inflicted on Trotsky's political influence in the Communist Party during the Civil War. It would have been remarkable indeed if the Bolshevik General Staff had not disputed appointments and strategy. Such conflicts did occur, and their outcomes were not always in Trotsky's favour. Resentment in the party against Trotsky's reliance on tsarist officers and his promotion of orthodox discipline, in which the military personnel had priority over party officials, ran deep. Stalin was not alone in suspecting the tsarist officers of sabotage. Trotsky was accused of being overly harsh on party members, blaming them rather than the specialists when military operations did not go according to plan. The feeling was widespread that Trotsky was acting independently of, or even against, the party, perhaps with the intention of staging a Bonapartist coup. Trotsky's military policy met with strong resistance at the Eighth Party Congress in the spring of 1919, from which he was absent. The main bones of contention were the employment of military specialists and the authoritarian policies of the military leadership. Alternative resolutions demanding more democratic control in the army and a partisan style of warfare received much support. Trotsky's recommendations survived, but only after some modifications were introduced. The slump in Trotsky's popularity is clear from the fact that only one-sixth of the several hundred delegates voted for his re-election to the Central Committee. In the months following the Eighth Party Congress Trotsky was on the defensive.

In the summer of 1919, for example, Colonel Vatsetis, promoted by Trotsky to be main commander-in-chief, was under attack following setbacks on the Eastern Front against the White admiral Kolchak. At a meeting of the Central Committee in early July Vatsetis, who enjoyed

Trotsky's backing, was replaced by Colonel Kamenev, who did not. Insult was added to injury when personnel changes at the Military Council of the Republic resulted in the demotion of appointments originally made by Trotsky. He showed his anger by storming out of the Central Committee and resigning as Commissar of War. The resignation was refused, but Trotsky's authority was visibly undermined.

Overall, Trotsky's relations with key members of the Central Committee were worsened by the vicissitudes of the Civil War. Trotsky accumulated some powerful foes. Most notably, his relations with Stalin were soured in the Civil War's early battles. Stalin had established his command centre in Tsaritsyn. Here he pursued an active policy opposed to the principles of military engagement advocated by Trotsky.[20] A series of Red defeats, despite numerical superiority, brought Trotsky into the fray. In September 1918 he was successful in having Stalin recalled to Moscow. Although the rivalry between the men mainly concerned different military principles, especially Stalin's opposition to the use of tsarist officers, there was also an element of personal hostility involved. Subsequent attempts by Lenin to smooth relations between Trotsky and Stalin failed. In an emerging one-party state and an ever more centralised Communist Party, no good was served to Trotsky's future political fortunes by his increasing isolation from other top leaders. A close study of Bolshevik military policy in the Civil War concludes that, 'for his contribution to the creation of the Soviet armed forces, Trotskii was rewarded with the distrust and hatred of a great many of his party comrades'.[21] This sense of isolation was magnified by the fate of Trotsky's proposals on how to set Russia's war-torn economy to rights.

BUILDING A SOCIALIST ECONOMY

In the economic sphere the Bolsheviks inherited an economy disrupted by war and revolution. These problems were to be magnified by the Civil War. There was a huge decline in industrial and agricultural output. The towns were depopulated as citizens fled hunger, disease and the military draft. By force of circumstance as much as ideological conviction, the Bolsheviks sought as far as possible to control production and distribution. Supplies, after all, had to be prioritised.

In the early months of 1920 Trotsky began to turn his attention away from military matters and focus more upon the tasks of economic construction in Russia. He was one of several commentators to note the negative impact of Bolshevik food policy. The peasants had adopted several strategies to circumvent the state requisition of surplus stocks. Cultivation of land was reduced so that it met subsistence needs only. Excess cattle were slaughtered in preference to their being seized by the state. Produce was sold illegally on the black market for higher prices. In proposals put to the Central Committee in February 1920 Trotsky warned that 'the food resources of the country are threatened with exhaustion, and no improvement in the requisitioning apparatus will be able to remedy this fact'.[22] He advised his comrades to ease pressure on the peasants in the grain surplus-producing areas. Here incentives to produce and sell to the state would follow the introduction of a progressive tax and better payments for grain. Although Trotsky's memorandum was rejected and no further action taken, he subsequently claimed great significance for his proposals, seeing in them the essence of the New Economic Policy adopted in March 1921 (of which more below; see pp. 113–16). Here, however, Trotsky was claiming far too much credit. His memorandum of February 1920 suggested only a modification of the agrarian policy of war communism, whose ultimate objectives of requisitioning and collectivisation he clearly supported. Outside Siberia, the Don and the Ukraine, for example, his memorandum urged the extension of requisitioning and the speeding-up of the introduction of collectivisation.

In their famous tract *The Communist Manifesto* (1848) Marx and Engels had outlined the eight-point programme of a socialist regime. This included the obligation of all to work, with each receiving back from the community an equivalent of what they put in, and the formation of Labour Armies for agriculture and industry. In December 1919 Trotsky was a driving force behind the establishment of Labour Armies for economic construction. The intention was to put detachments of soldiers no longer needed for army work into the domestic economy, then suffering from acute shortages of labour – and of skilled labour in particular. This early example of a hoped-for release of resources from a 'defence burden' was fraught with organisational difficulties. Lists would have to be drawn up of which army personnel had which skills, and where they could best be transferred. There was likely to be institutional rivalry. The army command would be reluctant to lose control of skilled soldiers, and local and central ministries would make conflicting assessments of what to prioritise. These obstacles notwithstanding, after an exchange of ideas with the army command of the Third Army on the Eastern Front, in January 1920 Trotsky announced that the Third Army was to be disbanded and transformed into the First Revolutionary Labour Army. As well as outlining the range of tasks that the Labour Army would carry out, from grain requisitioning to lumbering to repair work in the factories, Trotsky highlighted the role of discipline and communist enthusiasm. The whole operation was to be run on a centralised and strict basis, with rewards for the conscientious and punishments for the slack. The following instruction (16 out of 25) to the First Labour Army gives a flavour of Trotsky's vision of a socialist economy:

> Commanders and commissars are to forward to their superiors precise operational labour reports, stating the quantity of grain collected, loaded and transported, the number of cubic meters of firewood felled and cut up, and all other work. These operational reports are to be published in the daily newspaper of the First Labour Army, naming exactly each separate labour unit, so that the most diligent and zealous regiments shall be accorded the respect which they have earned, while other more sloppy or lazy units may strive to catch up with the best ones.[23]

Trotsky's commitment to the anti-market philosophy of war communism became even more apparent following his appointment in March 1920 as Commissar of Transport. The transport system was both vital to the recovery of the Russian economy and in a parlous condition. When Trotsky took over responsibility for the railways, locomotive production was less than 15 per cent of its 1913 level and wagon output less than 5 per cent. Trotsky responded with a series of measures. Above all, socialist central planning had to set sensible and achievable targets. Here Trotsky placed particular emphasis upon 'Order No. 1042' of May 1920. This outlined a repair plan for Soviet locomotives. From only 40 per cent of the locomotive stock being fit for operation in 1920, by 1 January 1925 this was to be increased to 80 per cent. If the modest improvements envisaged were to be attained, however, Trotsky stressed that bad practices in the railway industry had to be overcome. Bureaucratic indifference and laziness of the sort that had delayed one of Trotsky's journeys by nineteen hours because snow had not been cleared

from the tracks had to be remedied. In particular, the disease of absenteeism had to be purged from the workforce, partly by harsh punishments and partly by a broad propaganda campaign utilising theatre and
cinema as well as newspapers.

The railways should adopt measures that had proven their worth in
the military sphere, such as strict discipline ('the militarisation of body
and soul') and the employment of specialists. Given the centrality of
mending the railways to the healthy operation of the rest of the economy (the transport of food, supplies, raw materials, etc.), Trotsky
demanded that the party's and the nation's best workers be transferred
to work on the railways. He also called upon the workers to prepare
themselves for sacrifices. Not only would they not see an immediate
improvement in their everyday standard of living, but they should be
ready to undertake unpaid labour on communist Saturdays and Sundays.
Finally, the trade unions had to rid themselves of bourgeois prejudices
typical of their functions in capitalism. Trotsky drew a distinction
between trade unions under capitalism, in which there was no choice
but to battle for improvements in workers' living conditions against the
objections of employers and the state, and trade unions in a communist
workers' state, in which the very notion of a 'class struggle of the unions
with the state is senseless'. In a socialist planned economy characterised
by social ownership it was in the interests of all that production
increase. It was from this assumption that Trotsky saw the proper role of
trade unions changing from defending workers' employment rights to
promoting production. Trade unions should, he argued, become 'unions
for production'. They would, amongst other tasks, encourage workers to
reach higher levels of productivity, educate the workforce to view each
problem from the perspective of increasing output, help the administration to organise production better, and so on. Trotsky's ultimate goal for
the trade unions was a 'complete merger with the administrative apparatus, i.e., the formation of a single body, responsible in equal measure
for the administrative-technical needs of transport as well as the all-
round interests of its workers'.[24]

There is some evidence that the situation on the railways did
improve under Trotsky's guidance. Absenteeism became less prevalent,
repair targets were met and output increased. The number of opera-
tional trains went up from 4,000 to 7,500 between March and June
1920. Recent work has questioned, however, how much praise for these

improvements can be heaped upon Trotsky. More important than Trotsky's management in boosting the amount of healthy trains, perhaps, was the railway stock captured from the now defeated Whites.[25] Furthermore, the improvements of the spring and summer of 1920 were soon replaced by the transport difficulties evident in the winter of 1920. As well as being of dubious economic merit, Trotsky's economic policies almost immediately unleashed a furore of protest.

Railway workers, particularly the most skilled, resented the centralised and draconian industrial order introduced by Trotsky. Labour protest across the railway network sought to protect traditional shop-floor culture as well as to defend living standards at a time of shortages. In response to Trotsky's calls for revolutionary enthusiasm and a willingness to undertake unpaid overtime, at least one worker wrote to the railway newspaper *The Whistle* saying 'feed us first and then demand work'.[26] In the leading economic journal, *Economic Life*, several Soviet economists threw Trotsky's transport plans, including his much-loved 'Order No. 1042', into doubt. Some questioned the wisdom of prioritising transport. Others were critical of the plans produced by Trotsky's department, pointing out imbalances and probable falsification of statistical returns. A third source of hostility to Trotsky's economic policies suspected him of harbouring political ambitions. In the early summer of 1920, for example, the still active Menshevik leader Martov called Trotsky a potential 'economic dictator'. Central Committee members who suspected that Trotsky would like to use his military base to stage a Bonapartist coup no doubt shared this worry.

By the summer of 1920 there was already a broad-based reaction against Trotsky's militarisation of the railways. Of course, Trotsky did not remain silent. He upheld the integrity and coherence of his transport plans in a long article published in the official daily newspaper *Truth*. Protesting workers were offered a mixture of limited concessions and repression. It was opposition from the trade unions, however, that was to lead to Trotsky's downfall as a leading force in Bolshevik economic strategy.[27]

Discontent in the trade unions with the role assigned to them by Trotsky's militarisation orders rumbled in the background throughout 1920. It exploded into a full-scale party crisis from November 1920 onwards. Leading trade unionists, such as M.P. Tomsky, joined forces with fellow prominent members of the Central Committee, most notably Zinoviev, in an open assault. They accused Trotsky of riding roughshod over the trade unions, intending to eliminate them as institutions protecting the interests of workers. They linked his practice of the appointment of industrial officials over election from below to the growth of red tape and bureaucracy. The inevitable outcome of Trotsky's approach to the trade unions, they claimed, would be the alienation of the workers from the administration, a split between the party and the trade unions, and the growth of underground trade unions, most likely organised by Menshevik and Socialist Revolutionary agitators. Tomsky and Zinoviev called for the trade unions to be kept separate from the state, for their traditional functions to be maintained and for an extension of workers' democracy in the workplace.

Trotsky clashed with his critics at a series of meetings, from sessions of the Central Committee to debate forums attended by several thousand party members. At these events rhetoric could take precedence over serious discussion, with some insults aired in heated exchanges. During a debate held at the Bolshoi Theatre on 30 December 1920, for example, Trotsky called Zinoviev 'an apologist, defender, advocate and proponent of what is purely unproductive'. For Trotsky, the workers had to learn how to become producers, and the best way to ensure this was to merge the trade unions into the state. Indeed, at this time Trotsky saw the enlargement of the state and its functions as a natural part of the transition to communism. Lenin became less and less impressed with Trotsky's arguments and with his behaviour. He called him to book for insulting comrades, and blamed him for creating platforms and factions that threatened a split in the party. Although Lenin was keen not to censure Trotsky fully and openly, he sided with his opponents in agreeing that even in a workers' state the trade unions had to be independent so that they could defend the workers from their state. Lenin also gave prominence to the trade unions as 'schools of communism', a notion ridiculed by Trotsky for lacking a 'productionist perspective'.

The trade union debates of January to March 1921 resulted in a series of defeats for Trotsky. Regional party committees voted against his theses. Even those that had a majority of Trotskyists did not support him and were henceforth lost to his opponents. More seriously still, at the Tenth Party Congress of March 1921 Lenin ensured that advocates of Trotsky's line on the trade unions were demoted from important party bodies such as the Secretariat and that they would be in a minority on the Central Committee. The Congress devoted only one day to discussing rival motions on the trade unions and overwhelmingly backed the motion sponsored by Lenin. This not only marked the end of the militarisation of industry favoured by Trotsky, but was another indication of Trotsky's problematic relationship with a party he had only recently joined. Although Trotsky remained a prominent Bolshevik, his authority had once again been undermined. In the elections to the Central Committee his popularity showed little sign of recovering from the depths of 1919. He finished 'a humiliating tenth'.[28]

THE INTERNATIONAL REVOLUTION

The early Bolshevik regime shared Trotsky's enthusiasm for the cause of international proletarian revolution. There was a broad consensus in favour of Trotsky's long-held belief that a socialist government in Russia would depend for its success on the revolution spreading westwards. In order to encourage the outbreak of further revolutions, the Bolsheviks favoured the formation of communist parties in Western Europe and the joining together of these parties in a Third International. These processes were interconnected. The Third International, founded in March 1919 in Moscow, took a close interest in the creation of communist parties. In the case of the Communist Party of Great Britain, for example, it was on Moscow's insistence that Scottish suggestions that there should be a distinct Communist Party of Scotland were overruled.

It is somewhat ironic that the theoretician of world revolution, Trotsky, consumed with domestic tasks, performed largely decorative functions only in the first years of the Third International. At the First Congress, for example, he delivered a brief report on the Red Army, but otherwise would have chiefly been remembered for reading out the Manifesto of the Communist International. At the next year's gathering, apart from a brief intervention on the nature and functions of a communist party, his main speech was made at the Second Congress's closing rally. That Trotsky did not assume significant organisational roles in establishing the Third International is understandable given his responsibilities elsewhere. It did mean, however, that there would be limits to how much influence he would be able to exert over what was to become an important element of Soviet foreign policy. This was especially true as one of the driving forces of the Third International and its first chairman, Zinoviev, was hardly an ally in domestic matters.

Free of burdensome bureaucratic obligations to the Third International, Trotsky does not seem to have been a particularly sagacious commentator on the likely spread of the proletarian revolution. His prognoses were consistently over-optimistic. In January 1919, for example, he thought that the recent murder of Rosa Luxemburg during communist-led demonstrations in Berlin signalled the beginning of Germany's 'July Days', or the first, unsuccessful, movement of the revolution towards its culmination. He highlighted, however, one notable variation. Russia's 'July Days' had taken five months to emerge after the overthrow of the monarchy; in Germany they arose only two months after the fall of Wilhelm II. Trotsky used this comparison as evidence that Germany's 'October' was soon at hand. We now know how false this prediction was. Indeed, there were crucial differences between Russia in 1917 and Germany in 1919. The German Communist Party was much smaller and less significant in comparison to the centre parties, most notably the Socialist Party (SPD). Moreover, the pro-constitutional SPD was quite willing to employ the armed power of the state to crush communist uprisings. No doubt the Entente would have been far more proactive in defending German capitalism from a communist coup, especially when the Red Army was powerless to intervene in Central Europe. For these and other reasons it is highly unlikely that a German revolution could have unfolded along the lines desired by Trotsky.

Disappointed by reversals in the West, Trotsky was then too enthusiastic about the prospects for revolution in Asia. Following Red Army successes in the Urals in August 1919, for instance, he advised the Central Committee to draw up plans for a revolutionary assault on the East. No doubt the British Empire would have suffered a blow if India had turned communist in 1919–20, but there was little chance of Trotsky's new strategy for exporting the revolution coming to fruition. Apart from inhospitable terrain that would make the movement of any army tortuous, there was little sympathy for Bolshevism in Asian society. Moscow found itself mired in cultural difficulties in maintaining its power in Soviet Central Asia, without trying to magnify these problems by trying to push Bolshevism into India.

By the summer of 1920, when Trotsky had largely abandoned his hopes of further colonial revolutions as an immediate prospect, the

Russian Communist Party was debating the possible outbreak of a revolution in Poland as a consequence of the ongoing Soviet–Polish War. The conflict's origins lay in the fact that the Russo–Polish border had not been resolved by the post-war settlement. The British foreign minister had proposed the so-called 'Curzon line', but this fell short of Polish nationalist ambitions. In the spring of 1920 the Polish nationalist leader Pilsudski decided to attain his territorial objectives by force. For Trotsky, several factors had led to the invasion by Poland.[29] It was, above all, a means of settling discontent in Poland. Its gentry and peasantry were promised land, while the troublesome advanced workers would be crushed by the humiliation of Soviet Russia. Finally, France was encouraging Poland to declare war on Russia, hoping to avenge the Bolsheviks' refusal to recognise the debts run up under the tsars.

Trotsky accepted that the Polish army would not be easy to defeat, but he thought that strict discipline and the application of military science would be sufficient to deal a decisive blow to 'robber Polish gentry nationalism'. In this event, the Polish working class would be encouraged to stage its own revolution. If this was successful, Trotsky promised a socialist Poland territorial concessions on its eastern frontier that a nationalist Poland could only dream of. Throughout the campaign against Poland, however, he stressed that the first goal of Soviet Russia was peace. Under no circumstances would Russia impose a harsh peace settlement upon Poland.

The Soviet–Polish war was brief, with fortune favouring first the Polish, then the Soviet, and finally the Polish forces. At the height of Soviet successes, Lenin confidently awaited the fall of Warsaw to the Red Army. Trotsky was more cautious than this behind the scenes, but even he was furious with the extent of the Red rout when it came. For this, he blamed mainly Stalin's poor military leadership, adding one more bone of contention between them. By the Treaty of Riga, which ended the conflict, Soviet Russia had to concede yet more of its territory. Trotsky did his best to put an optimistic gloss on what he admitted to be 'very burdensome conditions'. The country had at last achieved peace, and the border with Poland was not as far into Soviet territory as the Polish army had at one point reached. But this attempt at consolation must have given the minimum of comfort. The resistance of the Polish workers to Soviet propaganda, despite the best efforts of Trotsky's journalism, illustrated the difficulty of exporting Soviet communism. Trotsky had long pointed out that an isolated revolution would face certain defeat, for it would be incapable of survival in inhospitable Russian conditions. Could the widespread social, economic and political discontent of the winter of 1920–1 be a sign that the Bolshevik experiment was about to end in failure?

CIVIL UNREST AND THE ADOPTION OF THE NEW ECONOMIC POLICY

With the Civil War and the conflict with Poland over, an exhausted Soviet people expressed their disappointments with the turmoil of the previous three years. There were widespread, if isolated, pockets of peasant rebellion. Although varying in scale and level of organisation, peasant protest was directed firmly against communist management of the countryside. The forced requisitioning of grain offended peasant perceptions of a moral economy, in which produce should belong to the producers. Furthermore, attempts by the Bolsheviks to win allies in the villages by relying on 'class struggle in the countryside' (i.e. poor peasants would support an attack on richer or 'kulak' peasants) were rejected by the peasants en masse. With the threat of a White restoration receding, from the autumn of 1920 onwards the peasants were more and more willing actively to resist communist governance. The largest-scale and most famous peasant rebellions include the uprisings in the Tambov province and the so-called Makhno movement in the Ukraine. Communist Party membership plummeted to new depths in the villages. There was a clear crisis of confidence in the regime in rural Russia.

Social and economic discontent with the policies of war communism was not confined to the countryside. In the crucial urban constituencies ordinary workers and soldiers took to the streets. Quite simply, there was not enough bread, insufficient work of good quality with good prospects, and a shortage of adequate rewards. Added to a harsh industrial and political order that allowed the workers limited opportunities to voice their grievances, the workers now felt that they had been betrayed by the revolution. Anti-government proclamations increasingly featured political as well as economic demands. For many commentators, the crisis in the urban landscape peaked in the spring of

1921 when sailors at the naval base of Kronstadt supported the protests staged by the Petrograd workers. The revolution's capital was ablaze with anti-Bolshevik feeling. Resolutions passed by the Kronstadt sailors offer particularly damning critiques of Bolshevik rule circa 1921. They highlight a society in which the most basic civil rights were absent. Moreover, the Kronstadters could not easily be presented as counter-revolutionary capitalists. They wanted a multi-party socialist democracy, with freedom of speech and of the press restricted to 'workers … peasants … Anarchists … and left socialist parties'.

If opposition from within society was not enough, the concerns raised by peasants, workers and sailors were reflected in political platforms within the Communist Party. The critiques put forward by groupings such as the Democratic Centralists and the Workers' Opposition were from a left-wing perspective. Supported by leading communists, including the much-admired Alexander Kollantai, they pointed out that the revolution was being taken over by a bureaucratic elite. This bureaucracy was acting in an anti-revolutionary fashion in several respects. It was ruling over the workers. It was creating special privileges for itself, privileges it wanted to defend from a hungry society. For Kollantai, if the revolution was to return to its guiding principles there had to be greater democracy in the party and in society, the workers had to be granted their full democratic rights, with complete accountability to the people for all bureaucrats and the party's central institutions.

The broad-based oppositions of the winter of 1920–1 are mainly presented as the 'conscience of the revolution', a sign that the promises of 1917 had now been betrayed. The government, headed by Lenin, presumably had an opportunity to reach out to the masses, to try to reconcile the gulf that had opened up between the regime and the society. Indeed the government did make concessions, some of them significant. In the countryside, for example, 'class struggle' was abandoned with the abolition of committees of poor peasants. More importantly, in the spring of 1921 food requisitioning was ended and free trade in grain was re-established. For one historian, at least, these concessions were so great that the peasants had actually 'won on the internal front of the civil war'.[30] The workers were promised better bread rations, and there was to be an overhaul in the urban economy, with greater opportunities for private enterprise in small-scale workshops.

The regime did not run away from the necessity of answering genuine economic grievances. It was far more reluctant, however, to countenance greater democratisation. Indeed, the government was unwilling to grant political protest the status of being reasonable. There was a harsh clampdown on opposition. The army was used to crush rebellion, unfavourable election results were quashed and camps were established to house political enemies. Trotsky did not shirk from these repressive measures, as is evident from his response to the Kronstadt uprising. Rather than accept that the Kronstadt mutineers had legitimate grounds for complaint, Trotsky linked the revolt at the naval base to extraneous causes. Above all, foreign counter-revolutionary agents had manufactured an anti-government revolt in the expectation that this would set Russia alight and bring down Soviet power. The evidence for this was to hand, for Trotsky, in how foreign stock markets rose when the rebellion first took off. In their counter-revolutionary machinations the agents of world imperialism were aided, according to Trotsky, by a quite fortuitous fact. The best sons of the Revolution of 1917 had been posted elsewhere, and replaced by 'casual elements ... who looked on their service as a temporary job and who had mostly played no part in the revolutionary struggle'.[31] Historical studies of the composition of the naval base's personnel have thrown doubt on Trotsky's claims, which undoubtedly bore the stamp of propaganda. The arguments adopted by Trotsky, coupled with his orders that Kronstadt be taken by force, nevertheless illustrate that the Bolsheviks were determined to uphold their dictatorship at all costs.

Indeed, now that the government was allowing the free market to operate, within certain limits, in Soviet Russia, the communists felt that they had to be even more wary of giving open rein to any political opposition. If, for Trotsky, Russia's 'economic, political and national independence' was safe only under a dictatorship of the Communist Party, the Communist Party now had to protect itself from potential counter-revolutionaries operating in its own ranks. The Tenth Party Congress of the spring of 1921 accepted that only a complete unity of the party with the policy of the Central Committee could guarantee the revolution's survival. The programme of the Workers' Opposition was defeated by 400 votes to 18. A 'temporary' ban, without an expiry date, was placed on factionalism within the party. Henceforth it was a crime to organise opposition to the official platform of the Central Committee.

Trotsky did not denounce the restrictions placed on political activity within the Communist Party. In this way he helped place himself in an impossible position when he began to raise concerns with the mixed market order of post-Civil War Soviet Russia.

Plate 1 Trotsky, aged 9, in 1888

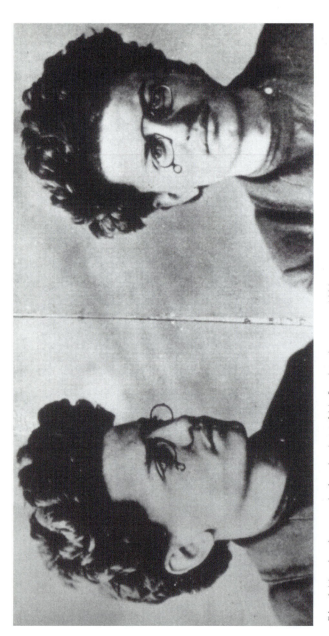

Plate 2 Trotsky photographed at the time of his first imprisonment, 1898

Plate 3 Trotsky reading his newly founded *Pravda* in Vienna in 1910

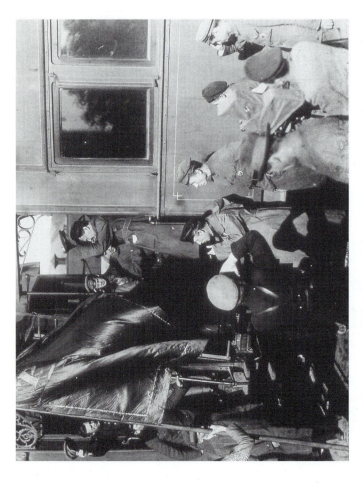

Plate 4 Trotsky visiting the Western Front during the Civil War

Plate 5 Trotsky's last holiday in the Soviet Union, 1927

Plate 6 Trotsky dictating to one of his secretaries in the 1930s

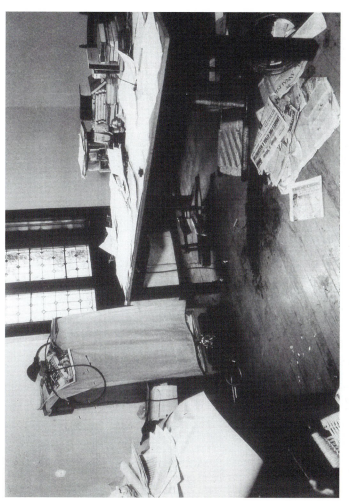

Plate 7 Trotsky's study after Ramon Mercader's attack, 20 August 1940

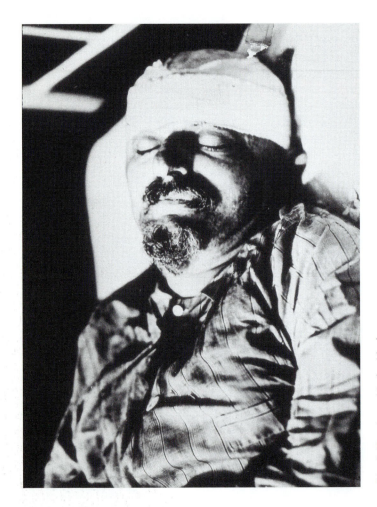

Plate 8 Trotsky on his deathbed

5

THE REVOLUTION IN DECLINE, 1921–4

In its first four years Soviet power was consumed first and foremost with the task of survival. The Bolsheviks – or more accurately Communists, as they had renamed themselves – had performed wonders to maintain and extend their grip on government. In the process of doing so, however, much had changed, not least the nature of the party itself. The cause of socialist pluralism had suffered irreparable damage. The Mensheviks, along with other left groups, had been outlawed from the Soviets and banned as organisations. The Communist Party was the sole surviving political party. It still felt itself, nevertheless, to be a party under siege. For example, it was surrounded by unsympathetic or overtly hostile capitalist states. And within Russia the NEP had unleashed market forces, albeit within certain limits. Would the seeds of capitalism flower to strangle the revolution? Compounding these difficulties were concerns about the Communist Party. How healthy was it as a vanguard? Its culture had inevitably been affected by the barrack mentality of the Civil War. With unity at a premium, the party had closed ranks so much that it had banned the formation of factions within itself. Did this leave sufficient freedom of criticism for healthy debates about how best to tackle pressing problems?

Finally, there loomed the issue of Lenin's health. This deteriorated sharply, eventually rendering him incapable of leadership. He died in January 1924. How would the Communists manage without Lenin? It was in these circumstances that the decline in Trotsky's political power and influence that had occurred during the Civil War continued its downward trajectory. From being an ardent centraliser of the Civil War, he became a critic of an overly oppressive control over the party by its central offices. Becoming ever more estranged from his colleagues in the Central Committee, and especially from its inner Cabinet or Politburo, Trotsky did not find a commissarial portfolio as important as Commissar of War had been during the Civil War. His became a voice on the margins.

A YEAR OF RELATIVE CALM, 1921–2

Following the disputes over military strategy and the 'trade unions' controversy, Trotsky managed to avoid further high-profile conflict in the first year or so of the NEP. He was given prime responsibility for the party's anti-religious policy, which was seen as an important part of the campaign to finish off one of communism's most dangerous foes.[1] Trotsky devised several strategies to weaken the Russian Orthodox Church (ROC). In the midst of the famine of 1921–2 he launched an assault on church valuables. Here he hoped to drum up popular support for the confiscation of church assets. After all, why should the church be exempt from helping out the poor at a time of dire social need? He also thought that any clerical resistance to the confiscation of church property could be used as grounds for the arrest of officials and their congregation. A final plank in Trotsky's drive to undermine the ROC was to encourage a split within its ranks between priests willing to work with the government and those vehemently opposed. Although a minority of the Central Committee thought Trotsky's anti-religious policies a might extreme, Lenin was an enthusiastic supporter of a harsh line against the ROC. Lenin applauded Trotsky's approach as 'True. 1000 times true!'

A mood of reconciliation between Trotsky and Lenin and the Central Committee was also evident at the party's Eleventh Congress, held in the spring of 1922. Despite having misgivings that the NEP was undermining the importance of state direction of the economy and state-led investment, Trotsky gave a speech in favour of the economic policies decided at the Tenth Congress. Lenin would have found it much harder to silence left criticisms of the capitalist NEP had Trotsky raised his voice in support, and he must have been grateful to Trotsky for his newly found tact. Trotsky was also careful about what he said in his contributions on the trade unions. True, there was an open clash of opinion with Tomsky about the extent to which trade unions should have control over management, but it was a minor storm. Trotsky was re-elected to the Central Committee, as were two of his supporters (C. Rakovsky and A.A. Andreev) who had lost out in the previous year.

In 1922 Trotsky added his weight to a growing cult of Lenin in the Soviet system. The publication in 1920 of Lenin's pamphlet *'Left-Wing' Communism: An Infantile Disorder* marked a new interpretation of the October Revolution, one that differed from that outlined in Trotsky's earlier essay *The Russian Revolution to Brest-Litovsk*. In 1918 Trotsky had presented the revolution as a response to pressures from below, in which there was not a hint of a dictatorial coup. Two years later Lenin, seeking to establish Bolshevism as the model for all communist parties to emulate, argued that the Russian Revolution would not have taken place had it not been for the leadership of the Bolshevik Party. The Bolsheviks, he pointed out, had acted as a classic vanguard of the movement, providing the workers with theoretical and organisational guidance. Lenin's message was that the type of body he had promoted since his essay *What Is to Be Done?* (1902) was the essential prerequisite to a successful seizure of power. In October 1922 the journal *Proletarian Revolution* published a fresh set of reminiscences from Trotsky about the October Revolution. These conformed fully to the requirements of contemporary Leninist thinking. The Bolsheviks were no longer reacting to events, but moulding them through a carefully planned conspiracy. Another noticeable feature of Lenin's *'Left-Wing' Communism* was its insistence that the Bolsheviks adhered to 'strict centralisation and iron discipline'. It was therefore important that no deviation from the leader's line should be tolerated. Trotsky contributed to the construction of a picture of harmony in Bolshevik ranks when compiling his collected works for publication. Between 1922 and 1924 his wartime journalism was issued in two volumes. However, overtly polemical articles directed at Lenin were either omitted or changed to give the appearance that Trotsky had agreed with Lenin as early as the Zimmerwald Conference of September 1915. In this way Trotsky could claim a much longer heritage of harmony with Lenin than was actually the case.

In several respects, then, the first year of the NEP marked something of a political rehabilitation for Trotsky. This comeback took place, however, within strict limits. In other crucial respects his influence in the party suffered further setbacks. Following the Eleventh Party Congress, for example, Stalin was appointed to the newly created post of General Secretary. This was a position of the highest importance, for the post-holder would ensure that local organisations carried out Moscow's directives and that the central institutions operated in a smooth and efficient manner. A General Secretary thus had much scope for interfering in every level of the party's operations, including the hiring and firing of key personnel. Lenin well understood the post's importance. That the job was offered to Stalin reflects the value Lenin placed upon his Commissar of Nationalities. The choice of a suitable candidate was not made lightly. Lenin already knew of Stalin's ability to manipulate the party in a way desired by Lenin.

In the run-up to the Eleventh Party Congress, for instance, Stalin had despatched his troops to the provinces to ensure that supporters of Trotsky were not elected as delegates. Lenin approved of Stalin's tactics, as he was uncertain how Trotsky and his followers would act. It was best to be cautious, he felt, and minimise the support the left might attract. After all, policy differences continued to plague relations between the party leader and the Commissar of War. Just two weeks before the Congress met, the Politburo received a Memorandum from Trotsky, in which he warned the party against excessive interference in economic management, something best left to specialists. This document was quickly confined by Lenin to 'the archives'.[2] When the Eleventh Party Congress met, Trotsky's most outspoken friends, including Preobrazhensky and Krestinsky, were not elected to the Central Committee. Lenin thus achieved his short-term goals with Stalin's support.

In the medium term, the manoeuvres favoured by Lenin to keep Trotsky in check would seriously hamper Trotsky's opposition campaigns of 1922–4. By this time some of Trotsky's concerns were shared by Lenin. The Bolshevik leader became increasingly disgruntled with aspects of a regime he had helped to create, but it was uncertain whether he had the strength to remedy matters. As Lenin's health deteriorated he was increasingly sidelined from active participation in politics.

LENIN, TROTSKY AND SOVIET POLITICS, 1922–3

The first potentially worrying development to catch Lenin's eye was the suggested changes to the state monopoly of foreign trade. Lenin consid-

ered it vital that the government maintain strict control over the interaction between Soviet enterprises and the world market. An open-door
policy would, he feared, permit capitalism to subvert Soviet socialism
via trade. Furthermore, peasants, seeking higher prices, would rush to
sell their produce to foreign over domestic markets. The country would
soon be drained of much-needed resources. Trotsky shared Lenin's basic
approach to the state monopoly of foreign trade, although for different
reasons. For Trotsky, the monopoly was crucial as a means by which the
state could redirect foreign trade profits into the development of domestic heavy industry. To speed up the efficiency of this process Trotsky
thought that the monopoly should be the responsibility of the State
Planning Commission, and not the Commissariat of Foreign Trade.

Lenin disagreed with the detail of Trotsky's proposals, but there was
sufficient agreement of principle for Lenin to turn to Trotsky with a
request that he uphold the foreign trade monopoly at the Central
Committee. The issue kept returning to the agenda as calls for the
monopoly's reform, if only as a temporary measure, won more support
amongst the party's top leadership. Eventually Stalin, Bukharin,
Zinoviev and Kamenev were all convinced that a relaxation of the
monopoly would expand Soviet foreign trade. However, they obviously
did not feel so strongly on this issue as to ignore Lenin's advice. When
Trotsky attended a key Central Committee meeting of 18 December
1922 Stalin and his cohorts had already resolved to keep the monopoly
in place. It was on Zinoviev's suggestion that the Central Committee
issued a statement reaffirming the monopoly. Little wonder, then, that
Lenin could write to Trotsky that they had won the day without a shot
being fired. With their opponents already in retreat, it was a relatively
small and hollow victory.[3] Lenin was to find Trotsky's aid of much less
help in the so-called Georgian Affair.

As a result of military victories in the Russian Civil War the
Bolsheviks had extended their control across the territories of the former
tsarist empire. This generated some discussion in the party about a constitutional settlement for the areas taken between 1918 and 1921. Two
basic options were suggested. Regions could be invited to join the existing Russian Federation, although with guarantees of some local rights
and responsibilities. Alternatively, the Russian Federation could be
granted no special status and enter a broader Union of Socialist
Republics on an equal basis with all other republics. Lenin and Stalin

shared the view that, whatever the exact constitutional arrangements, the regions should not enjoy a freedom that could be used to circumvent orders coming from Moscow. There was thus some understandable unease in the non-Russian republics that an overly centralised constitution would be enforced. To offset these objections Lenin and Stalin proposed that a Union of Socialist Republics be established. Whatever the constitutional talk of 'rights of succession' from the Union, however, the party leader and his Commissar of Nationalities intended a centralised chain of command from Moscow to the peripheries. Any undermining of Moscow's grip over the valuable resources situated across the Union of Soviet Socialist Republics (USSR) could only work to the advantage of world imperialism.

It was only after a constitution of a Union of Soviet Socialist Republics was granted formal approval in December 1922 that Lenin began to raise objections to a policy he had previously supported. It was events in Georgia that drew Lenin's concern. Lenin was as insistent as Stalin that Georgia should join with Armenia and Azerbaijan in a Transcaucasian Republic. In October 1922 he had informed the Georgian leaders that he rejected their criticism of Moscow's bullying tactics – which were evident in the actions of agents, including Stalin's deputy, S. Ordzhonikidze – when getting them to accept this plan. The rights of the localities were being taken into account, for example in the suggestion that the chair of the government should rotate between the various nationalities. In late December 1922, however, Lenin changed his mind, now accepting that Ordzhonikidze, and by implication Stalin, had been guilty of a 'truly Great-Russian-nationalist campaign'.

In March 1923 Lenin turned to Trotsky, asking him to insist that the Central Committee conduct further investigations into the fate of Georgian comrades whose pro-independence objections had been overruled and ignored by Stalin. Trotsky, however, displayed no great interest in the rights of Georgian comrades that may have been given short shrift. He told Lenin's secretaries that he was either too ill or too absorbed with economic matters to involve himself in the Georgian Affair. When, despite his earlier refusals, he did make noises about the dangers of Great Russian Nationalism, his suggestions were either incorporated by Stalin or so overwhelmingly rejected that Trotsky quickly dropped them. Trotsky may have been modest in his efforts on this issue because of a long-held prejudice against Georgia as a

Menshevik stronghold. At the end of 1921, for example, Trotsky had been commissioned to pen a pamphlet outlining the pitfalls of Georgian Menshevism. A review of Trotsky's *Basic Questions of the Revolution* (1923) noted with pleasure its critique of Georgian Menshevism and the fact that Georgia itself had finally been purged of non-Bolshevik influences.[4]

If we take the controversy over the state monopoly of foreign trade and the Georgian Affair, there is thus no startling evidence of a firm Lenin–Trotsky alliance. There was no great co-ordination of campaigns between the two, and differences in detail and in emphasis remained. This is also true of the third great issue that troubled Lenin's last political thoughts, the problem of bureaucracy in the state administration.

Surveying the structure and performance of party and government since 1917, the Lenin of 1922–3 saw little to commend and much to despair of. Most communists were incompetent and unsuited to their tasks. Party and state were riddled with petty-bourgeois prejudices and practices, including bribe-taking and tyranny. For Lenin, these serious deficiencies were rooted in Russia's low cultural and economic development, for which there were no immediate remedies. If Soviet socialism was to save itself from complete degeneration, Lenin reasoned that party and state had to be cleansed of ignorant, self-seeking bureaucrats and excessive red tape. These phenomena had mushroomed in the Civil War, as party membership grew to new heights. Lenin's response, and the title of one his last articles, was 'better fewer, but better'.

Lenin's aim was to downsize the administration, specifically to rid it of non-proletarian petty pen-pushers. Those fit to remain in post should, according to Lenin, be highly knowledgeable and well trained, and subject to constant re-examination and quality control. Lenin's remedy for bureaucratisation was the creation of small, specialised centres of expertise to guide the further course of the revolution. There was even to be a leading body to oversee all aspects of party and administrative life, a much-reformed version of the Workers' and Peasants' Inspectorate, which had initially been founded in 1919. As his intellectual biographer has recognised,

> [Lenin's prescriptions] rested entirely upon the exemplary qualities of what he recognised to be a tiny handful of able, devoted, totally incorruptible men grouped in one exemplary all-powerful institution. Here, at last, was the Jacobin solution, the rule of the men of Virtue.[5]

The dangers of bureaucratisation became the main theme of Trotsky's inner-party communications of October to December 1923, when a flurry of letters were exchanged between Trotsky and the Central Committee. He then made his views on bureaucratisation known to the wider public in a series of articles, first published in *Truth* in the last weeks of December 1923 and then in a brochure entitled *The New Course*. Trotsky first woke up to the perils of bureaucratisation when he returned to work in the autumn of 1923 after several months' rest for health problems. He immediately noticed a marked deterioration in several aspects of Soviet life since the Twelfth Party Congress. In the run-up to the Congress Trotsky had made several speeches to party organisations in which he emphasised the importance of careful and conscientious planning. Only on the basis of strict calculations could the party successfully manage political, economic and social developments in a socialist direction. However, instead of this Trotsky identified serious economic and political mistakes, which were rooted, he argued, in the growth of bureaucratic practices.

Although he offered no profound definition of 'bureaucracy', for Trotsky its mode of operation and its dire consequences were there for all to see. Bureaucracy was, he maintained, the mindless and unthinking carrying out of duties defined by superiors. It marked the separation of the bureaucracy from the party, the state apparatus from the people and ultimately the estrangement of the party from the working class. It had led to a series of economic convulsions, including widening differentials between industrial and agricultural prices that threatened to destroy any trace of equilibrium on the domestic market. Inside the party the rule of the bureaucracy had produced widespread dissatisfaction among the ordinary membership. The party's base was increasingly excluded from meaningful participation in economic and political decision-making, a situation that threatened to strangle the party's creativity, and especially that of its youth sections. For Trotsky, youth was 'the most faithful barometer of the Party, as it sharply reacts to the bureaucratism within the Party'. Accordingly he assigned youth an important role in maintaining the party's health, in particular guarding the elders against a hardening of their political arteries:

> Only the permanent interaction of older and younger generations within a framework of Party democracy can save the older guard as a

revolutionary factor. Otherwise the old men may ossify and become the most complete expression of the bureaucratism in the staff.[6]

Like Lenin, Trotsky located the origins of bureaucratisation in Soviet Russia's low economic and cultural level. However, for Trotsky bureaucracy would not have become such a problem were it not for the baneful practices of the party's Secretariat, headed by Stalin. According to Trotsky the Secretariat was systematically taking over the party from above, appointing local party secretaries on the basis of their loyalty to the 'centre' rather than on merit. Moreover, the principle of election, and with it a sense of the local secretaries' responsibility to their constituency, was lost. With the Secretariat's backing utmost in their minds, local secretaries felt that they could ride roughshod over local sensibilities. Little wonder that ordinary party members were either resigning or forming factions and groupings to oppose the unhealthy state of the party. Factionalism, undermining the essential unity of the party, was the natural outcome of the Secretariat's actions.

To heal this harmful situation Trotsky called upon his colleagues to reactivate the party's best traditions. If Lenin sought a remedy for excessive bureaucracy in a small elite, however, Trotsky argued that genuine democracy had to be reinstated in the party. He did not consider the possibility that he may have helped to extinguish democracy by his actions in the Civil War, that there may have been a contradiction between his current beliefs and his past actions. He simply emerged as the advocate of party democracy. The party membership had to feel free and able to make constructive criticisms, for which they would be thanked rather than placed under arrest. The party membership had to be given real roles and genuine responsibility in political and economic management. They should receive, for example, a genuine choice in elections. Only by broadening democracy, by placing trust in the cadres, could the party rectify the economic and political mistakes of the recent past and guarantee that the party's older and the younger generations worked in harmony to further the cause of socialism.

Trotsky took up his anti-bureaucracy programme with his usual sense of urgency and passion, believing that the party was entering a new epoch through which only his methods would ensure a safe passage. His colleagues on the party's leading bodies were, however, not convinced. They doubted whether matters were really as bad as Trotsky depicted. Yes, there were economic problems, but these were quite expected. In any case there was no imminent danger of collapse. The party anticipated several years of hard and steady work before it could claim to have fully rectified the economy. Looking at the party, Trotsky's comrades claimed that they could congratulate themselves on educating a new generation of cadres. The influx of this fresh blood would no doubt expedite the resolution of important tasks. Having rejected Trotsky's analysis of imagined ills besetting the regime, a majority of the old Bolsheviks wondered whether he could be trusted to develop sound and sensible policies. If Trotsky was prone to an exaggeration of difficulties, he was, they argued, remarkably vague in his solutions. For a majority of the Politburo, Trotsky was part of a problem, not an answer. For example, if he was concerned by an absence of systematic leadership why did he not attend important meetings of the Council of Labour and Defence and of the Cabinet? There was little evidence of conscientiousness in Trotsky's work habits. Furthermore, there was a marked absence of concrete proposals from Trotsky. This was hardly surprising, since his policy record was far from promising. In recent times Trotsky had suffered a series of defeats as he opposed Lenin over, amongst other matters, the Brest-Litovsk peace and the trade unions. For his colleagues, Trotsky's discontents were not rooted in reality, but in a hurt sense of pride stemming from personal disappointments. Thus, Trotsky could not have been pleased when, in April 1923, the Twelfth Congress shelved his more militant approach to religious affairs. In September 1923 Trotsky was certainly upset by personnel changes to the Military-Revolutionary Committee. Finally, and most annoying of all for Trotsky, came the Central Committee's refusal to grant him dictatorial powers. Trotsky was warned that his unfounded criticisms were encouraging anti-party platforms, sowing unnecessary disruption to important party work, and threatening a war between the older and younger generations.

TROTSKY'S DEFEAT, 1923–4

Beyond the narrow circles of the leading decision-makers, Trotsky's calls of alarm did meet with some sympathy and support. In early October 1923, for example, forty-six prominent old Bolsheviks wrote to the Politburo expressing their discomfort with a ruling clique whose 'incorrect leadership' was 'paralysing and breaking up the party'.[7] Recent archival research has also revealed evidence of widespread social interest in Trotsky's 'democratisation' programme.[8] In Moscow, for example, citywide and individual factory-focused studies have suggested that as many as one-quarter, or in some instances a majority, of workers' cells approved 'Trotskyist' resolutions. The opposition's support base was even stronger in the party's cells in the military, with a minimum of one-third backing calls for reform. Trotsky held most appeal, however, for student youth. Several of the capital's educational institutions were won over to the opposition.

Despite an emerging coalition in the opposition's favour, Trotsky was unable to convert this support into tangible political gains. On the contrary, he was to suffer further losses throughout 1924. The Thirteenth Party Conference of 16–18 January 1924 set the tone for what was to be a torrid year. With Trotsky absent through ill health and Lenin on his deathbed, the conference evaluated Trotsky's recent campaigns as 'ultra-factional', a 'petty bourgeois deviation', all of which added up to an attack on the Central Committee 'unprecedented in our party's history'. The delegates agreed to 'politically annihilate anyone who makes an attempt on the unity of the party ranks'.[9] V. Antonov-Ovseenko, a high-ranking Trotskyist in the military, was an early victim of this 'political annihilation'. The Thirteenth Party Conference dismissed him from his post for distributing a circular letter to party cells in the military on inner-party democracy without the prior approval of the Central Committee.

Trotsky was sufficiently recovered to meet his critics at the Thirteenth Party Congress of 23–31 May 1924. Here he faced a largely hostile audience. His main Congress speech was conciliatory in tone. It was, it has been argued, 'the most inept speech of his career'.[10] On the one hand, it attempted to justify Trotsky's recent statements as a reaction to an overly oppressive atmosphere in the party's leading bodies. On the other, it offered a complete capitulation to party resolutions that condemned Trotsky as a factionalist. Trotsky rejected what he called the 'margarine democracy' of bourgeois parliaments, in which matters were resolved by mathematical majorities and minorities. He simply refused to recognise that only formal guarantees of abstract rights (speech, franchise, association, etc.) are the best methods to secure democracy. Instead Trotsky made it clear that if the

party censured him he would have to submit. In a passage amazing for
its blind loyalty, he claimed:

> [N]one of us wants to be or can be right against the party. In the last
> analysis the party is always right, because the party is the sole histori-
> cal instrument that the working class possesses for the solution of its
> fundamental tasks ... I know that no one can be right against the
> party. It is only possible to be right with the party and through it since
> history has not created any other way to determine the correct posi-
> tion ... if the party passes a resolution that one or another of us con-
> siders unjust, that comrade will say: Right or wrong this is my party,
> and I will take responsibility for its decision to the end.[11]

Trotsky could thus have no grounds for complaint when the Thirteenth
Congress affirmed the anti-Trotsky resolution of the Thirteenth Conference. He had been truly routed, something he must have been all too
painfully aware of. There are several reasons why his fall was so severe.

First of all, in late 1923 there was evidently a complete breakdown
in political and personal relations between Trotsky and the vast majority of the Politburo and the Central Committee. This fracture merely
widened and hardened over the course of 1924. Although Trotsky
protested in public that he desired a close working relationship with
his fellow senior colleagues, this was impossible. This is clear from an
examination of Trotsky's acrimonious correspondence of late 1923
with the Central Committee. Its tone could hardly have sunk much
lower.

Trotsky accused his top-ranking comrades of using just about every
conceivable political dirty trick against him. There were, he stated,
secret sessions of the Politburo to draw up policy and strategy without
his knowledge. The core of this secret 'inner Cabinet' was composed of
Stalin, Zinoviev and Kamenev, subsequently known as the 'triumvirate'.
It was the inner Cabinet, claimed Trotsky, that dreamed up a story of
battles between Lenin and Trotsky and ascribed artificial, extreme views
to Trotsky with the intention of discrediting him. When party cells
nevertheless backed Trotsky, official publications, including the party
daily *Truth*, either hid or falsified the results. In his defence, Trotsky
claimed that there was 'no better Bolshevik' than he, and that this was
evident above all in the way he passed the revolutionary tests and tur-

moil of 1917. In reply, the Politburo pointed to Trotsky's consistent 'anti-Leninism', his factionalism and an 'absolute ignorance of the actual state of affairs'. Finally, the Politburo made plain its intention to prevent Trotsky from committing further anti-party acts. These accusations and counter-accusations were to be repeated in the debate that followed the autumn 1924 publication of Trotsky's essay 'Lessons of October' (a debate covered in the Introduction, pp. 6–8).

Second, in what was a battle between two irreconcilable sides Trotsky had no trump cards. It is not clear whether party members who approved his resolutions in the winter discussions of 1923–4 actually shared his outlook, or whether this was merely a convenient opportunity to express discontent over other issues. Thus workers angry with pay and employment prospects may have joined their protest to Trotsky's. Similarly, a party youth alienated from their organisation because of its failure to address issues such as youth unemployment during the NEP may have added their voices to Trotsky's bandwagon. However, for every oppositionist, however committed, there were far more who associated their political careers with the Central Committee. Take, for example, the highest leaders of the youth body, the Komsomol, who remained in post partly because they supported Stalin. Indeed, the decision to support the triumvirate was made easier by the way the Central Committee adopted elements of Trotsky's programme. The famous 'On Party Building' resolution of 5 December 1923, for example, accepted the need for 'workers' democracy' but upheld the ban on factions. In essentials this did not differ from Trotsky's formula of greater democracy whilst preserving 'the organisational principles of Bolshevism'.[12] With the opposition and the Central Committee employing very similar language there was no particular reason why party workers should stick their necks out by backing the opposition. As early as 17 December 1923 Stalin could write with some justification to Kirov stating that Trotsky, Preobrazhensky and others had 'lost the battle on principled ground'.[13]

Faced with a weak and fragmented opposition, the Politburo majority was able to manipulate the party in its direction. At no point did the party slip out of the Secretariat's control. We are now able to read the reports sent to Stalin by his lieutenants, reassuring the General Secretary that the local party bodies were in his pocket. In a communication sent from Kiev in December 1923, for example, I.M. Vareikis informed Stalin that, despite local Trotskyism being 'strong', party meetings were giving firm approval to the Central Committee. Moreover, the 'press is wholly in our hands'.[14] This picture of a landslide for the Central Committee is confirmed in a remarkably detailed account of the politics of the town of Iuzovka, Donbass. Known as a centre of radicalism, for several months in 1923 this town was called Trotsk. However, in the discussions of late 1923 the town's party committees voted 67 against 12 in favour of the Central Committee. This clear defeat nevertheless contained the largest support the opposition mustered. In the spring of 1924 the town's name was changed once more, this time to Stalino.[15] With the party firmly under control the Secretariat was able to purge members of the opposition from its ranks, and especially from the youth sections, without too much difficulty.

A similarly depressing picture for Trotsky emerged in the army. In the aftermath of the Civil War Trotsky had progressively lost interest in military affairs, other than to pen some articles on military doctrine. He had not used his position as Commissar of War to foster undivided loyalty to him amongst generals and the rank and file alike. Any remaining influence he may have enjoyed was swept away by the personnel changes of early 1924. Antonov-Ovseenko's dismissal was soon followed by an overhaul of the army's top leadership. The changes were partly a response to an alarming report on the parlous state of Russia's armed forces. Added to these legitimate concerns were political motivations whose consequences were drastic for Trotsky. Effective leadership of the army fell to his prominent opponents, especially M. Frunze. In the months leading up to his formal removal in January 1925, Trotsky was Commissar of War in name only.[16]

Finally, with the odds stacked clearly against him Trotsky was unable to draw upon Lenin's influence. This was not only because of the leader's ill health and death, but also because Lenin's relationship with Trotsky was highly problematic. It is clear that Lenin wanted to retain Trotsky's services as a leading Bolshevik. The party leader would not accept an offer of resignation from the Commissar of War, nor would he countenance an attempt to sack Trotsky from the top leadership. At the same time, however, Lenin was frequently upset by Trotsky's policy recommendations. Indeed, he had serious doubts regarding Trotsky's political skills, noting on one occasion that 'Trotsky is a temperamental man with military experience ... but, as for politics, he hasn't got a clue.'[17]

This mixed assessment of Trotsky's talents was also expressed in Lenin's famous Testament of December 1922, in which Trotsky was not given a recommendation higher than any other comrade. Trotsky was put on a par with Stalin, and the party warned that a split might be in the offing if their clash of personalities was not restrained. In writing in this way, Lenin may have encouraged Stalin and his cohorts to close ranks further to block Trotsky's ambitions. Lenin was unlikely to have given his stamp of approval to Trotsky for the post of leader because, even in 1922–3 when he relied upon the Commissar of War to present some of his views, he remained suspicious of him. Lenin's biographer has emphasised that he would have dropped Trotsky at the next available opportunity.[18]

The absence of any firm seal of approval from Lenin left Trotsky vulnerable to charges that he was exaggerating his closeness to Lenin, mainly to mask his long history of conflict with the genius of Bolshevism. Trotsky's failure to return to Moscow immediately after he received news of Lenin's death is accepted as one of his many political miscalculations. After all, this left the ground free for the triumvirate to dominate the scenes of grief and mourning, adding to their reputation for carrying on Lenin's mantle. However, given the dire state of Trotsky's relations with the triumvirate and other leaders, his preference for continuing his journey south for rest and recuperation is quite understandable. It was a recognition of Trotsky's exclusion from the corridors of power.

INTERNATIONAL AFFAIRS AND WORLD REVOLUTION, 1921–4

The period between the end of the Civil War and Lenin's death was characterised by contradictory trends in Soviet Russia's foreign affairs. It remained on the whole isolated, a pariah state. However, there was a reluctant admission by some of the Great Powers, most notably the United Kingdom, that the Bolshevik regime had stabilised itself in power. Russia was simply too large and rich in resources to ignore indefinitely. It had to be dealt with, whatever the nature of its government, for geo-strategic and trade purposes. The USSR thus entered into limited forms of traditional diplomacy, a development welcomed by its Minister of Foreign Affairs G.V. Chicherin. On the other hand, powerful

Bolshevik voices desired, above all, the downfall of the Western powers via a series of communist coups. Funding the revolutionary activities of foreign communist parties may have been the responsibility of the Comintern, but no one was fooled into thinking this a non-Soviet, non-governmental organisation. The USSR trod a fine line between traditional diplomacy and socialist internationalism, favouring first one and then the other. But these were two irreconcilable principles, and the attempt to combine them left the USSR open to charges of betraying them both. Soviet Russia could thus be considered an unreliable partner for Western governments and foreign communist parties alike.

For Trotsky, the fundamental problems of Russian socialism were linked to delays in the outbreak of the international revolution. Such delays were not, he argued, the fault of an absence of fertile ground or suitable opportunities. He thought post-war Europe ripe for communist revolutions. For Trotsky, the European bourgeoisie was no longer a progressive force. It was incapable, most importantly, of developing the continent's productive forces. The continuation of the old order promised further economic and cultural decay. He dismissed the notion that Western capitalism had successfully stabilised itself following the destruction and turmoil of World War One. Long-term growth on capitalist foundations was possible, he reasoned, only in an unlikely combination of events:

> If a million Europeans were to die from cold and hunger, if Germany were converted into a colony, if the Soviet power were to fall in Russia and the latter also converted into a colony, if Europe were to become a vassal state of America and Japan, then a new capitalist equilibrium would be restored.[19]

Overall, Trotsky foresaw capitalism going through its usual boom–slump cycles, with a tendency towards deepening and more critical crises.

Despite outlining capitalism's bleak prospects, Trotsky argued that Europe's bourgeois rulers would not easily give up power. Indeed, the more hopeless their situation, the more tenaciously would they seek to maintain their privileges. With a rich experience in centuries of diplomatic trickery and government intrigue, the European bourgeoisie would employ every trick in their rich arsenal to keep communism at bay. Europe's communist parties, Trotsky warned, would have to be careful, inventive and above all in touch with the moods of the masses if they were to stage their own Octobers. Trotsky's writings on international affairs of the early 1920s thus sought to warn Soviet Russia of diplomatic entanglements with a desperate and rapacious West, whilst advising foreign communist parties on how to manipulate a revolutionary epoch into actual revolutions.

For Trotsky, the bourgeois world was divided between and within itself. Some sections, particularly in Britain, were willing, under certain conditions, to engage in limited forms of economic co-operation with the USSR. On the other hand, there were powerful interests, represented above all by France, that desired the immediate downfall of Soviet communism, possibly by new military campaigns. Trotsky argued that Soviet foreign policy had to respond to both tendencies. It had to encourage progressive elements by stressing the USSR's peaceful intentions, which were evident in its efforts at mutual disarmament. It should seek separate and collective deals where appropriate. Certainly Trotsky was not opposed to sending a Soviet delegation to the Genoa Conference of April to May 1922, which was called, on Britain's initiative, to discuss Europe's economy. He was less enthusiastic than some colleagues as to what such negotiations could achieve. After all, as a Marxist he believed that capitalism by its nature leads to war. The USSR was under constant threat of attack. Furthermore, a genuine concern with trade with the USSR had to be based on a long-term perspective, something he doubted the crisis-ridden West was capable of. Indeed, Trotsky's writings on the international diplomacy of the early 1920s reveal quite clearly why nothing of substance was achieved in the reconciliation of East and West. There was too much mutual suspicion and hostility in a battle both sides were eager to win.[20]

Trotsky believed that the USSR would be secure in peace and have meaningful international trade relations only after the downfall of capitalism. Soviet communism had been forced to make compromises with market forces mainly because of delays in the world revolution. If German comrades had been successful in 1918–19, he claimed, Soviet Russia would not have dreamed up the NEP. Fortunately, however, these setbacks could be forgotten because recurrent booms and slumps would present further opportunities for communist revolutions. Unfortunately, Trotsky was unable to report any actual success for the communist parties of Western Europe in the early 1920s. He berated the French Communist Party (PCF) for failing to implement the resolutions of the Communist International's Executive Committee. In particular he accused French comrades of being insufficiently rigorous in rooting out reformist currents from party ranks. The French party was speaking with insufficient revolutionary clarity and as a consequence was failing to win over the French working class. The many letters of advice he sent to the leadership of the PCF amounted to a call for a root-and-branch overhaul of the party's key political activities, from its dealings with youth to its tactics in parliament. If the PCF was guilty of insufficient revolutionary zeal, Trotsky thought German comrades too willing to call for revolutionary onslaughts when the necessary preconditions were absent. In March 1921, for example, the German Communist Party (KPD) had bungled a promising situation by attempting to seize power when the majority of workers were not prepared. The inevitable outcome was depression amongst the workers and a fall in the prestige of the German vanguard.

Trotsky's appeals to his foreign comrades reveal the profound difficulties contained within his strategy for world revolution. So damning were Trotsky's critiques of the leadership of the Western communist parties that they must have been demoralised if they took them to heart. Trotsky gives the impression that only he possessed the genius to lead the masses whilst nevertheless warning Moscow not to adopt too haughty an approach to the brother parties of the Third International. Trotsky never doubted that delays in the world revolution were mainly due to problems of party leadership, but this was surely a simplistic approach.

Perhaps workers were discouraged from entering communist politics by the constant threat of a purge should they stray from the correct line. Nor were Trotsky's recommendations always as well reasoned as he thought. He was, for instance, too optimistic about the tactic of the united front. According to this strategy, communists should enter into pacts with reformist socialists, but only as a means of reaching more workers. In these deals, the communists would retain complete independence of organisation and programme with the intention of revealing the bankruptcy of the reformist parties. He did not consider the fact that the reformist socialists would resist such tactics, and that they and ordinary workers would be further alienated from the communist groupings.[21] Trotsky was not immune from the crime of rushing into proclaiming a revolution at hand when this was an exaggeration. Most famously, in 1923 he encouraged the KPD into another disastrous and ill-prepared attempt on power.[22] Finally, even had a communist revolution being successfully staged in Paris or Berlin, Trotsky held unrealistic expectations about how this would transform the situation in the USSR. He gave no full and sustained analysis of what quantity of free technological aid would have been sufficient to overcome Russian backwardness or whence such resources would have issued. Thus, even with a German revolution on its side, Soviet communism may all the same have had to make an accommodation with market forces. Trotsky could not escape the problems associated with communist modernisation of Russian conditions so easily.

LOW AND HIGH CULTURE

In the midst of these inner-party disputes, the Politburo expressed its amazement that Trotsky found the time to publish two works on culture. One, *Problems of Everyday Life*, examined the relationship between communism and everyday existence; the other, *Literature and Revolution*, focused on higher creative endeavours and their interaction with the construction of socialism. The Politburo used these publications as further evidence that Trotsky preferred his hobbies to serious political work. For Trotsky, however, these two texts addressed concerns that were central to the building of socialism, for what was communism if not a new era of possibilities for human behaviour, both high and low?

Trotsky was far from impressed with the general mores of Russian society. He viewed the mass of Russians as uncultured. He described them as illiterate, inefficient, dirty, unpunctual, prone to swearing and abusive language, and under the sway of superstition. The root of these evils lay, he thought, in the poverty of Russian existence coupled with a natural human trait to abide by accepted customs and habits. However, if socialism was to progress and the masses discover respect for themselves and for others, Russians had to become everything that they were not. Trotsky's articles on everyday living emphasised and re-emphasised the importance of elementary hygiene, good grammar and correct speech, self-discipline and punctuality, and a rational approach to life and its problems. If these attributes could not be developed within each and every individual there was little hope that society could be recast into socialism. Trotsky accepted that such a radical transformation of the Russian soul could take decades to achieve. He was confident, however, that the October Revolution had made a solid beginning.

First of all, it had guaranteed an eight-hour working day. The working class had sufficient leisure time to concentrate on its self-education. Second, the workers' state was promoting the growth of a new and better everyday culture. Libraries were being provided, textbooks written and the means of production rationalised as the necessary precondition for the rationalisation of morality. Legislation and propaganda encouraged people to be sober, atheistic and punctual. Trotsky lauded the prohibition of the sale of vodka and a decree, made on his initiative, that banned late attendance of meetings. He called on the nation's journalists to expose poor and uncultured behaviour, to use court reportage of family and other individual acts of injustice to mount more general campaigns. Trotsky saw cinema as an especially effective branch of propaganda. Its simplicity (even illiterates could follow its messages) and power of entertainment could be combined with socially useful themes to break, for example, the attraction of the church as a forum of hymn and colour.

Despite the variety of means by which the state could encourage good conduct, Trotsky recognised that all these efforts would come to nought if ordinary people lacked the desire to change and adopt new habits. The final and perhaps decisive factor in the success or failure of socialism would be the 'voluntary initiative of the worker and peasant'. Newspapers and books would continue to be poorly produced and bound so long as ordinary citizens did not complain about slapdash proofreading and shoddy workmanship. Even the revolution's most radical goals, including the full equality of the sexes, would be merely paper decrees if their intent did not become an accepted part of everyday behaviour. Trotsky argued, for example, that the political emancipation of women had been easy enough to legislate but would be deprived of real value if domestic responsibilities held back women's participation in politics. Furthermore, the family would become a relationship based on mutual respect, equality and love only when men learned to 'see life through the eyes of women'. For Trotsky, then, the emergence of a free, just collective order depended on a combination of good governance and example from above and of popular pressure and self-activity from below.

There is coherence and a certain attraction to Trotsky's writings on everyday life. No doubt the common weal would have improved if only people in their everyday existence were more caring and socially responsible. However, this thought, like so many others, is nothing more than a banal truism. Despite Trotsky's strictures against 'empty moralising' one cannot help thinking that his ideal human type consisted of his own habits writ large. His advice is littered with its own brand of simplifications and over-generalisations. For example, it may be reasonable to claim that 'a man who is always late because he is "frightfully busy" works as a rule less and less efficiently than another who comes on time whenever he is due'.[23] But how meaningful would this be to a person suffering from a poor diet, shortages and the time spent hunting down goods and services, deplorable housing and a dangerous work environment? This is just one indication of how far Trotsky seems to have underestimated the scale of the difficulties facing ordinary Russians. Women, for instance, were hampered in their political ambitions not only because of domestic duties, low-paid work and a dearth of collective childcare and other public services. There was also a serious problem of sexism within the regime itself. The extent to which the Bolsheviks had imbibed patriarchal assumptions is evident in its propaganda. Gender analyses of early Bolshevik poster campaigns, for instance, show that women were portrayed primarily in 'backward' or subservient roles.[24] Perhaps this was to be expected from a government in which men occupied the leading positions. There seems to have been little recognition of how unattractive the Communist Party was to women, beginning with its youth organisations and continuing to the Central Committee.[25] One can even claim that Trotsky was as dismissive of his female compatriots as any other egocentric man. In the following memoir from a librarian, for example, we discover Trotsky using his wife as a (unpaid?) secretary:

Yesterday there appeared in the Museum a person of short height, with a Southern accent and a turned-up nose who, it turned out, was Mrs Trotsky. She wished to receive *Kievan Thought* for 1915 and 1916 for her 'husband'; she was very polite. I informed her that certain formalities were necessary to which she agreed. She appeared today, well dressed but tastelessly, in a car with a soldier who stood to attention before her. She received her *Kievan Thought* in return for a letter, 'To the Citizen Librarian ...' in which, with all the bourgeois conventions such as 'I have the honour to request' and 'I beg you to accept my assurance', Mr Trotsky asked about the issuing of journals to him for no longer than two weeks.[26]

It may not be surprising that Trotsky did not take his own advice to view reality through women's eyes very seriously. Certainly he did not advocate a female candidate to replace Lenin; nor did he produce the promised fuller account of what he thought a woman's perspective on the world might be.

A final critical thought on Trotsky's writings on popular culture is the manner in which he misunderstood the potential of cinema. Trotsky considered this a relatively unproblematic medium for propaganda and entertainment purposes. However, the screen is not so easily manipulated, and there is a much more complex relationship between movie and audience than Trotsky bargained for. Recent research has suggested that there is an issue of 'cinema literacy' quite overlooked by Trotsky and other Bolsheviks.[27] Furthermore, judging by attendance figures and magazine sales, audiences preferred films of a non-Bolshevik variety and were quite competent at rejecting what they did not approve of in any cinematic spectacle.[28]

Yet, for all their flaws, Trotsky's musings on everyday life and socialism were a new aspect of his thought. Some of the more recent historical writing has interpreted them as embodying the regime's fundamental concerns about the health of NEP Russia.[29] His volume surveying literary trends and the revolution reflected a much deeper tradition within his writing. In *Literature and Revolution* he championed the Marxist method of literary criticism as the only means of explaining the rise and fall of literary schools. Once one understood the social context of artistic endeavours one would appreciate, for instance, how Shakespeare's tragedies would have been 'unthinkable without the Reformation'. Trotsky was careful to be wary, however, of a simplistic approach to art. Aesthetic judgements should not be based on materialist analysis only. After all, a 'work of art should, in the first place, be judged by its own law, that is, by the law of art'.

In his literary reviews, however, Trotsky was incapable of following such distinctions. He praised and condemned according to a work's relationship to the revolution, not by a set of purely artistic criteria. For example, of pre-October or contemporary writers who had fled into emigration he writes:

> October entered into the destinies of the Russian people, as a deci-
> sive event, and gave to everything its own meaning and its own value.
> The past receded at once, faded and drooped, and art can be revived
> only from the point of view of October. He who is outside of the
> October perspective is utterly and hopelessly reduced to nothing.[30]

Indeed, in successive chapters examining, amongst other themes, the so-called 'fellow-travellers', and the schools of Futurism and Formalism, Trotsky's criticism becomes a predictable series of high-sounding but tendentious statements. The flaws in each and every artist are reduced to failings to express the revolution in all its magnitude, inner develop-ment and grandeur. Particularly short shrift is given to critics who do not share similar assumptions. Here, for example, is how Trotsky dis-misses Chukovsky's interpretation of the poet Alexander Blok:

> [Chukovsky's] booklet on Blok is not worse than his other books. They
> reveal an external vivacity combined with an inability to bring the least
> order into his thoughts, an unevenness of exposition, a provincial
> newspaper rhythm, as well as a meagre pedantry and a tendency to
> generalise on the basis of external antitheses.[31]

One could, if one chose, apply similar sentiments to Trotsky's own efforts.

For the most part *Literature and Revolution* is a highly unsatisfactory work fraught with contradictions.[32] On the one hand, for instance, it argues that the Communist Party should not prescribe the future course that art should take. It holds out little hope for the formation of a spe-cific proletarian art demanded by some comrades. Proletarian art was a misnomer, for Trotsky, partly because the transition to communism is dominated by political and economic tasks, and mainly because the ulti-mate goal is to produce art that has no class basis but is truly human. On the other hand, however, the possibility for an anti-revolutionary art is dismissed. The Communist Party would have to maintain a 'cautious censorship' against any literary attempt to disrupt the revolution. One may wish to congratulate Trotsky for the limits he sought to place on censorship, but such limits are notoriously difficult to define. His for-mulation of 'in the interests of the revolution' left broad scope for severe and restrictive party censorship – for who, by his own admission, guarded the revolution's interests better than the party?

Trotsky is at his most vague when he outlines what the human art of the communist future will consist of. His intention is to be bold and affirmative, to offer reasons why someone should believe in the beauty of the communist future. He is certain that it will be atheist, dominated by rationality and reason. However, the vision of this Godless existence becomes less attractive the more its details are revealed. Trotsky has humankind controlling the environment so as to move mountains and change the course of rivers. In the realm of biology, artificial selection will create a race of supermen in which the average human being will be an 'Aristotle, a Goethe, or a Marx'. Such thoughts harbour environmen-tal and ethnic dangers of which post-Holocaust and post-industrial gen-erations are only too aware. In any case Trotsky knew well that between the society of his time and that of his imagination there lay a potentially unbridgeable gulf. In the ensuing years his warnings to the party became graver as the revolution faced yet more difficulties.

6

OPPOSITION AND DEFEAT, 1925–9

The last four years of the 1920s were filled with sharp turns in the fate of Soviet socialism. For instance, Stalin downgraded the commonplace assumption that the future of the Soviet experiment was dependent upon foreign revolutions. In works such as the second (1926) edition of *Problems of Leninism* he put forward a theory of 'socialism in one country'. The USSR, this notion proclaimed, had sufficient resources to embark on the building of socialism in isolation. How this would happen in an economic sense was outlined initially by Bukharin, a prominent figure in the Stalin camp from 1925 to 1927. According to Bukharin, a socialist economy could best be constructed in the USSR as a slow process. Above all, the development of industry had to follow the tempo of an expanding agricultural sector. The key slogan of the Bukharin path was for the peasants to 'enrich themselves' within the mixed market model of NEP. From 1928 onwards, however, Stalin ditched this programme, and Bukharin along with it. Henceforth the USSR was to follow a programme of rapid industrialisation in the form of the First Five-Year Plan, to be financed largely by robbing the peasants. The 'great leap forward' in economic policy was accompanied by political and cultural campaigns. The whole country was to be mobilised in a gigantic effort to 'catch up' with the West in the shortest time possible.

Throughout this period Trotsky proclaimed himself head of a genuine Bolshevik–Leninist class outlook. Although he welcomed some of the about-turns in government policy, he was a consistent critic of Stalin's leadership. There were two main stages in Trotsky's anti-Stalin campaigns of this period. In the first, covering most of 1926 and 1927, he was a leading member of the so-called United Opposition. Other key figures in this coalition included his recent critics Kamenev and Zinoviev, who had now come to share his misgivings about Comrade Stalin. This alliance ended in failure following the Fifteenth Party Congress of December 1927. This condemned the United Opposition as an anti-party tendency and confirmed the expulsion of its members, including Trotsky, from the party. Kamenev and Zinoviev sought immediate re-entry into the party, offering a full recantation. Trotsky could not countenance a refusal to propagate views he felt to be correct, and was accordingly sent into internal exile. A move to Alma-Ata, deep in Soviet Central Asia, did not prevent Trotsky from continuing his political work. As unofficial head of the so-called Left Opposition, he wrote numerous commentaries on Stalin's shift to the left, and through a massive correspondence tried to maintain contact with sympathisers spread across the USSR and abroad. In these trying circumstances Trotsky was no immediate threat to Stalin. However, his stubborn refusal to abandon the hope of a political comeback, combined with biting commentaries on Stalin, was a constant thorn in Stalin's side. Convinced that he would not recall Trotsky to Moscow, Stalin could see no use in keeping his arch enemy within the USSR. Early in 1929 Trotsky was quietly deported to Turkey. In this way Trotsky began a last period of exile and a new stage in his political struggles.

TROTSKY AND THE UNITED OPPOSITION, 1925–7

The year 1925 was one of political solitude and quiet for Trotsky. The circumstances of his resignation from the Commissariat of War marked a complete break with the Politburo. Rest and recuperation from the fevers and headaches that marked the return of his frequent but undiagnosed illness kept him away from the Fourteenth Party Conference of April 1925. Upon his return to work in the following month he was offered what was for him a minor job as member of the Supreme Council of the National Economy. In this capacity he chaired, amongst other bodies, the Concessions Committee. The advocate of world revolution was expected to conclude trade deals with the world bourgeoisie!

Indeed from time to time he would meet with foreign capitalists, but the work was infrequent and not overly demanding. Trotsky used his time principally to further his study of the NEP. In works such as *Towards Capitalism or Socialism?* (August 1925) he outlined possible paths of development for the USSR.

During a period in which the Soviet economy had reached 1913 levels of production and was increasingly becoming integrated into the world economy, Trotsky argued that the criterion for further Soviet economic success would be the extent to which it achieved higher growth rates than capitalism. It was the battle for greater output and quality of output that would resolve the USSR's ability to resist 'the economic pressure of world capitalism as well as the military-political pressure of world imperialism'. At the time of writing Trotsky admitted that Soviet socialism was lagging behind capitalism in key economic indicators. However, he dismissed the notion that the far stronger capitalist economies would inevitably overwhelm the Soviet economy. He listed several advantages of socialist economic management that would enable the Soviet Union to expand at a faster rate than that possible in the free-market west.

First, with its parasitic classes eliminated, the Soviet Union could reinvest a much higher percentage of any surpluses. Second, planning enabled a more efficient use of resources than the invisible hand of the free market. Third, Soviet production was not disrupted by boom–slump cycles. Finally, the Soviet economy could exploit the world market for its own benefit. With the money earned by the sale of Russian grain on the world market or by loans raised on international stock exchanges, for example, the USSR could purchase equipment needed by its internal urban and agricultural markets. By these methods the world market would be utilised to cement the alliance between Soviet workers and peasants; capitalism would become a 'creditor of socialism'. Trotsky thought that the strategy of interacting with the world market carried limited dangers for Soviet socialism. A versatile system of socialist protectionism would cushion the Soviet economy from the fluctuations of the world economy. Trotsky dismissed the proposition that increased links with the world economy would leave the Soviet Union vulnerable to economic blockades by hostile capitalist powers. First of all, he reasoned, by exploiting the world market the Soviet economy would become stronger than it could in isolation, and it would thus be much better placed to withstand any deterioration of international relations. Second, he pointed out that the more capitalism invested in the USSR, the less likely it would be to impose a blockade.

Although Trotsky's observations on Soviet economic growth envisioned a role for market forces, his main intention was for the USSR to strengthen the socialist, non-market elements of its economy. He was thus fundamentally opposed to the current pro-NEP thinking of the Stalin–Bukharin-dominated Politburo. Trotsky attended the Fourteenth Party Congress of December 1925 with a consulting vote only. He took no active part in its debates. From the sidelines, however, he observed the acrimonious falling out between the now disintegrating triumvirate. Kamenev and Zinoviev had at last decided to air their long-simmering discontent with Stalin.[1] They criticised the pro-peasant orientation of the NEP and objected to Stalin's one-man dictatorial rule of the party. As ever the composed master of inner-party intrigue, Stalin had managed the selection of Congress delegates to guarantee his own victory in advance. Shortly afterwards, Zinoviev's power base as head of the Leningrad party organisation was shattered. Kamenev was demoted down the ministerial ladder.

With their political ambitions in tatters, there was sufficient common ground in policy thinking and in sharing defeat at Stalin's hands for Kamenev and Zinoviev to seek an alliance with Trotsky. A key event in cementing the new grouping was a Central Committee meeting of April 1926. Here Trotsky and Kamenev, without success, spoke of the need to increase the tax burden on the wealthy kulak peasants to fund a more rapid expansion of industry. The formation of the so-called United Opposition had to wait several more months, however, until Trotsky returned from Berlin, where he had undergone medical treatment for his still mysterious maladies.

As an alliance the United Opposition was not so united. There were understandable reservations on both sides, amongst leaders and followers. Only a few months earlier, Kamenev and Zinoviev had demanded Trotsky's expulsion from the party. This call was rejected by Stalin; but, even with his party card still intact, Kamenev and Zinoviev must have known that they were aligning their political careers with a man already in the dead end of Soviet politics. Trotsky, on the other hand, had firsthand experience of Kamenev's and Zinoviev's failings. There was a long history of ideological struggle with his new stablemates. In the recent political infighting Trotsky had made much of Kamenev's and Zinoviev's political wavering in 1917, while Kamenev and Zinoviev had pointed to Trotsky's non-Bolshevism. As well as personal resentments and suspicions, there continued to be political differences over how far and to what extent the Stalin leadership was going astray in domestic and international affairs. These difficulties notwithstanding, the formation of the United Opposition did at least breathe new life into Trotsky's political activities. He may have been impressed with the zeal with which Zinoviev initially entered battle against Stalin. Such was the strength of Zinoviev's protestations at the Politburo, particularly over Soviet foreign policy, that Stalin took Zinoviev as his main enemy. Over the course of 1926 and 1927 the United Opposition presented a series of co-authored and jointly signed documents. Taken together, these amounted to a damning critique of the ruling clique's record in internal and international policy.

According to the United Opposition, the fundamental problem with the majority line was its increasing departure from proletarian and Leninist thinking. This was evident above all in current economic policy. For socialism to progress, heavy industry had to increase its weight in the national economy. Without this there would be no growth of the working class. Furthermore, the alliance between the workers and the peasants would be undermined. Peasants would not willingly grow and market their produce if they could not purchase industrial goods. Nor would the socialist agricultural policy of collectivisation stand a chance of acceptance in the countryside until the regime was able to supply tractors and other mechanical goods to the farms. Finally, socialism would only prove itself on a world scale if it could out-produce capitalism. To do this the USSR had to industrialise. There were thus many reasons why the regime had to prioritise investment in heavy industry. The United Opposition also perceived the means of doing so. Through sensible and rational planning there were numerous avenues for efficiency savings. There was also a substantial amount of taxable revenue that could be taken from the excessive profits made by kulaks (rich peasants) in the villages and by NEP capitalists in the towns. If a coherent, flexible and planned economic policy were devised with these priorities in mind, the United Opposition claimed that the USSR could experience economic growth with an improved standard of living for workers and poor peasants. (These claims will be evaluated below; see pp. 151–3.)

Instead of this proletarian and Leninist outlook, however, the Stalin leadership was favouring petty-bourgeois elements of the national economy. Industry was given no particular preference. Its growth rates lagged dangerously behind the expansion of the economy as a whole. The workers were under constant pressure to produce more for less reward, with a continual squeeze on their basic standard of living. In contrast, NEP capitalists were making super profits from the trade of scarce items. In the villages the kulaks benefited from tax breaks, while the tax burden on the poor and middle peasants increased. Not only was Bukharin economics shoring up difficulties for socialism, but it also contained pernicious political consequences.

The United Opposition noted that Bukharin economics was accompanied by an abandonment of Leninist principles of party organisation. Lenin had insisted above all upon democratic centralism. This meant, amongst other things, that party members would have the right to discuss all issues, conducting a fair and open debate. In particular, in the run-up to important events such as party congresses and conferences, rival platforms would be able to print and distribute conflicting programmes and advice. However, once a decision had been taken, all party members would unite around that decision and implement party policy in unison. In between conferences and congresses, however, the rank and file had the right and a duty to inform the party if they felt that its policy was not adapting itself to new circumstances. Ultimately the party remained the property of its membership. If sufficient comrades were convinced that the leadership had gone astray, the party could call its Central Committee to account. It was little surprise, then, that for the United Opposition the period of Lenin's rule was full of debate and controversy over issues ranging from the peace of Brest-Litovsk to the trade unions.

The rule of Stalin and Bukharin, however, formed a marked contrast to the party under Lenin. Now the party was terrorised so that the ordinary membership was afraid to voice its criticisms of the leadership. The principles of a fair and open debate had been lost. Rival platforms were denied access to the party's printing presses. The leadership ascribed false views to its opponents, with the purpose of outlawing them as illegal and anti-party. Scheduled party meetings, including the national congresses and conferences, were suddenly and unlawfully postponed if the ruling clique felt that it was in its interests to do so. The official justification for these 'anti-Leninist' actions was the need to preserve party unity. Their actual impact, for the United Opposition, was to push honest and conscientious communists into factional activity.

It was clear to the United Opposition why the Stalin majority had to ride roughshod over the best traditions of Bolshevism. The more it departed from a proletarian class line, the more it was isolating itself from the working class and leading the regime into a blind alley. Discontent was an inevitable result, as the working class abandoned the party in droves. The only way the majority could maintain its grasp on power was to silence its opponents and rely on the petty-bourgeois beneficiaries of current economic policy. This was why good communists were being persecuted and their places in the party taken by NEP traders and kulaks.

The United Opposition claimed that the national and international bourgeoisie was delighted by Stalin's repression of his left critics. The more confident the bourgeoisie became, the more pressure it exerted on Stalin to shift further to the right. Ultimately, for the United Opposition the doctrine of socialism in one country was the ideology of Menshevism. Stalin replicated his crimes against the Russian Communist Party in the international communist movement. Sympathisers of the United Opposition were hounded out of communist parties in Europe and beyond. The inevitable result of Stalin's wager on the bourgeoisie, however, was disaster for the communists of Great Britain and China. The defeat of the working class in the British General Strike of 1926 and in the Chinese Revolution of 1925–7, in no small part down to Stalin's mistakes, served to reinforce the pessimism of the international working class and to strengthen Stalin's belief in socialism in one country.

Despite painting a depressing picture of the state of affairs in the Soviet and international workers' movements, the United Opposition did not think that all had been lost. The processes of degeneration had not reached the point at which one had to call for a new revolution against the ruling clique to save Leninism. Stalin could return the party to the right path through reform, but only if he adopted a true Leninist class policy. The first steps in this direction would be to reassert the rights of open and free criticism, and to hold a party congress in this spirit. From its side, the United Opposition offered its services and good will.

There is much in the platforms and pronouncements of the United Opposition that is common to subsequent commentaries on the nature of the inner-party struggle of the 1920s. One of Stalin's personal secretaries who later defected to the West, Boris Bazhanov, confirms that it was behind-the-scenes manoeuvres, not the amassing of support through superiority in debate, that assured his boss victory.[2] The post-Stalin Soviet leadership itself, most notably Khrushchev and Gorbachev, accepted that many of the party's mistakes in the period of Stalin's rise to power stemmed from the General Secretary breaking the democratic norms of party life. It is hard to deny the claim that there was a far from healthy situation in the Soviet Communist Party at this time. An atmosphere of persecutions, false accusations and recriminations no doubt impeded sensible evaluations and resolutions of pressing political problems.

In these difficult circumstances Trotsky did what he could to maintain a standard of honesty in debate. He went to the podium at national and international conferences armed with a series of quotations to show that Lenin denied that socialism could be built in isolation. In no way did Trotsky submit meekly to the campaign against him. He repeated a tactic he had previously employed in his battles against tsarism, turning the tables to put the accusers in the dock. In June 1927, for example, the Central Control Commission met to consider a recommendation for Trotsky's expulsion from the Central Committee. He replied to the charges of anti-party acts with a series of robust denials and counter-accusations. He called for the removal of several of the Commission's members for their part in Stalin's anti-party conspiracies. He presented the United Opposition as the true standard-bearer of Bolshevism, most notably for its advocacy of a proletarian line in domestic and international policy. This was contrasted with Stalin's government, described as a 'worthless regime, a regime of back-sliding, an ideologically emasculated, narrow-minded and short-sighted regime'. If, he declared, the Central Control Commission was truly interested in fulfilling its functions honestly, it would be 'duty-bound to put an end to the dirty, abominable, contemptible and purely Stalinist campaign against the Opposition'. With the benefit of hindsight, when time had proven the Opposition's criticisms correct, Trotsky warned the Central Control Commission that it might find itself concluding that it 'parted company with those whom we should have preserved, while preserving those from whom we should have parted company'.[3]

The damning speeches at the Central Control Commission were followed, in October 1927, by a lengthy refutation of officially sponsored slanders on his role in the revolution and regarding his relations with Lenin. The cause on this occasion was a request from the Commission for the Study of Party History for reminiscences to celebrate the revolution's tenth anniversary. In Trotsky's reply Stalin was accused of orchestrating a ten-year campaign against him. Several documents were cited to illustrate Trotsky's skills as a leader and Lenin's appreciation. This contrasted sharply with the examples offered to illustrate Stalin's 'opportunism', culminating in Lenin's decision to break off relations with his General Secretary and to recommend his removal.[4] However compelling this version of the party's history may appear, it remained unpublished until Trotsky could issue it in exile.

Hidden from the general public and the ordinary party membership, Trotsky's speeches at the Central Control Commission and the letter to the Commission for the Study of Party History did have an impact on the inner-party struggle. They probably strengthened Stalin's determination to banish from the capital a man who described him in such unflattering terms. Certainly, in a letter to his friend and colleague V. Molotov, Stalin responded angrily to Trotsky's outbursts at the Central Control Commission:

> I had a look (very quickly) at the 'transcript of the Central Control Commission session' on the Zinoviev and Trotsky affair. The impression given is one of utter confusion on the part of the Central Control Commission. Zinoviev and Trotsky, not the Commission members, did the interrogating and the accusing. ... I resolutely protest against the fact that the commission to charge Trotsky and Zinoviev has turned into a forum for charges against the Central Committee and the Comintern, with an emphasis on the 'case' against Stalin.[5]

Although Stalin was less than happy about his colleagues' inability to clamp down on Trotsky's rhetorical flourishes at key meetings, it was the case that the struggle for power would not be resolved by persuasiveness of arguments. In the heat of battle, polemics took precedence over calm analysis. The fact is that Trotsky had no adequate response to the fundamental problem of how to further his programme in the absence of much-needed gestures from Stalin. Trotsky readily admitted that Stalin held a majority in the party. The state's not insubstantial repressive apparatus was also in Stalin's hands. And yet Trotsky remained incredibly naive about how to overcome Stalin. Initially he expected ordinary party members to raise the concerns of the United Opposition at cell meetings across the country. If this happened simultaneously the Opposition would ride to the top on a groundswell of discontent from below. When he realised that repression and fear made such a scenario unlikely, he claimed that the workers' anger with Stalin's pro-bourgeois policy would eventually force them to act, by way of strikes and other protest activity, to defend the gains of October. In this event, the United Opposition would return to power. In the meantime, he urged his supporters not to abandon the party and to remain loyal to its decisions, even when the United Opposition was condemned.

In the circumstances of the time, Trotsky thus sentenced himself to political impotence, beyond the modest propaganda efforts he was able to mount. After all, Stalin was highly unlikely to undergo a sudden change of heart. He could not have been impressed by how the United Opposition described Stalin's political role. He was maligned as a man and as a thinker, labelled variously as disloyal and stupid. In the writings of the United Opposition Stalin was presented as having no core beliefs of his own. He merely reacted to external stimuli, turning now to the left and now to the right, but with the trends of a series of zigzag policy changes favouring the right. Stalin may have possessed no great intellect, but his speeches of the time show a clear determination not to offer any concessions to Trotsky. Stalin was able firmly and steadily to demote his critics, first from the Politburo, then from the Central Committee, and ultimately from the party.[6] The morning and evening sessions of a meeting of the Joint Plenum of the Central Committee and the Central Control Commission of 23 October 1927, for example, were dedicated to a discussion of the United Opposition. The debate did contain policy issues, but it was dominated by a familiar mixture of accusations and insults. Trotsky and co. were called 'neo-Mensheviks', whose clear intent was to found a second party to derail the revolution. Trotsky recalled a comment made by Lenin at the Tenth Congress, that Stalin knew only how to prepare 'spicy dishes', and went on confidently to predict his enemy's 'inevitable political failure'. His speech was continually interrupted by cries of 'shame', 'Menshevik chatter', 'lies' and so on. Such was the furore that the chairman resolved on a temporary halt to the proceedings. The meeting broke up as Trotsky continued at the podium. In contrast, Stalin's careful condemnation of the United Opposition was met with respectful interjections of 'correct' and 'absolutely right'. When a vote was taken, only 11 out of 219 delegates objected to Trotsky's and Zinoviev's expulsion from the Central Committee.[7] At a further Joint Plenum of 12–14 November 1927 the vote to expel them from the party was just as decisive: 210 for, 2 against and 1 abstention.[8]

Faced with insurmountable difficulties in the party's higher institutions, Trotsky lacked the popular support and appeal he needed if he was to make a sudden political comeback by the *vox populi*. The United Opposition's programme was consciously rejected by party members, who saw it as an attack on their interests. In Siberia, for example, the white-collar bureaucrats and peasants who dominated the local party organisations were particularly unresponsive to the propaganda of the United Opposition.[9] Indeed, such difficulties notwithstanding, in the absence of open politics there were few means by which Trotsky could campaign for a mass following amongst the party and non-party workers. The level of politics undertaken by Trotsky and his adherents was, of necessity, extremely limited. The United Opposition issued statements confirming its loyalty to the party, promising to refrain from 'factional' activity. As 'factional' politics included any public meeting or statement that criticised the Central Committee, the party majority was handed all the grounds it needed to clamp down immediately on any signs of oppositional politics. In turn, rank-and-file followers of the United Opposition understandably became disillusioned with the hopeless situation of its tightrope politics. Under pressure from party loyalists in the workplace, it was not uncommon for ordinary oppositionists to recant their views and to seek an accommodation with the party majority.[10] What was true of the rank and file became increasingly common amongst the United Opposition's leadership. By the time of his sentence to internal exile at the end of 1927, Trotsky not only lacked a mass following but stood more or less alone in refusing to apply for readmission to the party.

Of course, even if by some miracle Trotsky had been able to grasp the reins of power, there are many reasons to doubt whether he would have enjoyed the sorts of policy successes his programme promised. One can question, for example, whether a Soviet economy managed by Trotsky could have provided industrial expansion and improved living standards. After all, the sources of potential additional state revenue identified by the United Opposition, chiefly nepmen (private traders) and kulaks, were either insufficient or likely to react adversely to renewed economic pressure. Trotsky's complaints that the Stalin–Bukharin regime was overly soft on the nepmen ignored the range of new taxes and restrictions heaped upon Russia's urban bourgeoisie in 1926–7.[11] It is unlikely that additional resources could have been squeezed from this sector without fatally undermining its profitability. This subsequently happened, with a loss of tax revenue and a worsening of the situation for the poor Soviet consumer. Trotsky's estimates regarding the kulak danger and the additional taxation available here were also too high. It is generally recognised that the agricultural economy of the mid-1920s was far less stratified than in the pre-war era. Put simply, there were fewer rich compared to middle peasants. Since the revolution there had been a process of 'middle-peasantisation'. Comparative prices for grain were also lower. There was much less grain marketed and traded on the internal and world market. Trotsky nevertheless expected to take extra resources from a far from healthy Soviet agriculture. He does not seem to have considered the possibility that such measures would have acted as a disincentive for the peasants to up production. After all, why should peasants produce more merely to have it taxed by the state? The peasants also had a history of resistance to unfair taxation, for example in the form of further restrictions of marketing and tax evasion. Of what Trotsky's response might have consisted in these circumstances there was not one clue. If one ruled out the option of a return to Civil War-style requisitions, as Trotsky did, then he would have to operate within the limitations of the NEP, something Trotsky did not desire![12]

Having overestimated the resources that could be taxed from the NEP bourgeoisie, Trotsky was also overly optimistic in his plans to reap profits from international capitalism. Several commentators have praised Trotsky for insisting that the Soviet Union should integrate into the world market. In influential studies, both Baruch Knei-Paz and Richard Day have argued that, had Trotsky's plans for economic integration into the world market been followed, there would not have been such pressure to squeeze resources from agriculture to fund industrialisation. Much of the repression that took place under Stalin could thus have been avoided. Yet there are good reasons to question such arguments. It is doubtful whether the Soviet economy of the mid-1920s had much to offer foreign buyers, and certainly it did not have the capacity to earn the level of profits needed for investment to industrialise the USSR. Furthermore, Trotsky held too rosy a picture of a super-efficient Soviet bureaucracy knowing how and when to exploit trends in the world economy. Greater integration with the global market may well have undermined the bureaucracy's plans. The Wall Street Crash of 1929, with its concomitant effects on loans and interest rates, is one notable example of how even Trotsky might have been forced to rely more on internal resources than he bargained for. After all, he accepted the fact that only a stable and expanding capitalism could offer the USSR the economic aid it required. But Trotsky consistently stressed that capitalism was fraught with contradictions and in Europe was certainly in decline. Such assumptions were an important part of his case for revolutionary possibilities, but they undermined his economic programme of utilising the world economy. Indeed, capitalism was duly wary of doing business with a man and a system that sought its overthrow.[13]

An important element of the United Opposition's critique of Stalin's rule was, of course, the view that the world revolution was being betrayed by socialism in one country. In the autumn of 1926 Trotsky famously called Stalin 'the grave-digger of the revolution'. If by this it was meant that Stalin wilfully wasted revolutionary opportunities, the criticism is clearly unfair. In the British General Strike of 1926, for example, Stalin insisted that communists work within the Anglo-Russian trade union committee established in 1925, not so that reformism should triumph (as he was accused by Trotsky), but so that the reformists could more easily be unmasked. One may question the sense of the united-front strategy employed here, but Stalin sincerely thought that it would bring the communists more influence than any alternative. After a close reading of some of Stalin's correspondence touching on international developments of the mid- to late 1920s, Lars Lih has reasonably concluded:

The letters refute the Trotsky-derived interpretation of 'socialism in one country' as an isolationist rejection of revolution elsewhere. To be sure, Stalin never ignored the interests of the Soviet state and he was often cautious to the point of pessimism about the prospects for immediate revolution. But the letters show that he was also capable of hope and enthusiasm when revolution seemed to be on the move and ready to put his money where his mouth was. The letters also document his unremitting hostility toward and suspicion of the capitalist world even when he was forced to deal with it. He was vigilant lest the foreign policy professionals succumb to the disease of rightist degeneration and lose the ability to see the revolutionary aspect of diplomacy. All in all, Stalin comes out of the letters with his revolutionary credentials in good order.[14]

Despite Stalin's undoubted commitment to expanding the base of revolutionary conquests, an accumulation of setbacks for the world communist movement has lent Trotsky's 'grave-digger' comment an enduring appeal. Indeed a 'Trotskyist' narrative on the pitfalls of Stalin's international leadership has long influenced the historiography of the Comintern. This is evident above all in discussions of the fate of the Chinese Communist Party (CCP) in the 1920s.

The CCP was founded in 1921. Since Comintern theorists considered China ripe for a nationalist revolt, the CCP was encouraged to join the national independence forces of the Kuomintang. With a social revolution ruled out, the CCP was advised to subordinate its longer-term goals to the short-term battle to oust the conglomerate of feudal-minded warlords and the imperialist powers from China. In the meantime, much Soviet military aid was offered to the Kuomintang's army, as well as advice on how to organise politically. The tactic of co-operating with a broader movement of national liberation did bring some benefits to the CCP. During 1925–6, for example, party membership mushroomed in the urban areas. Here the CCP became a genuine mass party. The growth of CCP strength did not go unnoticed by the nationalist leadership of the Kuomintang. In the first half of 1926 its leader, Chiang Kaishek, took measures to reduce CCP influence in Kuomintang ranks. Despite these warnings, Moscow ordered the CCP to remain within the Kuomintang-dominated alliance. The possibility that the Kuomintang would wipe out communist forces when they were no longer considered necessary was not taken seriously by the Comintern. Yet in spring 1927 this was exactly what happened. A communist-led strike in Shanghai had prepared the eventual fall of the city to the Kuomintang. Once firmly in control, the Kuomintang used its superiority to massacre thousands of Chinese communists. Trotsky, who had called for the CCP to retain its independence of slogans and organisation to deepen the revolution by establishing Soviets of Workers' Deputies, took the unfortunate turn of events as confirmation of his strategy. Had his advice been heeded, he claimed, the CCP would not have so easily fallen victim to Kuomintang subterfuge and the revolution could have been saved.

Although Stalin cannot escape a proportion of the blame for the disaster that befell Chinese communism in 1927, matters were not as clearcut as Trotsky-inspired historiography has claimed. Indeed, a close study of the many views propagated amongst Soviet leaders on Chinese developments has pointed out that Stalin and Trotsky shared similar hopes for a socialist China, even if they differed on tactics. Stalin thought that the CCP could grasp power by taking over the Kuomintang from within. In this process, Stalin argued that the CCP had to be as independent and as flexible as possible, advancing and retreating as circumstances dictated. Stalin may have held to this strategy for too long, but it did have its logic. Stalin worried that if the CCP abandoned the Kuomintang, as Trotsky demanded, the fruits of the 'entryist' tactic would be lost in one fell swoop. Trotsky, it has been argued, underestimated Stalin's 'leftist intentions'.[15] The gulf between Stalin's gambits and Trotsky's revolutionary recommendations was also breached to some extent by differences within the United Opposition. Zinoviev, for example, was unwilling to reject all forms of CCP–Kuomintang co-operation, even if he accepted the argument that the CCP had to be completely independent. Trotsky often tempered his own stance on China to maintain the unity of the United Opposition. By the time Zinoviev's thinking had been radicalised along Trotsky's lines, i.e. by the spring of 1927, and the United Opposition's critique of Stalin's Chinese policy had become more strident and urgent, it may have been too late to save the CCP from its fate.

In some respects, then, one may legitimately claim that Stalin and Trotsky shared similar views on the necessity of a socialist China. Both may also have overestimated the potential strength of the CCP. For too long, the compromises demanded of Trotsky within the United Opposition masked some of his key differences with Stalin. Putting these nuances to one side, there are other key assumptions of the case against Stalin that must be examined. These are, chiefly, that the CCP blindly followed a policy set in Moscow and that it was this policy that led the CCP unarmed into the Kuomintang's rifles. Further recent research on the Chinese Revolution of the 1920s has questioned both of these claims. To begin with there was a variety of Comintern advisers in China offering conflicting messages. Debate amongst Comintern officials was matched by scepticism and conflict within the CCP. On the ground the Chinese communists displayed far more independence than is accounted for within Trotsky's narrative of events. Furthermore, even had the CCP abandoned the Kuomintang in 1926, there is no evidence to suggest that it could have enjoyed any greater success in 1927. The Soviets that Trotsky thought the CCP could have founded would not have possessed sufficient resources to maintain power. The fact was that the Kuomintang held the advantage in terms of military prowess and popular appeal. What the CCP could have achieved in these conditions would have been limited under any leadership.[16] Indeed, in a recent interview a surviving Chinese Trotskyist of the 1920s claimed that the best that a Trotsky-inspired strategy could have attained would have been a CCP in a better state to recover from a defeat, not that defeat could have been avoided altogether.[17]

In the polemics of 1926–7 Trotsky thus overestimated the influence the Comintern could exert over local communist forces and underestimated the complexities of the reality in foreign countries. One could claim that to expect a more dispassionate analysis from a politician in his situation is to expect too much. He had to use any opportunity for political point-scoring. Even outside the arguments intimately affected by the power struggle, however, Trotsky overstressed extreme tendencies and developments. A notable instance of this is contained in his analyses of inter-imperialist relations. In several speeches surveying the post-war world economy and international relations, Trotsky combined some sharp insights with some blatant wishful thinking.[18] For instance, comments regarding the growth of American capitalism as the main superpower rival to Soviet socialism are well taken. The view that the USSR had to prove its superiority over the USA in peaceful economic competition or be buried in the attempt became the main theme of Soviet politicians from Stalin to Gorbachev. But from the ascendancy of American capitalism as the main Western power Trotsky drew several erroneous conclusions. Prominent amongst these are the notions that

Great Britain, defending its world position, would declare war on the USA; or that the rise of America had pushed European capitalism into terminal decline and hence proletarian revolution; and that, finally, the loss of Europe to socialism would, in turn, put America on the road to a workers' revolt. Trotsky may have felt it the duty of revolutionary socialists never to ignore revolutionary possibilities, but here his main theses were culled from the rich store of his revolutionary imagination rather than rooted in reality. This undermined his power of analysis and prediction, and made of him a less appealing politician and a less sagacious commentator.

EXILE IN ALMA-ATA, 1928–9

In January 1928 Trotsky was sent to Alma-Ata, the capital of Kazakhstan. His departure from Moscow, sanctioned under article 59 of the criminal code for 'counter-revolutionary activities', was marked by a protest demonstration at the capital's railway station. This delayed the implementation of the internal exile order by one day. The journey to Alma-Ata took eight days, with the final section by truck, sleigh and then car. After spending several uncomfortable weeks in a hotel the Bronsteins were offered housing accommodation. The problem of finding adequate living quarters was compounded by Alma-Ata's climate, 'a realm of horrifying dust' in Trotsky's description. Harsh winters alternated with scorching summers. In the latter, one had to leave the town to escape the mosquitoes. A summer dacha was eventually procured, but in the two-year stay in Alma-Ata there were recurrent bouts of malaria. The most striking feature of their new residence, however, was its isolation. This brought with it difficulties of communication. At the best of times the post would be slow; the authorities had ample opportunity to tamper with the mail. Despite these annoyances, Trotsky was soon able to receive letters, books, and journals and newspapers from Moscow and abroad. This enabled him to continue his calling as a revolutionary.

In Alma-Ata he divided his energies between several tasks. He accepted commissions from the Marx–Engels Institute in Moscow to translate some of the classics of Marxist literature. He conducted some research for a planned autobiography, writing to his first wife to enlist her help. He answered the slanders heaped upon his name and the theory of permanent revolution. He corresponded with publishers for contracts. Above all, however, he evaluated the political situation in the national and international workers' movements. Trotsky saw a close connection between Soviet and world developments. A favourable event in international affairs would ease the task of building socialism in the USSR and vice versa.

A major theme of his correspondence, apart from reassuring friends as to his safety, was to note a series of resignations from the opposition's ranks. Trotsky met each recantation with disdain and disgust. Labelling such people 'traitors', he despatched each prominent 'capitulator' with a damning portrait of their political foibles, long known to himself and Lenin. Of Yu. Pyatakov, an oppositionist from 1923 to 1927 who capitulated in 1928, he wrote:

> [A] political corpse who pretends to be alive and invents all sorts of slapdash sophisms to give himself the appearance of a revolutionary politician. ... Lenin was right again when he wrote that in a serious political matter Pyatakov cannot be relied upon.[19]

There was little appreciation of the pressures and factors that led his former allies back into the party. For many, recantation was a natural step to take given Stalin's seeming adoption of key elements of the United Opposition's economic recommendations.

The market-based compromise of the NEP assumed that peasants would voluntarily produce and market sufficient grain to pay state taxes and to sell surpluses via private trade. There would be equilibrium between the needs of the government for revenue for investment in state priorities, the interests of the peasants for self-enrichment, and consumer demand. Economic historians have identified that the NEP was undermined from 1926 onwards. Most importantly, government price policies were set far too low, both for scarce industrial resources and for the grain sold to the state. The main result was a goods famine. Traders bought state goods at low prices to sell them on in the villages for super-profits. The natural way for peasants to offset the difference between higher buying prices for industrial goods on private markets and the low prices offered for their produce by the state was to withdraw from government grain markets. Peasants could make more money by selling on the private market or by trading with the government in items that carried a higher purchase price. The inevitable consequence, by the winter of 1927/8, was a significant shortfall in the government's grain quotas. It was in these circumstances that leading government figures went to areas of healthy farm surpluses to implement a forced requisitioning of grain. Most notably, Stalin in Siberia and the Urals, Zhdanov in the Volga, Kosior in the Ukraine led attacks on the kulaks and the nepmen so that the state could gather the resources to fund a much more rapid expansion of industry. Was the so-called 'Urals–Siberian method' not close to the programme of the United Opposition? Was not a recantation of past errors a small price to pay in order to participate in policies that one approved of?

Such were the conclusions drawn by many former members of the United Opposition. Yet throughout 1928 Trotsky refused to take the shift to the left in economic policy seriously. He noted its superficial crisis-driven character. To the extent that an anti-bourgeois line had been proclaimed, the Left Opposition, formed to replace the United Opposition, could congratulate itself, for without its ideas and theses the Stalin group would not have had the policies to combat the right. Stalin's shift to the left was not, for Trotsky, sufficient grounds to abandon a strictly oppositionist stance. In no sense could Stalin's borrowing of some left measures be taken as a genuine, fully committed left-orientated policy. Indeed, Trotsky considered the centrist epigones incapable of firm leadership. The likelihood remained that the Stalin 'centre' would capitulate to the right. The duty of the Left Opposition remained that of critical support of every move towards its programme. At the same time it had to insist that the CPSU could only become a healthy vanguard party if the Left Opposition was recalled to the helm.

One may wish to applaud the consistency of Trotsky's insistence on 'no surrender'. He would only return to Moscow if certain conditions were met, most importantly a guarantee of open debate before a democratically elected party congress. The logic of Trotsky's advice to the Left Opposition may have been clear, but it did nothing to overcome the failings of the United Opposition.

Despite a damning appraisal of Stalin's shortcomings, Trotsky did not think that the party had degenerated to the point at which one needed to form a second party. If the Left Opposition stood firm, refusing to capitulate and compromise, then eventually it would recapture the CPSU and return the USSR to a truer path to socialism. It would do so by winning over what Trotsky called the proletarian core. He admitted that at the time of writing the proletarian core was largely deaf to the Left Opposition. However, beyond blind faith he had no answer to the problem of how the Left Opposition would reach this proletarian core. This was a key weakness in Trotsky's writings of 1928. It is also a surprising omission from a politician who had long stressed the importance of knowing the correlation of forces. In contrast to his analysis of the class structure of tsarist Russia, Trotsky's references to the proletarian core contain no hint of who made up this group, where its regional and strategic strength lay and how the Left Opposition would gain its trust. To reiterate, in terms of practical politics Trotsky appeared to be living on blind faith.

There were also several strong convictions in the propaganda of the Left Opposition for which evidence is lacking. The claim that Stalin's turn to the left would not have occurred without the pressure exerted by the Left Opposition, for example, is spurious. It ignores the fact that there were anti-market prejudices shared by all Bolsheviks, from Bukharin to Stalin and Trotsky. Even Bukharin argued that the free market would one day be abolished. Disagreements occurred over means and tempos, not fundamental principles. Thus Stalin would have had an anti-market option even without Trotsky's writings of the mid- to late 1920s. When historians discuss the emergence of the 'Urals–Siberian method' they do not assign any prominence to the demands of the Left Opposition. There are a host of factors that carry more explanatory weight. Here one can include the heritage of the Civil War, with its nationalisations, grain requisitioning, and an offensive on all fronts, military, economic, political, social and cultural. It is also possible to place Stalin's left turn in a much longer historical pattern, to interpret it as a revival of the peasant levies typical of Muscovite Russia. It has further been claimed that Stalin's policies developed on his foray into Siberia had an appeal rooted in the history of that region. Without favourable local conditions Stalin would not have concluded that the 'Urals–Siberian' methods could be applied to the whole country. Finally, one should not overlook the work of planners within Soviet economic institutions. By 1928 they had elaborated several planned options for economic growth, one of which assumed measures against the richer peasants to help fund industrialisation.

No doubt Trotsky claimed an excessive influence for himself and the Left Opposition because he held such a low opinion of Stalin. How could the dullard and anti-party Georgian conduct a truly Marxist strategy? With such a prejudice against the General Secretary it must have seemed quite natural for Trotsky to write of the 'inevitable decline of the centre', of its defeat at the hands of the right (and therefore of the national and international bourgeoisie). What has struck subsequent historians, however, is how Stalin remained in control of the party and state throughout 1928. At no point did it seem probable that the party-state would fall under Bukharin's leadership. The ever-masterful Stalin overcame Bukharin's rivalry with a mixture of well-timed concessions followed by fatal blows.

As in previous periods, there are also strong grounds for doubting whether, had he made a triumphant return to Moscow, Trotsky would have made a positive difference. This applies above all to his demands for inner-party democracy. Trotsky may have claimed that he was for the restoration of the party's rights, but this would have clashed with his obviously sincerely held belief that truth was on his side and his side only. After all, a prominent feature of his writings from Alma-Ata is that only Trotsky possessed the acumen to devise correct policies, both domestically and internationally. It was this belief that, in turn, drove the conviction that the party could not do without him. The day would come when Trotsky would have to be recalled. One gains the impression that Trotsky raised the issue of democracy as a means of reinstating himself in the party and ultimately of assuming the mantle of leader. Once these goals had been achieved, however, it is hard to see what use Trotsky would have had for the rights of the ordinary membership. If Trotsky alone was correct, any alternative view would of necessity be incorrect. If Trotsky alone was the true representative of the left, any dissident would of necessity be 'centrist' or 'rightist'. Trotsky's tendency to dismiss his critics as political nonentities has already been noted.

The final aspect of Trotsky's writings of 1928 that must be considered is his ongoing critique of Stalin as head of international communism. Over 1927 and 1928 Bukharin, now leader of the Comintern, had undertaken a re-evaluation of the world situation and communist tactics. The post-war era was divided into three main periods. The first, from 1918 to 1923, was marked by revolutionary upheavals, all of which suffered defeat. This was followed by a trend of capitalist restoration and stabilisation. This lasted from 1923 until 1926, during which time communists were advised to seek blocs, united fronts, with reformist socialists. From 1927, however, a so-called 'Third Period' had emerged, characterised by an increasing likelihood of imperialist tensions and wars, and also of class conflict and revolutions. In the Third Period communists should capture a majority of working-class backing through vehement struggles against social democrats, seen as a major prop of a decaying capitalist order.

Several factors have been identified as underpinning the adoption of more radical strategies in Comintern thinking in 1927–8. There was a worsening of the international situation for the USSR. In May 1927 the British government broke off diplomatic relations, leading to a war scare in the Soviet Union. Several months later, in September, the British trade union leadership resigned from the Anglo-Russian Trade Union Committee. This reinforced impressions among, for example, German communists that socialist reformists could not be trusted to keep to agreements. Finally, the experience of the CCP in the Kuomintang dealt a fatal blow to the united front. In this context it has been suggested that Trotsky's writings on the Chinese Revolution may have had an influence on the Comintern's leadership:

> It can plausibly be argued that Trotsky's critique of the united front from above in China was sufficiently damning to impel Bukharin and Stalin to rethink their Comintern strategy. To this extent, it influenced the shift to the left.[20]

However, as with the shift to the left in domestic policy, Trotsky was less than impressed with developments in the Communist International. He had no objection to the slogans of greater independence of communist parties, of winning over the masses to communist banners and so on. His chief ire was directed at a leadership that, for him, was clearly incapable of giving real content and meaning to these slogans. The bureaucratisation of the CPSU was reflected, he claimed, within the Comintern. In both instances cadres were appointed, not according to talent, but by their willingness to follow the latest line set in Moscow. In an epoch in which objective circumstances could be converted into actual revolutions only if given correct guidance from above, Trotsky lambasted Bukharin *et al.* for their intellectual and political deficiencies. 'A Bukharinist manner of treating questions', meant, he claimed, treating them 'in a literary, pedantic, didactic, and not in an active revolutionary way'.[21]

On Trotsky's understanding, the Comintern could become a genuine centre of revolutionary leadership only if the Left Opposition headed it. He outlined several scenarios by which this could occur. First in preference would be a reform of the CPSU. In the absence of such reform, the Left Opposition could capture the Comintern from within. This would then be used as a base to exert pressure on the CPSU. Finally, a radicalisation of the masses in the coming economic and political struggles could generate a momentum for the recall of the Left Opposition. The chances of each of these scenarios becoming real were quite weak in 1928. The CPSU was firmly in Stalin's hands; the Left Opposition was scattered and weak. A similar situation prevailed in the Comintern. The leaders of the main communist parties applauded the tactical turns of 1927–8. If anything, their alliance with Stalin had been strengthened. The international Left Opposition had been purged from the mainstream of the foreign communist parties. As for the workers, there was little sign of a mass upsurge in Trotsky's favour.

Despite bleak prospects in the domestic and international arenas, Trotsky continued to believe that the future would confirm his prognoses. The Stalin clique could not keep him from power for long. It was from a position of strength, not weakness, however, that Stalin decided, some time in the latter half of 1928, to have Trotsky exiled from the USSR. For Trotsky, Stalin was motivated by several factors to issue an expulsion order. Above all, he was worried by the growth in the popularity of the opposition. With Trotsky in exile, not only would internal discontent lose an obvious figurehead, but it would be easier to condemn the leader of the Left Opposition as a traitor to the USSR. It is likely, though, that Stalin resolved upon exile for more pragmatic and mundane reasons.

To keep Trotsky in the confines of the USSR was to admit that the Soviet authorities were responsible for his general well-being. Recalcitrant communists and awkward regimes would turn to the USSR for information about its most famous prisoner. To deprive Trotsky of Soviet citizenship and to set him free would liberate the Soviet authorities of all responsibility. Stalin could also quite safely gamble that Trotsky would have precious little influence abroad. Devoid of state support, it would be difficult for him to conduct the world revolution. Trotsky soon discovered that the West was all too willing to collude silently with Soviet wishes for his isolation. When Trotsky was told that his new home would be in Turkey he immediately sought permission to settle in Europe, where he expected the next round of revolutions to take off. Requests for a visa to Germany were quickly refused. In the event, the best Trotsky could do was to offer a decorative protest to the Turkish authorities as the Bronsteins were taken over the border. Despite this harsh twist of fate, Trotsky had no intention of ending his political career. Convinced that the workers of the world were in as urgent need of his leadership as ever, his first task was to find new avenues to spread his words. After all, there was the rising threat of fascism to repulse, world capitalism to bury and a Stalin clique to overthrow.

7

AGAINST STALINISM AND
FASCISM, 1929–33

Other than a brief trip to Denmark in late 1932 to deliver a speech on
the Russian Revolution, Trotsky spent the period from his exile from the
USSR in February 1929 to the summer of 1933 in Turkey. For the first
few weeks of the 'Turkish interlude' Trotsky was the 'guest' of the Soviet
Consulate, after which the first of several private lodgings were found.
The most comfortable of these was a villa on the island of Prinkipo,
which provided a home for the majority of the Bronsteins' stay.
Although Trotsky was piqued at being so far from Western Europe, he
had no serious grounds for complaint about his new surroundings. The
Turkish authorities were not inhospitable. No obstacles were placed in
the path of visitors; there were regular meetings with foreign journalists
and publishers, friends and comrades. Each day the post brought a large
correspondence. When the Soviet government deprived the Bronsteins
of Soviet citizenship in February 1932, the loss of Soviet passports was
made good by the issue of Turkish travel documents. It was on these
papers that the trip to Copenhagen was made. Alongside a benign
regime, Trotsky also basked in the beauty of the locality. He particularly
liked the evening view from his office balcony, 'the play of light in the
sky and over the water' as one guest described this 'nightly enchant-
ment'.[1] Weather permitting, there were frequent fishing trips and, from
time to time, hunting excursions. The household had a cook, a cleaner, a
secretary and a permanent Turkish police guard. In these many ways,
Trotsky enjoyed the perfect retreat in which to combine rest and work.

He opened the next stage of his political career by establishing a new publication, the journal *Bulletin of the Opposition*. It was originally issued, in July 1929, from Paris, but its editorial offices were transferred, along with Trotsky's student son Lev, to Berlin in February 1931. The *Bulletin* provided a focus for Trotsky's scattered supporters, some of whom met in Paris in April 1930 to found an International Left Opposition as a faction of the Third International. These manoeuvres would not return Trotsky to power, of which there was little or no hope. They did, however, establish a base from which Trotsky could comment on Soviet and international developments. It is as an observer of important and groundbreaking events such as industrialisation and collectivisation in the USSR and Hitler's rise to power in Germany that Trotsky the outcast continues to lay claim to our interest. Apart from current affairs, Trotsky also used the seclusion of Turkey to complete his magnum opus on October, the three-volume *The History of the Russian Revolution*.

STALIN AND THE USSR

Trotsky's quiet retreat in Turkey contrasted sharply with events in the USSR. Driven by the imperatives of the First Five-Year Plan (1928–32), the Soviet Union's economy and society underwent a rapid and fundamental change. The regime prioritised the expansion of the USSR's heavy industrial base, alongside the collectivisation of agriculture. The urban environment mushroomed. There was movement on a vast scale, from country to town and also within the countryside itself. Some industrial centres were built from scratch. The pace of the transformation was as noticeable as its scale. There were ever-present shortages, the formation of 'storm brigades' of workers to help put priority schemes back on course, and countless orders and counter-orders. It was a chaotic and confused attempt to 'catch up with the West'. Some groups profited and were in favour of the changes. Material advantages, promotions and social mobility could combine with ideological zeal, a sense of purpose and grand hopes for the future. Others were less impressed. There was near civil war in the countryside as peasants sabotaged their stocks rather than have them incorporated into the alien state-sponsored collective farms. And yet despite the undoubted and hard-felt costs, especially the drastic plunge in the ordinary standard of living, there were notable achievements. An industrial base was created. There was an expansion of the working class. In at least one historian's estimation, the workers learned to 'speak Bolshevik'.[2] It was with good reason, perhaps, that the eminent historian E.H. Carr wrote of Stalin as the 'great westerniser'.[3]

Trotsky could not help but be intrigued and fascinated by events in the USSR. Here was Stalin solving in his own fashion the fundamental riddle of permanent revolution: how could a socialist revolution survive in isolation? After all, the key idea with which the Five-Year Plans were inaugurated was to make good a gap of fifty to 100 years with the West in five to ten years. Otherwise, Stalin warned, the Soviet Union 'would be crushed'. Trotsky expressed conflicting emotions on Stalin's 'economic revolution from above'. Its positive aspects, collectivisation and rapid industrialisation, were seen as direct borrowings from the programme of the Left Opposition. Indeed, Stalin's 'turn to the left' in economic policy, Trotsky believed, would have been unthinkable without its previous elaboration by the Left Opposition. Its adoption was a reflection of the Left Opposition's strength, derived from its understanding of the real interests of the proletariat. To the extent that this policy had been implemented, the undoubted superiority of socialist planning had been amply demonstrated. The USSR, Trotsky asserted, would not have made such progress under capitalism. Had Soviet communism fallen to capitalism, the former tsarist empire would enjoy no more than semi-colonial status, an exploited and ravished rump on the margins of more developed capitalist systems. Fortunately, state-led industrialisation and collectivisation had taken the USSR further down the road of socialism. It had thus strengthened its position as the home of the international proletariat.

Alongside such clear praise, however, Trotsky presented numerous criticisms of the methods by which Stalin implemented the Left Opposition's recommendations. A chief criticism concerned the regime's 'adventurism'. The rate set for the collectivisation of agriculture, as much as two-thirds of all farms in a matter of months, was clearly unrealistic. For Trotsky, collectivisation could only proceed on a voluntary basis. The peasants had to be convinced of the advantages of collective farming, for example in its higher yields, greater profits and so on. The regime would only be able to demonstrate this when it could guarantee the complete mechanisation of collective units with farm machinery, and the free exchange of agricultural and industrial goods on state-regulated markets. In other words, collectivisation was a long-term policy, predicated upon a much more highly developed Soviet industry.

Stalin, in contrast, had ordered mass collectivisation in the absence of these important material preconditions. The upshot was a demoralised and resentful peasantry anxious to do anything to avoid state-imposed burdens. Even the collective farm system that had appeared, Trotsky warned, had done so largely in name only. Inside the collectives, constructed on a low economic base, the peasants would fight one another for control over scarce resources. Differentiation would inevitably occur and, along with it, fresh reservoirs of kulaks would emerge. The regime could not claim, therefore, to have eliminated the kulaks as a class. Apart from the terrible harm done to Soviet agriculture's productivity, forced collectivisation had also broken the link, the *smychka* that Lenin had set such store by, between worker and peasant. The countryside was no longer willing to contemplate voluntary exchange with the state, something that had proven difficult even in the best of times. Stalin had to rely on coercion to guarantee grain. This carried with it the constant threat of rebellion in the villages.

The strains and tensions typical of Stalin-led collectivisation were for Trotsky also evident in the industrial sphere. Here the planning agencies expected far too rapid an expansion of the nation's industrial plants. The levels of targeted growth far exceeded those set in the Left Opposition's programme. The Five-Year Plan's mad dash produced several notable negative economic consequences. With the achievement of output targets put at a premium, little attention was given to the quality of the goods produced. This resulted in much wasted production, as some items were not fit for use. Trotsky pointed to examples of roof iron that cracked the moment it was set in place and tractors that continually broke down. There was thus much demand for repairs, and an economy that did not have the spare capacity to meet these demands. Problems of quality also inevitably had an impact on the future progress of the plan. Defective goods were bound to hold up construction schemes. One could not build a four-storey building if the foundations had not been laid correctly. Little wonder that the economy was riddled with half-finished projects, lying in waste as the workers waited for the next deliveries. Soviet heavy industry was not the only victim of poor-quality output. Light industry had a lower priority in the Five-Year

Plan, but even its modest targets contained the disease of low quality. The sufferings of the Soviet consumer were all too apparent.

Apart from issues of quality, a rapid leap in output would also result, Trotsky warned, in serious imbalances in the economy. It would be impossible to guarantee equilibrium of growth across all the various branches of the national economy. In part, this was a consequence of Russia's uneven development under the tsars. The revolution had inherited a largely backward economy, with pockets of advanced industry. Problems of backwardness had been compounded by the USSR's isolation. The Five-Year Plan did not envisage substantial imports to fill the gaps in the nation's own output. A key complicating factor identified by Trotsky, however, was the imperfect knowledge possessed by the planning agencies. It was beyond the capacity of the planners to know precisely which resources would be needed by whom and when. There was inevitably a large element of guesswork involved, especially when a relatively small group of central planners were expected to draw up a plan for a huge country over a five-year period. There would be inevitable gaps and unforeseen complications.

These issues notwithstanding, the Soviet bureaucracy proclaimed the Five-Year Plan real and realistic, and demanded that its targets be met. Indeed, targets were continually revised upwards and a decision was taken to achieve the Five-Year Plan in four years! The overly centralised nature of the whole experiment meant that mistakes made in Moscow carried grave implications for the rest of the country. This served to guarantee that imbalances and halted production remained as constant features of the Soviet industrial landscape. Of course, money invested in incomplete projects was essentially money wasted. Once again, the foundations for further sustainable growth were being put in jeopardy.

The greatest crime of Stalin-led industrial growth, for Trotsky, was the deteriorating position of the working class. It had to accept a worsening diet, partly as a consequence of collectivised agriculture's lower output, inadequate housing, shopping and so on, and a draconian order in the workplace. Higher industrial output should have been sanctioned, according to Trotsky, on the condition that it was accompanied by a raising of the workers' standard of living.

If the economics of the Stalin leadership was not flawed enough in itself, Trotsky pointed out how the situation was made much worse by the political context. Criticism of all too obvious flaws in the economy was dangerous, if not impossible. Official propaganda presented Stalin as an omnipotent and omnipresent leader incapable of wrong-headed decisions. Ordinary workers and managers were thus placed in the awkward position of having to pretend that everything was proceeding according to the plan. Indeed, rewards were distributed if the plan was not merely met but surpassed. Instead of telling the truth and helping the regime obtain a clear picture of the actual state of the economy, managers and workers were encouraged by the reward system to fabricate their work reports. In Trotsky's apt description:

> The coefficients of growth have become questions of bureaucratic prestige. Where is the place for calculation? The director or chairman of a trust who 'completed and exceeded' the plan, having robbed the budget and laid a mine in the form of bad quality of production under adjacent sectors of the economy, proved to be the hero. On the other hand the economist who tried to estimate correctly all the elements of production and did not push for the sacred bureaucratic targets constantly fell into the ranks of the penalised.[4]

The fundamental flaws in the methods of planning in the USSR were, Trotsky believed, producing a crisis in the Soviet economy. He thought, however, that the timely application of a series of interrelated measures could rectify the situation by reform. In one article, he listed a twenty-four-point programme affecting several broad areas of policy. First of all, a halt had to be called to the nonsensical practice of ever-higher projected growth rates. The economy needed a breathing space in which projects at various stages of completion could be finished. The collective farm system had to be curtailed to sustainable proportions. An inventory should be conducted to ensure that only farms that were feasible as collectives would remain so. All other peasants should be given the option of leaving the collective farms. The kulak danger should be kept in check by economic measures such as the taxation system.

Second, economic policy should not abandon free-market practices at one blow. In the transition to socialism there had to be a role for capitalist economic indicators, a lesson that lay behind the introduction of the NEP in 1921. The budget had to be brought under control. Excessive spending had resulted in inflation, which was just as harmful to socialist planning as it was to the free market. The currency should be stabilised by cuts in state spending. Profit-and-loss considerations should guide the operation of state business. It was a mistake, Trotsky argued, to try to outlaw the free market *tout court*. The best way to illustrate the efficacy of planning, for instance, was to see how far planning could balance supply and demand via market transactions. Given Trotsky's warnings about the 'right danger' in Soviet politics it is important to quote his own words to show how far he contemplated a combination of plan and market in the transitional economy:

> The innumerable living participants in the economy, state and private, collective and individual, must serve notice of their needs and of their relative strength not only through the statistical determinations of plan commissions but by the direct pressure of supply and demand. The plan is checked, and to a considerable degree, realised through the market. The regulation of the market itself must depend upon the tendencies that are brought out through its mechanism. The blueprints produced by the departments must demonstrate their economic efficacy through commercial calculation. The system of the transitional economy is unthinkable without the control of the ruble. This presupposes, in its turn, that the ruble is at par. Without a firm monetary unit, commercial accounting can only increase the chaos.[5]

Reading this, one may conclude that Trotsky was one of the first thinkers to call for free-market solutions to remedy the ills of planning. Indeed, one enthusiastic commentator has taken Trotsky as an early proponent of 'market socialism', the model of reform communism that became famous for its role in events such as the Prague Spring of 1968.[6] This is going too far, however. Trotsky resorted to free-market methods only to the extent that they supported planning. He made it clear that planning had to resume, but on firmer foundations. This would hasten the day when planning would replace all forms of free-market activity. Above all, there should be democratic planning. Successful planning could not issue out of a narrow circle of central bureaucrats, however intelligent. It required the active participation of millions of ordinary workers. Those who implemented the plan would know best its shortcomings. There had to be some mechanism by which those at the bottom could convey information to those at the top. If this information was to be true and useful, the outlawing of criticism had to be repealed. Democratisation of society would be meaningless, however, without democratisation of the political system. By this Trotsky did not mean bourgeois democracy, with several competing political parties. He called for the rejuvenation of the one-party state. The election of party officials by the secret ballot and the convocation of a genuine party conference were the first vital elements of a renewal of the CPSU with genuine Bolshevism–Leninism. Trotsky despatched several offers of co-operation to the Politburo. In return for an amnesty for both factions, the Left Opposition would take up its rightful place in the party, helping it to rediscover its true vanguard role.

Trotsky's writings on the First Five-Year Plan contain much intelligent and valuable criticism. The failings highlighted by Trotsky, from the lack of quality, an absence of consumer choice, a disregard of care and concern for the workers, to the predominance of coercion and the hounding of dissident voices, are now common to critical accounts of Soviet economic history. It was a system that seemed to have stood common sense on its head, with rewards for bad practice and punishments for outspoken, if potentially good, suggestions. For example, Stalin described the distinguished economist N. Kondratiev, who developed a market-based model for Soviet industrialisation, as a 'scoundrel' who 'must definitely be shot'.[7] This was obviously far from the approach needed to encourage a sensible discussion and resolution of pressing economic problems.

Given a clear understanding of what was wrong with Stalin's revolution from above, it is somewhat surprising that Trotsky retained an undoubtedly high opinion of the changes underway in the USSR. Most important for Trotsky was the absence of large-scale private ownership in the Soviet economy. As long as the means of production were state property, the bureaucracy, even with its mismanagement and illegal usurpation of the party's functions, could not be a true possessing class. The state thus remained a workers' state, and it was the first duty of any revolutionary to defend this key gain of the October Revolution. It is likely, however, that he may not have been so positive about the wonders of planning had he been more aware of the real economic and social consequences of the Five-Year Plan.

Trotsky doubted the success of collectivisation because he saw it as running ahead of the nation's technical capabilities. He nevertheless welcomed even the perverted form of collectivisation as marking 'a new development in the epoch of humanity, the beginning of the liquidation of the "idiocy of rural life" '.[8] There is no evidence to suggest that Trotsky knew of the extent of the damage caused to the Soviet countryside by crash-course collectivisation. It was, in J.R. Millar's study, an 'unmitigated economic policy disaster'.[9] It would take much more than a limited retreat on the regime's behalf to remedy the dire state of agriculture. Trotsky's intended palliatives to the peasants may therefore have been just as unsuccessful in raising productivity and reconciling state and peasants as Stalin's introduction of neo-NEP market incentives. In the summer of 1932 the Soviet government reduced state grain-collection plans and allowed peasants to trade surpluses at market prices. Against the background of a severe decline in production, however, the peasants could not meet even the reduced targets voluntarily, and the state felt it had no alternative but to resort, once again, to repression. 'Neo-NEP' was incapable of breaking the cycle of peasant protest and state violence.

Peasant hostility towards collectivisation was not only based on economic considerations. Recent research by social historians has revealed how the peasants' misgivings about collectivisation also came out of cultural concerns. Rumours circulated concerning the Godless nature of communism and of the moral abominations typical of the collective farm order. It was reported, for example, that women and children became state property, with everyone sleeping under one huge blanket. Furthermore, worried peasants interpreted the introduction of the collective farms as a portent of the world's end. Divine retribution, or death at the hands of foreign armies invading Russia, would be laid upon those who voluntarily joined the collective farms. Such rumours tended to cement peasant hostility to collectivisation. The peasants devised several strategies of passive and active resistance, with women often leading the rebellions.[10] A powerful combination of the peasants' economic and cultural concerns about collectivisation may have rendered even Trotsky's plans for limited collectivisation redundant.

If Trotsky had at best a partial understanding of the horrors of collectivisation, even because of problems of inadequate information, it can also be claimed that there were serious limitations to his appreciation of the flaws of planning. Trotsky thought that the USSR had made gigantic progress, even under the regime of 'imperfect' planning. Some commentators, in contrast, have described this as a period in which the USSR's faulty economic foundations were well and truly put in place.[11] From such accounts it is not at all clear that, as Trotsky assumed, Soviet planning could have been easily rectified by reform. Indeed, the Soviet government did implement some of the measures advocated by Trotsky. The summer of 1932 marked an attempt to bring excessive spending under control and to move from over-ambitious to more sober planning. Despite these reforms, the economy continued to be plagued by problems of inflation and imbalances throughout the 1930s and beyond. Serious doubts have also been expressed as to whether democratic, or 'perfect', planning as advocated by Trotsky is in fact possible, especially if, even as Trotsky himself would have recognised, it is introduced in an isolated and relatively backward economy. Alec Nove is one prominent economist who has pointed out how and why democratic planning would be no substitute for the free market:

> A view is held by some on the left that Soviet planning is not planning at all. How can it be 'real' planning, when ... distortions occur and when the outcome frequently fails to conform with the intentions of the planners themselves? ... underlying this view is the belief that there could now exist a 'real' socialist democratic planning system which would dispense simultaneously with market, bureaucracy and hierarchy, based upon some undefined form of mass democracy. Those who hold this view are usually quite unaware of the complexities of the modern industrial structure, with its innumerable complementarities and interdependencies. It is not clear where, in this process, is the place for political democracy as an alternative to both market and bureaucracy. Democratic procedures are indeed essential, but these cannot be meaningfully applied to multiple-millions of micro-economic decisions; an elected assembly can vote on broad priorities (e.g., more for primary education, or housing, or developing a region), but hardly on whether 3 tons of constructional steel should be allocated to this or that building site, or that production of red dyestuffs be increased by 3 per cent.[12]

Finally, there are problems associated with other aspects of Trotsky's reform programme. It is doubtful, for example, how far the condition of the workers could have been improved, even under Trotsky's less ambitious growth targets. The requirements of budgetary control, a stable currency, and profit and loss may have meant the workers continuing to pay a heavy price for industrialisation, even if it was limited to a few sectors of the economy only. Trotsky's reliance on the 'proletarian core' to reform the CPSU also looked increasingly unlikely to produce results. In a political system that brooked no opposition there was no obvious answer to the problem of how the party could be captured from Stalin. Trotsky's proposals for democratisation may have foundered on the central dilemma of all subsequent attempts, from Khrushchev to Gorbachev, to open up the Soviet political system, i.e. how to combine democracy and a one-party state. Certainly, his appeals to be brought back into government by an invitation were quite feeble. They were not graced with a reply.

Of course, all of Trotsky's recommendations were premised upon the belief that sooner or later there would be an international revolution. He consistently argued that the Soviet regime could not survive in isolation. If it could not be rescued from the contradiction of building socialism in a backward environment by revolutions in the advanced West it would collapse. Trotsky had highlighted a major obstacle to accomplishing an international revolution. The issue was not capitalism's resilience, but the failings of the international proletarian vanguard. It is not surprising, therefore, that he devoted much of his attention to fighting for a correct proletarian line in the Comintern.

THE THIRD INTERNATIONAL AND HITLER'S RISE TO POWER

Even before the Wall Street Crash of 1929 the notion that European capitalism was in terminal decline had been an established feature of Trotsky's world outlook. It was the insistence that the death-knell was tolling for capitalism that underpinned his certainty that a European socialist revolution was an immediate and real possibility. The fact that a golden opportunity was to hand did not mean, of course, that a socialist revolution would actually occur. For the potential of revolution to be converted into an actual event the proletariat would require firm and flexible leadership. Should the working class fail to resolve capitalism's crisis, the free market would limp on, but under the directorship of the workers' deadliest foes. For Trotsky, this scenario was played out in all its drama and tragedy no more clearly than in Germany between 1929 and 1933.

For Trotsky, the key task in Germany was to save the country from capitalism, not to prop up the bourgeois Weimar constitution. He argued that as soon as the Weimar order could no longer guarantee capitalism a peaceful environment in which to exploit the workers, German finance capital would rely on more openly anti-proletarian forces. In the first instance this would take the form of German Bonapartism, or a government dictatorship standing above a society drifting towards civil war, established to keep the workers from power. Should Bonapartism prove unable to stabilise the situation to capitalism's advantage, it would make way for the most violent form of rescuing capitalism, namely German fascism. According to Trotsky, the defining feature of Germany's numerous political crises of 1929 to 1933 was the battle between socialism and extreme right-wing capitalist politics for the fate of the nation.

It was a struggle that, on Trotsky's reading, the German working class could have every expectation of winning. After all, the workers were the vast majority of the population, holding the key strategic positions in the country's economic life in their own hands. Furthermore, the workers were ready and willing to fight to defend the political, economic and social gains threatened by the collapse of the Weimar Republic and a fascist takeover. All the German Communist Party (KPD) had to do was to lead the workers to power through a correct reading of unfolding events and by applying the correct strategy. In fulfilling these tasks the KPD could have no better guide than Trotsky himself and the German Left Opposition. In numerous articles Trotsky laid down his tactical prognoses, railing against the deficiencies of the German party's leadership.

At each stage of the events that led to Hitler becoming Chancellor in January 1933, Trotsky accused the German communists of doing precisely the opposite of what was required. For German communism to progress it had to capture a majority following amongst the workers. To do this it had to convince them that the KPD was their best hope of preventing a fascist victory. This could be achieved by the application of the united-front strategy, as developed in the first years of the Communist International. By this Trotsky meant that the communists would take the initiative in offering reformist socialist organisations, including the Social Democratic Party (SPD) and the trade unions, a broad-based agreement to join forces to defend the workers' rights from the fascist threat. Should the flawed reformist leaders place obstacles in the way of joint action, Trotsky thought that previously reformist-minded workers would become revolutionary. Apart from the united front, Trotsky argued that the KPD should unify the working-class constituency through other policies and slogans. He thought it vital, for example, that the German communists should bring together employed and unemployed workers. In this context, the party should convince all workers that it had the policies to guarantee full employment. Here Soviet planners should produce outlines of the fantastic growth levels a planned and integrated German and Soviet economy could expect.

Instead of the onward growth of influence a KPD under his guidance could achieve, Trotsky experienced the agony of watching a communist party in retreat. Instead of the timely application of the united front, German communists held Social Democratic organisations at arm's length. The Sixth Congress of the Comintern (July–September 1928) had identified social democracy as the communists' chief enemy, as a form of social fascism determined to keep the workers from revolution. When this outlook was belatedly abandoned, the united front was adopted in the worst form possible. The SPD was told that it could sign up to a joint anti-fascist coalition only if it accepted stringent conditions. This form of 'ultimatism' served to alienate reformists the communists had not only to attract but also to win over.

As his advice was rejected and his criticisms not given serious attention, Trotsky emphasised that German communism would discover its true voice only if it was freed from the pernicious influence of Soviet tutelage. One could not expect an organisation from which freedom of criticism was absent and whose leaders were appointed from Moscow on the basis of loyalty and not ability to lead a revolution. Trotsky urged the KPD to adopt the model of reform he had long recommended for the CPSU, namely a genuine party conference for the election of a new, Bolshevik–Leninist leadership. Such a conference should be preceded by the opening of the party's journals to the programme of the Left Opposition. Given its correct policies, the Left Opposition could not fail to win a majority backing from the workers.

In the absence of the German party's willingness to concede to Trotsky's demands, there was little the Bolshevik-in-exile could do, marooned on his Turkish island. The Left Opposition was too thin on the ground in Germany to undertake the sort of broad-based campaign advocated by Trotsky. He applauded and encouraged any signs of workers taking the initiative to conclude anti-fascist fronts from below, and hoped (forlornly as it turned out) that these would grow to engulf the leadership. When Hitler was offered the job of Chancellor Trotsky put all the blame on the Communist leadership, in Germany but ultimately in Moscow. The list of Stalinist-inspired crimes was long and depressing:

> Since 1923 ... the Stalinist leadership ... restrained and hindered the workers when the conditions dictated a courageous revolutionary offensive; it proclaimed the approach of the revolutionary situation when it had already passed; ... it replaced the serious struggle by leaps, adventures or parades; it isolated the Communists from the mass trade unions; it identified the Social Democracy with fascism and rejected the united front with the mass of workers' organisations in face of aggressive bands of the National Socialists; it sabotaged the slightest initiative for the united front for local defence, at the same time it systematically deceived the workers as to the real relationship of forces, distorted the facts, passed off friends as enemies – and drew the noose tighter and tighter around the neck of the party, not permitting it to breathe freely any longer, nor to speak, nor to think ... the Stalinist bureaucracy has succeeded in converting the crisis of capitalism and of reformism into a crisis of Communism. That is the total of ten years of uncontrolled command by the epigones![13]

Trotsky's analysis of German politics from the Wall Street Crash to Hitler's appointment as Chancellor has found numerous admirers. Deutscher rated the 'attempt to arouse the working class of Germany to the danger that threatened it' as his subject's 'greatest political deed in exile'. More recently a collection of eye-witness accounts of the immediate background to Hitler's rise to power confirms Trotsky's claim that a mixture of typical SDP defeatism and a hollow KPD leadership combined to sap the undoubted fighting capacities of the workers, paving the way for German fascism's success.[14] Finally, an examination of the KPD based on freshly released materials from the archive of the Comintern reveals that the party chief, E. Thaelmann, paid more attention to upholding the cult of his personality than to answering his critics' claims that he was ignoring the party's inadequate response to Hitler. Thaelmann was so blind to the actual developments taking place outside his immediate orbit that on the very eve of Hitler's appointment as Chancellor he was sending soothing reports to Moscow about how the threat from fascism had already passed. At least one contemporary scholar's conclusion echoes that of Trotsky's drawn some seventy years' earlier: 'if progressive forces seeking cooperation with Social Democrats had captured the KPD, Germany's fate would have been altered, and the world would have escaped the horrors of the Second World War'.[15]

There is a certain attraction to Trotsky's account of KPD blunders and the possibility that had the German communists adopted a different course Hitler's triumph could have been avoided. The support such a case has received in subsequent studies is hardly surprising. After all, who does not wish that the National Socialist German Workers' Party (NSDAP) had never taken power? One can still question, however, whether history would have been so different had Trotsky had a greater influence upon events. It has been suggested, for example, that sectarianism on Trotsky's behalf, a refusal to work with those who would not tender unconditional acceptance of his leadership, blocked joint action amongst even the several small splinter groups that operated on the far left.[16] Such squabbles did not bode well for Trotsky's calm assumption that he could have reached vital agreements with the SPD.

The mutual suspicions that divided the far left were also apparent in the relations between reformist and revolutionary socialists. It has been made clear that the SPD's anti-communism was as much at fault as the KPD's social-fascist line in maintaining the united front as a low priority on the left's agenda. Indeed, the concept of social-fascism was not invented by the Comintern as a deliberate ploy to hand victory to Hitler, but because it made sense in view of the SPD's unquestionable hostility towards communism. Had not Lenin himself spoken of the crimes of 'social patriotism' in World War One?[17] Here one should note that Trotsky was as dismissive of the SPD as he was of Stalin. He described Social Democracy as 'the hanger-on of the bourgeoisie' and 'doomed to wretched ideological parasitism'. He set clear limits to the type of united-front activity he would countenance. Indeed Trotsky dismissed out of hand the sorts of united-front efforts that might have made most difference to the politics of the time. This is clear from his stance on the presidential elections of 1932. Trotsky insisted that the communists field their own candidate, informing his supporters to campaign for Thaelmann 'to their utmost'. With the left devoid of a serious contender and in disarray, Social Democrats preferred Hindenburg to Hitler. The man who (ironically) was soon to offer Hitler the job of Chancellor was re-elected.

Of course the case against Trotsky's assumptions can be taken one stage further. He tended to be very dismissive of National Socialism as a political movement. In November 1931 he wrote of its membership as 'human rubbish ... the great bulk of the fascists consists of human dust'. In retrospect, Trotsky denied Hitler any political genius. It was merely the case that 'Hitler played checkers and his opponents played to lose'. Little wonder, then, that Trotsky thought that the difference between Hitler winning and Hitler losing was the fact that his own recommendations had been overlooked. In an article of February 1933, for example, he wrote of a pamphlet written 'two and a half years ago': '[t]here is not the slightest doubt today that if this policy [the united front etc.] had been adopted in time, Hitler would not be Chancellor at the present time and the positions of the German proletariat would be unassailable'.

In making this bold claim Trotsky overestimated the power of the workers and underestimated the strength of fascism. It is possible that Hitler would have risen to power even over a coalition of communists and social democrats. German socialism had taken a severe blow from the Great Depression. Its organisations were weakened by the growth of unemployment. It is not so persuasive to claim, as Trotsky did, that fascism was the means employed by finance capital to see off the workers' assault on capitalism. Workers still in employment tended to become more defensive, thinking in the first instance of holding on to their jobs. As much as two-thirds of the KPD's membership was drawn from the unemployed. Little wonder that the party's appeal for strike action fell on deaf ears. This was a reflection of the party's social base, of its political and social weakness, and of apathy in the face of a seemingly hopeless situation, rather than incorrect tactics as outlined by Trotsky. On the other hand, the NSDAP went from strength to strength. Its highly efficient and inventive electoral machine was very successful at mobilising Germans in their many millions to vote for Hitler. Despite Trotsky's claim that the German army would not be decisive in the battle between socialism and fascism, the fact that the military leadership swayed to the right was another factor in Hitler's favour. Also, a strong case has been made for the fact that without the machinations and miscalculations made by Germany's traditional conservative power elites Hitler would not have become Chancellor. There were thus numerous factors that produced a Nazi Germany. A change in KPD policies as demanded by Trotsky might have been insufficient to keep the NSDAP from government.

Finally, it is not at all certain that, out of all of the commentators of the time, Trotsky, as Deutscher claimed, 'like no one else, and much earlier than anyone, grasped the destructive delirium with which National Socialism was to burst upon the world'. Hitler also troubled some traditional German conservative voices. In January 1933, for example, Ludendorff told Hindenburg that 'this accursed man will cast our Reich into the abyss and bring our nation to inconceivable misery. Future generations will damn you in your grave for what you have done.'[18] Indeed, Trotsky held a one-sided conception of fascism. This weakened even his understanding of what it boded, despite his early prophecy that in government it would inevitably produce a second world war.

For Trotsky, fascism was primarily a device employed by a decaying capitalism to atomise and crush the workers. Its main tasks were merely assigned it by 'monopoly capitalism'. Its triumph was therefore the workers' 'greatest defeat'. This was true in that the Nazis soon took repressive measures against socialist and communist organisations. Against this, Nazi employment and social policies did undoubtedly buy some worker support, at least in the short term. Nazism was also harmful, and in some instances more harmful, for so many other groups and interests, including capitalism. In denying that Nazism's 'historic role' could permit it to take 'a single thought to its conclusion', Trotsky missed National Socialism's self-radicalising and ultimately self-destructive essence. In this context, Trotsky largely ignored the racial aspect of Nazi ideology. Nazi anti-Semitism appalled him. However, Trotsky would strike today's reader as an extremely perspicuous and farsighted commentator on fascism if he had foretold a likely Holocaust, but he issued no specific warnings on this regard. Indeed, in a most unfortunate analogy he compared the programme of National Socialism with 'a Jewish department store in an obscure province. What won't you find here – cheap in price and in quality still lower!' Had he conceived of National Socialism as more than an economic category, his perception of its evils and dangers would have been broader, and his political response might have looked beyond communist and socialist workers to build an even broader anti-fascist coalition (to include, for instance, Jewish organisations troubled by Hitler's anti-Semitism).

Whatever the merits of Trotsky's view of fascism, the Nazi victory did convince him of the final bankruptcy of the Third International and of the CPSU. He ceased to believe that they could be reformed from within. The masses would have to be won over to newly founded communist bodies, both national and international, led by the Left Opposition. Trotsky did not underestimate the difficulties involved in establishing a fresh network of communist organisations. But, he reasoned, there were several factors that would work in his favour. After the experience of Moscow's blunders, the workers of Germany and elsewhere would surely abandon Stalin forever. To whom else could they turn but the real representative of Bolshevism–Leninism? Convinced that he was armed with a correct politics, Trotsky was certain that the future belonged to him.

HISTORIAN OF THE REVOLUTION

In many ways Trotsky was ideally suited to write a lengthy treatise on the Russian Revolution in quick time, just one year in fact. He had a large store of existing texts to draw upon, from his study *1905* to his numerous attempts to address what really happened in October during the struggle for power. Much of this was simply recycled into the three-volume *The History of the Russian Revolution*. As a historian Trotsky already had a conceptual framework to hand; he knew whom to write out of the story and whom to praise. In Trotsky's version of October there was a hero (Lenin) and a villain (Stalin). Prior to the hero's return to Russia in April 1917, the villain was leading the Bolsheviks according to the Menshevik stance of supporting the Provisional Government. It took the hero's harsh and urgent intervention in the April Theses to rearm Bolshevism with a truly revolutionary strategy. A footnote reminds the reader that only one other Russian socialist (Trotsky) reached the hero's conclusions independently of the master. Anyone familiar with Trotsky's account of the October Revolution before 1931 would thus find little of surprise in the three-volume history. Chapter 1 did reformulate Trotsky's long-held beliefs on the peculiarities of Russian history into a grand sounding 'law of uneven and combined development', but this was just another instance of Trotsky responding to Stalin. After all, Stalin had referred to Lenin's use of a law of uneven development to give a Leninist kernel to the formulation of socialism in one country. The appearance of the 'law' in *The History of the Russian Revolution* was another attempt to link it to permanent revolution, and hence Lenin to Trotsky.[19]

Apart from the absence of a new interpretation, *The History of the Russian Revolution* is a profoundly idiosyncratic work. It is not based on any new sources. Its author was proud of the absence of a formal scholarly apparatus. Existing accounts, for example the remembrances of the Menshevik journalist N.N. Sukhanov, are at times dismissed as unreliable and at others used as supporting testimony. At key moments the interpretation of events is clearly contradictory. In answer to the question 'Who led the February revolution?', for instance, we are told: 'Conscious and tempered workers educated for the most part by the party of Lenin'. Later the text makes it clear that by these 'conscious and tempered workers' is meant those who had 'decisively risen to their feet during the upward years of 1912–14'. And yet at other points we are informed that during the war the class-conscious workers were sent off to the front and replaced by new stock to the extent that 'the war produced a new working class'. Furthermore, during the hostilities the Bolshevik organisation in Russia had been smashed to the extent that 'the revolutionary succession had been broken', and Bolshevism reoriented itself and 'began to speak out loud ... with its own voice' only after Lenin's return in April 1917. In the light of these factors the reader is left to puzzle over where exactly the Leninist workers of February 1917 had come from! The periodisation of the October Revolution is carefully truncated to fit a particular interpretation. By concentrating almost exclusively on 1917, Trotsky is able to present October as an 'authentic popular revolution'. Histories that look beyond this year, even if they accept the popular support given to the Bolsheviks in 1917, then recount how the Bolsheviks betrayed these popular aspirations. Small wonder, then, that some critics have denounced *The History of the Russian Revolution* as the justification of a profoundly anti-democratic coup, or as dramatic art, as theatre, in which literary devices give a reader little choice but to agree with the text's teleology.[20]

There are numerous instances in which *The History of the Russian Revolution* produces its own myths of the revolution, in this way obscuring its history. In order to magnify Lenin's genius, Trotsky downplays his own role. Hints of his greater importance are to be found, but one has to undertake further research to bring out the full extent of Trotsky's impact. If the author minimises his own contribution, the variety of outlook in the Bolshevik faction prior to Lenin's return are not faithfully reproduced. In order to lend the April Theses a greater importance the whole of the pre-April Bolshevik leadership is dismissed as Menshevik, advocating the war as a war of defence and being sympathetic towards the liberal Provisional Government. In actual fact there were several Bolsheviks who, prior to April 1917, were anti-war and sought to overthrow the Provisional Government. There was far more heterogeneity of outlook in the pre-April Bolshevik leadership, and therefore more continuity between pre- and post-April Bolshevik thinking, than Trotsky accounted for. There were thus several prominent Bolsheviks (including 'Shlyapnikov, Kaiurov, Chugurin and other members of the Vyborg District Committee') for whom the April Theses would not have represented a bolt from the blue, but a welcome confirmation of current thinking.[21] In the more recent period there has also been a robust defence of Stalin's actions in 1917. *The History of the Russian Revolution* is highly dismissive of Stalin, claiming that

> [He] was neither agitator nor orator. He never appeared as spokesman at party conferences. But did he appear so much as once in the mass meetings of the revolution? In the documents and memoirs no record of it has been preserved.[22]

However, a close reading of Stalin's actions and writings of 1917 has shown that *The History of the Russian Revolution*'s villain shared with Trotsky a view that the bourgeois Provisional Government had to be replaced by rule by the Soviets with a Bolshevik majority. Moreover, Stalin had expressed his hostility to the Provisional Government before April 1917. Finally, in October Stalin 'did not hesitate to work towards such a take-over by the Soviets, and harmoniously participated in the venture. He did not need to be convinced of its timeliness. It was a perspective he had stood for all along.'[23] In the disagreement between Lenin and Trotsky over the tactics and the timing of the revolution it is highly likely that Stalin backed Trotsky (something both men would subsequently not wish to recall, for similar polemical purposes).

Despite its numerous shortcomings, *The History of the Russian Revolution* has exerted a profound influence on the general study of the Russian Revolution. Richard Pipes, for instance, dismisses *The History of the Russian Revolution* as 'partly political tract, partly literature'. But even Pipes on occasion relies upon *The History of the Russian Revolution* for a factual version of events.[24] The conclusions of several recent accounts of Russia in the revolutionary period broadly defined are very similar to those of *The History of the Russian Revolution*. To mention just a few of the key examples, *The History of the Russian Revolution* argues that tsarism fell because it failed to update itself to meet the needs of a modernising society:

> Although the monarchy did under compulsion make concessions to the new forces, nevertheless inwardly it completely failed to become modernised. On the contrary it withdrew into itself. Its spirit of medievalism thickened under the pressure of hostility and fear, until it acquired the character of a disgusting nightmare overhanging the country ... [Nicholas II's] ill-luck flowed from the contradictions between those old aims which he inherited from his ancestors and the new historical conditions in which he was placed.[25]

This is a conclusion reached by Peter Waldron in his (1998) consideration of the fate of the reforms of the tsarist reforming prime minister, P.A. Stolypin:

> Stolypin needed to persuade the traditional political elites of the empire that the long-term interests of the state required them to forgo their power and privileges ... the tsarist political establishment was determined to make as few concessions as it could. The Russian autocracy possessed no mechanism by which it could respond to social and economic change ... Nicholas II and his coterie took a short-sighted view of Russia's future, believing that antiquated political structures could successfully cope with a society and economy that were rapidly modernising.[26]

In *The History of the Russian Revolution* Trotsky recounts the winning of majorities by the Bolsheviks in the Soviets and other bodies over late August and September as evidence of the popular base of Bolshevism's rise to power. In Ronald Kowalski's (1997) textbook of 1917 we read: 'Bolshevik majorities in the Petrograd Soviet on 31 August and the Moscow Soviet on 5 September testified to their rapidly growing support'.[27] According to *The History of the Russian Revolution* the peasantry's experience of service in the army, combined with their return to the villages in 1917, produced their radicalisation, which was a key element of the Revolution of 1917:

> [I]n the matter of direct influence upon the village the soldiers were still more important. It was only in the artificial conditions of the front or in the city barrack that the young peasants, overcoming to a certain degree their isolation, would come face-to-face with problems of nation-wide scope. ... An infinitely greater work was accomplished by those hundreds of thousands and millions of soldiers who quit the front and the rear garrisons of their own accord with the strong slogans of mass-meeting speeches ringing in their ears. Those who had sat silent at the front became garrulous at home in the villages. They found no lack of greedy listeners. ... The men from the front introduced into the business the heavy determination of people accustomed to handle their fellow-men with rifle and bayonet.[28]

Orlando Figes' (1996) award-winning study of 1917 concurs:

> Military service has always been a form of upward mobility and psychological transformation for the peasantry. The army broadens the peasant's horizons, acquaints him with new technologies and methods of organisation, and often teaches him how to read and write. ... The return of the soldiers on Easter leave, and indeed of deserters from the army, also had a lot to do with this increased peasant militancy. The peasant soldiers often took the lead in the march on the manors.[29]

If, despite the consideration of many factors, Trotsky places special emphasis on the Bolshevik Party for making the October Revolution happen – 'the Russian proletariat was headed by a party of extraordinary political clarity and unexampled revolutionary temper. Only this permitted that small and young class to carry out a historic task of unprecedented proportions' – then, most recently, for John Eric Marot, 'The Bolsheviks *alone* ... steered the revolutionary process to a successful conclusion, and made history.'[30] Indeed Trotsky's summary of the factors he had highlighted to account for 1917 still forms our research agenda of the Russian Revolution:

> Step by step we have tried to follow in this book the development of the October insurrection: the sharpening of discontent of the worker masses, the coming over of the soviets to the Bolshevik banners, the indignation of the army, the campaign of the peasants against the landlords, the flood-tide of the national movement, the growing fear and distraction of the possessing and ruling classes, and finally the struggle for the insurrection within the Bolshevik party.[31]

Measured against *The History of the Russian Revolution* most 'modern' research does not seem so 'modern' after all. Any student of 1917 would be foolish to overlook *The History of the Russian Revolution*. It is essential reading.

Trotsky was not, however, motivated to write *The History of the Russian Revolution* as a textbook for future student use. It was a key component of a wider political campaign to uphold a particular view of Bolshevism. It was a manual of sorts on how to make a revolution. Surveying the balance sheet of the socialist movement's fortunes since his arrival in Turkey, Trotsky would probably have admitted that setbacks outweighed successes. On the plus side, the USSR had undergone some positive developments thanks to the limited implementation of the programme of the Left Opposition. The chief disappointments were Stalin's continued bureaucratic stranglehold over the CPSU and the Third International, not to mention the fall of Germany to fascism. But Trotsky the optimist did not abandon all hope. Political connections in Western Europe finally managed to secure a French visa. Trotsky had just identified France as the country in which Europe's immediate political outlook would be resolved. If genuine socialism could triumph there, then the spectre of communism could once more haunt the continent. It was with his revolutionary head held high that Trotsky finally escaped his Turkish idyll and moved to France.

8

THE FINAL EXILE

THE FOURTH INTERNATIONAL AND WORLD EVENTS, 1933–40

For Trotsky the period of Turkish exile, 1929–33, had not been unproductive. Several important books were completed, including an autobiography and the three-volume *The History of the Russian Revolution*. A new journal, *Bulletin of the Opposition*, was established as a fighting organ against Stalin and for the world revolution. Despite these advances and the beauty of his surroundings, Trotsky was clearly frustrated by being so far from the key political developments of the time. In 1933 there was at last the opportunity to return to Western Europe. He settled first in France, from 1933 to 1935, and then in Norway from 1935 to 1936.

Any expectations that a move to France would provide more fertile ground for the spreading of Trotsky's political influence were to be disappointed. It was easier to meet with other Trotskyists, but there was little chance of Trotsky stepping onto a broader political stage. It even proved impossible to locate a permanent residence free from the public eye and controversy. In the two years they were to spend in France, for example, the Bronsteins had no less than a dozen addresses of varying leases. The all too frequent changes of abode occurred despite Trotsky's efforts to avoid upsetting his governmental hosts. For the most part, the French state was content to keep contact with Trotsky to a minimum. He was, after all, a marginal figure, with no large following or mass organisation at his fingertips. Even so, there was always the likelihood that he would become a political hot potato, a potential embarrassment to any government. The increasing polarisation of European politics into left and right helped, amongst other factors, to ensure that his future was always under question. A turn to the left could result in an invitation and a visa; a turn to the right or a worsening of the international drama could produce an exit order. In requesting that Trotsky find another country of residence, Paris could at least object to his articles on the radical left and the possibility of a French revolution. After all, was it not a condition of his visa that he abstain from political activity?

With this lesson in mind, as part of his next visa application Trotsky promised the Norwegian authorities that he would not enter its national life as a revolutionary. Given these guarantees, the newly elected social democratic government at first welcomed Trotsky to Norway in 1935. However, his writings on non-Norwegian affairs were controversial and his hosts were made uncomfortable by Soviet objections to Trotsky's presence so close to its borders. The Norwegian government thought it best to place Trotsky under house arrest. He was rescued from this awkward situation by an invitation to live in Mexico. The offer was gratefully received. The move to North America, where the Bronsteins arrived in mid-January 1937 after a month-long journey by boat, was made possible by representations made on Trotsky's behalf by, amongst others, the famous artist Diego Rivera to the then radical government headed by General Lazaro Cardenas. In Mexico Trotsky had a freedom of expression and movement that he could no longer enjoy in his old stomping ground of Europe. There were even some celebrity visitors, including the novelist André Breton. The relative openness of this existence, however, also created opportunities for Trotsky's enemies. It was in his own study that a Stalinist agent carried out a successful assassination attempt in August 1940.

The constant movement and uncertainties must have upset Trotsky's work patterns and routines. Nevertheless he maintained a healthy output of newspaper articles, pamphlets and books, as well as a vast correspondence with fellow Trotskyists. His political activities were dominated by the struggle to expose Stalin's crimes, typified above all in the series of public show trials brought against old Bolsheviks that began in August 1936. A related task was the foundation of a new international Marxist body, the Fourth International. Much of Trotsky's energy was spent adjudicating the factional infighting between various shades of Trotskyist opinion. He devoted so much of his time to issues affecting the Fourth International because he considered its creation to be the major task of his remaining political life. The stakes were set very high, for Trotsky believed that only a new Bolshevik–Leninist international vanguard could carry out a world revolution, in this way saving the Russian Revolution from Stalinist degeneration, and humanity from fascism and war.

STALIN AND STALINISM

For several years following the return to Europe Trotsky wrote less on the USSR than at any other time of his career. On New Year's Eve 1935 he issued a press communiqué responding to readers' requests for more articles on the Soviet Union. Of course, developments in Russia had not escaped his attention altogether. He had devoted several articles to a defence of his conception of the USSR as a workers' state, so defined because state ownership of the means of production was the dominant form of property. At the same time, Trotsky was keen to expose all aspects of its bureaucratic deformations, including the privileged lifestyles of the top state officials and the constant police surveillance and repression of opposition.

For Trotsky, there was a basic contradiction in the centre of Soviet society. The workers were growing in numbers, culture and self-confidence as a consequence of planned industrialisation. Therefore they could not help but become increasingly dissatisfied with the caste of bureaucratic overlords. At some point the workers would seek to rid themselves of paper-pusher parasites in the cause of deepening and furthering the country's socialist foundations. It was every Bolshevik–Leninist's duty, according to Trotsky, to hasten the day when the workers would turn against the bureaucracy.

Indeed, Trotsky saw some evidence of cracks appearing in the facade of Stalin's harmonious utopia in the famous assassination of the Leningrad party chief Sergei Kirov in early December 1934. Trotsky did not deny that Stalin would use this event as a pretext for further repression. The principal blows, he thought, would be directed against some wavering sections of the bureaucracy to keep the state apparatus in line, and against the remnants of the Left Opposition to weaken opposition against another likely turn to the right. But from the fragments of information that were released about Kirov's murder he did not for one moment suggest that Stalin had issued a death warrant as a means of seeing off a potential rival. The assassin may have had links with the State Political Administration (GPU), but no official, Trotsky was convinced, had ordered Kirov's elimination.

Whether it was carried out for personal or general motives, Trotsky believed that the assassination was a reflection of social discontent with Stalin's bureaucratic terror. In the absence of open political channels for the expression of complaints such acts of individual terror were to an extent understandable and even unavoidable. But, Trotsky warned, they could not in themselves bring about a fundamental change in the political landscape. Only class struggle, the joint and concerted efforts of the vanguard workers, could topple the Stalinist bureaucracy. Before they could reach this conclusion, however, the workers would need a correct Marxist education and leadership. This was the task that Trotsky set for his propaganda. When Stalin and his cohorts announced a new constitution in 1936 as the most 'democratic in the world', Trotsky's immediate riposte was an article highlighting the fallacy of Stalinist democracy. The workers could smash this facade of a socialist heaven and turn it into a reality, Trotsky advised, only if they joined the Fourth International.

In the summer of 1936 Trotsky completed his fullest single study of the USSR, published the following year under the title *The Revolution Betrayed*. Of all of his exile writings, this was the book most likely to reach a wide audience. Its publication, in a paperback English translation, came hot on the heels of the famous Soviet show trials that made world headlines. Just after Trotsky had finished the manuscript in August 1936, some sixteen leading old Bolsheviks, including Zinoviev and Kamenev, were indicted at public show trials for terrorist crimes against the socialist state. After admitting the prosecution's case, the defendants were shot. There were to be two more centrepiece show trials, both of which featured Trotsky's former allies. In January 1937 the 'leftists' Yu. Pyatakov and K. Radek were among seventeen accused. In March 1938 the twenty-one defendants included Trotsky's longstanding associate C. Rakovsky. Against this background, interest in Trotsky's tract on the fate of the October Revolution was understandably high.

The Revolution Betrayed did not mark a new development in Trotsky's views on the USSR. It contained a summary of previously held beliefs and conceptions. This would not necessarily have struck a contemporary reader, most likely unaware of the Russian-language *Bulletin of the Opposition*. The deepest impression the work makes is the extent to which Trotsky thought the Stalin regime had betrayed the Bolsheviks' original aims and intentions. It was a betrayal, he argued, that affected all aspects of Soviet life. In politics, the Bolshevik programme of 1917 was proletarian democracy, including freedom of criticism within the party and the Soviets. It had been replaced by a totalitarian order, characterised most obviously by the rule of an unelected bureaucracy and police repression of any critical voices.

For society, the Bolsheviks had desired, if not absolute equality, something which lay in the complete communist society of the future, then at least that inequality be kept within certain limits. For example, Lenin had famously insisted that the wages of the state officials should be no higher than the pay packet of a skilled worker. In the Soviet Union observed by Trotsky, however, there was gross and increasing inequality, both between and within social groups. The most marked contrast lay in the lifestyle of the bureaucracy compared with the experiences of ordinary citizens. The bureaucrats could expect spacious accommodation, including a holiday home in the countryside. The workers were provided with cramped and inadequate housing, and could even be reduced to sharing a bed on a shift basis in a workers' dormitory. The bureaucrats enjoyed access to specialist shops carrying a range of choice consumer goods. Ordinary citizens had to resort to survival strategies such as scouring the black market or stealing from state enterprises to meet their basic needs. Society was thus clearly divided between a privileged elite and a citizenry suffering from want. Trotsky highlighted the divide-and-rule tactics employed by the bureaucracy against the working class, mainly to prevent an impoverished mass from uniting in revolt. It favoured, for example, the formation of a labour aristocracy, partly via wage differentials and partly via the distribution of benefits in competitive work schemes. One of the most famous examples of Stalinist pandering to a labour elite was the Stakhanovite movement. This rewarded workers who emulated the achievement of the coalminer Aleksei Stakhanov, who in August 1935 overfulfilled a workshift norm by more than fourteen times.

In cultural life, the October Revolution had, Trotsky stated, initially taken gigantic strides towards the liberation of women and the elimination of religious superstition. Stalin's USSR, in contrast, had abolished a woman's right to abortion and was developing a cult of the bourgeois nuclear family. The attack on religious belief had been abandoned in favour of a 'positive neutrality' or reconciliation between church and state. The priesthood would now enjoy greater freedom to fool the people with their non-scientific, superstitious nonsense. In international affairs, Lenin had welcomed the October Revolution as the first step of an unfolding world revolution. Stalin had a narrowly nationalist outlook, summed up in the policy of socialism in one country. Stalin's diplomats were no longer the soldiers of world revolution, but had adopted the dress codes and manners of traditional bourgeois diplomacy. In 1934 the USSR had even joined that arch imperialist club the League of Nations. The foreign communist parties were tolerated only insofar as they were useful for domestic Soviet security goals. Even in the one area in which the original gains of 1917 had been offered some protection – the nationalisation of the economy and the instigation of planning – the Stalin leadership had committed gross policy errors, including crash-course expansion, that were undermining the economy's socialist foundations.

The system described by *The Revolution Betrayed* was clearly not socialist. Trotsky defined the USSR as a 'transitional regime' lying somewhere between capitalism and the beginnings of the lowest form of socialism. Current Soviet claims to have completed the first stages of socialist construction were, he argued, clearly exaggerated. But why had the revolution ended up in such a sorry condition? Trotsky highlighted several interlocking factors. Some were clearly outside the control of the Stalin leadership, most notably the heritage of Russia's poverty, the hostility of international capitalism and the crimes of reformist social democracy, which sought accommodation with the factory bosses instead of their overthrow in a socialist revolution. These objective difficulties had, however, been compounded by the political mistakes of the Soviet bureaucracy. In a self-interested defence of its numerous privileges it had followed a conservative anti-revolutionary policy at home and abroad. For the workers of the USSR and the world one key question remained. Would the Soviet Union correct its deformations and return to socialism, or would its degeneration continue to the restoration of full-scale capitalism? For Trotsky, the USSR's fate would be decided by a living struggle of forces, domestic and international. At home, the workers had to overthrow the bureaucracy by a political revolution. This would only bring benefits, however, if it was supported by the international proletariat. Outside a world revolution, Trotsky saw no hope for the long-term prospects of a communist USSR.

As a critique of current Soviet boasts to be a socialist paradise, evident in the 1936 constitution's statement that the 'exploitation of man by man' had been eliminated, *The Revolution Betrayed* has much to recommend it. It has stood the test of time far better than the panegyrics of the then Western-based friends of the Soviet Union. The British socialists Sidney and Beatrice Webb, famous for their book *Soviet Communism: A New Civilisation?*, were the rightful target of Trotsky's biting humour. Modern research, with its access to archives and Soviet police reports, can give a much fuller picture of life in the mid-1930s' Soviet Union, but its detail often confirms rather than refutes many of Trotsky's claims of the time. Recent work on everyday life, for example, paints a depressing picture of the trials and tribulations of the ordinary Soviet man, and more often woman, in search of scarce resources. Similarly, studies of popular opinion in Stalin's Russia also stress the gulf that citizens felt separated the bureaucratic 'them' from the ordinary 'us'. Understandably, the privileges enjoyed by the bureaucracy and its favoured workers were the source of widespread social resentment. It is less clear, however, whether the population wanted to right these wrongs via socialism or by its overthrow. Trotsky felt that the Soviet proletariat remained sympathetic to socialism, and that its socialist aspirations were a serious hindrance to the bureaucracy's preference for capitalism. Today's historians differ over the extent to which the population genuinely believed in socialist propaganda, or whether ordinary citizens employed socialist language as a convenient ploy to convince their political superiors to grant the people a larger slice of the social cake. Studies of Stalinist ideology and culture lend some support to Trotsky's assertion of a 1930s' 'conservative reaction' against radical Bolshevism 1917-style. This viewpoint was expressed in a revised form in N.S. Timasheff's popular thesis of 'The Great Retreat', first formulated in the aftermath of World War Two. It is still common to read accounts of Stalin's brand of 'national Bolshevism' as opposed to an earlier commitment to 'proletarian internationalism'. It is thus not surprising that *The Revolution Betrayed* continues to be extracted in anthologies of classic writings on Stalin and Stalinism.[1] A contemporary review in a leading American academic journal noted that in exiling Trotsky the Soviet authorities had deprived the regime of an original and inspiring mind. On the whole, *The Revolution Betrayed* was received as a 'brilliant book'.

Of course *The Revolution Betrayed* could not avoid criticism. Some of its fundamental propositions were questioned. The most severe attacks focused on its most basic premise that there was a pristine period in the revolution's history, under Lenin's command. Some object that Lenin was as guilty as Stalin of extinguishing democracy and establishing the rule of a bureaucratic elite. Others doubt early Bolshevism's commitment to liberation, especially of women. There could hardly be a 'betrayal' of the revolution, as Trotsky was suggesting, if Stalin's rule did not differ from that of Lenin.

Trotsky's definition of the USSR as a workers' state, despite its degenerated features, has also not commanded universal acceptance. If one takes the forms of distribution of wealth, rather than ownership, as the system's defining feature, other models or descriptions will carry more appeal. One of the most recent scholarly accounts of state and society under Stalin, for example, discusses three alternative ways of conceptualising its subject: as a form of 'prison or conscript army', as a 'boarding school', or as a 'soup kitchen or the relief agency'.[2] Another leading expert prefers to view Stalin's USSR not in isolation, but as part of a pan-European trend towards a welfare state.[3] Finally, it is worth noting one contemporary reviewer's response to Trotsky's call for a new political revolution to be led by the Fourth International against the Soviet bureaucracy. Did this not provide 'a convenient justification for Stalin's recent ruthless use of the firing squad'?[4]

Trotsky was certainly troubled by the frequent reference to a 'Trotskyist' conspiracy in the charge sheets used in the Moscow show trials. On the long boat journey from Norway to Mexico that lasted from mid-December 1936 to mid-January 1937, he wrote several articles analysing and refuting Stalin's 'frame-ups'. He detailed the processes by which the GPU brought the accused to confess to blatantly false charge sheets. To begin with, compromising confessions were extracted from friends and colleagues. Once under arrest, defendants were then subjected to a barrage of promises of some leniency in the event of co-operation and threats if any objections were raised, levelled at themselves and family members. With the necessary signed confession to hand, the stage was set for the final public humiliation. Courtrooms were packed with secret police masquerading as honest and outraged citizens. Prosecution lawyers and judges – there was to be no defence – then acted out pre-prepared scripts to the announcement of the inevitable verdict of guilty. The fact that such a spectacle was beyond belief would not, Trotsky warned, prevent the outbreak of further trials. Indeed, there was a logic that suggested that one trial would lead to another. In order to lend a semblance of reality to the fantastic claims of a dangerous anti-Soviet terrorist plot the authorities would be obliged to bring more 'terrorists' to justice. But why start the trials in the first place? Trotsky discerned base, but familiar, motives. The elaborate show trials were put on to provide a justification for a reign of terror aimed at the elimination of all opponents. At stake was not so much Stalin's personal rule as the privileges of the bureaucracy. The trials were evidence of the deep unpopularity of the totalitarian regime, and that it was living through a profound crisis. The physical extermination of the old Bolsheviks also provided a graphic illustration of Stalin's betrayal of original, Leninist Bolshevism.

To expose the sham nature of the Moscow show trials in print was Trotsky's initial and understandable response. But however persuasive his case, it was not sufficient proof of his own innocence. To establish this, a more concrete and objective forum, one approaching a legally constituted courtroom, was required. Once in Mexico it became a top priority to set up a quasi-official examination of the accusations levelled against him. The Soviet authorities did not take up his offers to be extradited and cross-examined in Moscow. Instead, Trotsky asked his followers in the United States to organise a counter-hearing. The quickly formed American Committee for the Defence of Leon Trotsky soon arranged a Committee of Enquiry into the Moscow Trials. In this venture they were aided by a leading American liberal philosopher, John Dewey, who agreed to chair the investigation into Moscow's allegations. Dewey had a longstanding interest in the USSR, particularly its education system, and had even visited the country in the late 1920s. Trotsky thus secured an air of objectivity and authority for clearing his name. After all, what interest, apart from a sense of fair play, could a liberal political opponent of Trotsky and Stalin have? The so-called Dewey Committee worked primarily from the United States, but since Trotsky was denied an American visa the chief witness's deposition had to be taken in Mexico.

The counter-show trial was held over a full week in April 1937, with no less than thirteen separate sessions, lasting a total of over forty-one hours. It was held in Trotsky's study in Rivera's house, where the Bronsteins were lodging. A subsequent publication of the verbatim transcript of the hearings runs to some 600 pages. Apart from Trotsky, his lawyer and the Committee, room was set aside for members of the press and interested public associations. The result was a gripping spectacle. Trotsky was subjected to a rigorous examination and cross-examination. He fielded questions not only about his supposed headship of an anti-Soviet conspiracy, but also concerning his pre- and post-revolutionary career more generally. At times the minutes read as if the Committee was using its investigation to satisfy a student-like curiosity about the Russian Revolution. Dewey was particularly interested in Trotsky's relationship with Stalin. Why did 'the prophet outcast' lose to the 'gravedigger of the revolution'? And, if the tables were turned, would Trotsky guarantee his rival the rights he was currently seeking for himself?

To Trotsky's credit, he responded freely and readily to all queries, whether they bore a direct or indirect relevance to the task at hand. A standard Western legal courtroom may have been less willing to enter into a broader historical discussion. As it was, Trotsky stood the test of the witness stand well. The Moscow-based claims that he had created a terrorist, fascist-sponsored network in the USSR were refuted. Indeed, how could Trotsky have met with Pyatakov to pass on counter-revolutionary orders, as was claimed in the January 1937 trial, for example, when it was clear that neither Trotsky nor Pyatakov was at the appointed airport, and when the relevant authorities could confirm that no planes had landed at the supposed times? After several months of further investigations, in late 1937 the Dewey Committee announced its findings. The Moscow trials were declared an unreliable guide to the truth, the accusations against Trotsky unproven.

Trotsky was understandably pleased with the Dewey Committee's conclusions, claiming them as irrefutable proof that Stalin had staged 'the greatest legal forgery in world history'.[5] This favourable outcome for Trotsky would not have come as a bolt from the blue to the rest of the interested world, for scepticism about the veracity of the Moscow show trials was already widespread. The London *Times*, for example, duly noted the Dewey Committee's findings in a short report published in December 1937.[6] However, independently of Trotsky's efforts, earlier in the year it had carried an editorial statement on the Moscow show trials. This contained a sceptical view of events in Moscow and a frank portrayal of the trials' negative consequences. Trotsky would surely have applauded most of the bourgeois newspaper's analysis:

> [I]t is clear that M. Stalin is bent on consolidating his position ... eliminating, on whatever pretext, any of his comrades who are or who may be potential sources of opposition to his aims. ... Dictatorships need enemies for internal consumption. ... The villainies of the Trotskyists ring with wearisome redundance in the ears of the Russian public. The world has ceased to be stirred by news of events in Russia. ...
>
> The damage which these ultra-Georgian tactics have done to the Soviet Union has been enormous. France contemplates without enthusiasm her alliance with a country where treason appears to be a national pastime. ... The lives of prominent servants of the state are cheaper than they were in the darkest days of Rome's decline; and the charges brought against them imply, whether they are true or false, a fundamental unsoundness of the administration.
>
> And there have been other changes as well. ... To watch M. Stalin lopping off the heads of the tallest and reddest poppies is intriguing rather than edifying; for his ruthless prescriptions are not in part condoned, as perhaps Lenin's were, by fanatical devotion to a fixed ideal. The old revolutionary tenets have gone, together with, but more unobtrusively than, most of the men who made it possible to put them into practice; they have been replaced by a botched tissue of dogma, as shifting, adaptable, and elusive as a mirage.[7]

Reading this, Stalin, who followed the *Bulletin of the Opposition* closely,[8] could have been forgiven if he perceived Trotsky's influence at play. The *Times'* sentiments are more indicative, however, of the fact that Trotsky was not alone in doubting the validity of the Moscow show trials. One should not belittle the Mexico exile's determination to prove his innocence, but against a background of general disbelief in Stalin's stage-managed trials the Dewey Committee's verdict did not make headline news. Trotsky himself was disappointed that his supporters were not able to make more political capital out of the Dewey Committee, perhaps by turning it into a more permanent institution. But, as the *Times* pointed out, the public had already become desensitised to more episodes of the Russian *fantastica*. An American Trotskyist subsequently recalled having tried to raise the interest of a local journalist in Russian developments, only to be asked: 'What do the Moscow Trials mean in Kokomo, Indiana?'[9]

That Stalin's Great Terror might turn people, and specifically workers, away from socialism troubled Trotsky greatly. He thought it crucial that the bureaucratic assault on socialism underway in the USSR should not be mistaken for the genuine article. In this dark hour for communism, it was of vital importance to expound and defend real Marxism. While Trotsky was grateful to Dewey for his work on the Committee of Inquiry, he was keen to stress his differences with the kind professor about the merits of Marxism over liberalism. It was in this context that, in February 1938, he completed a short but passionate essay, 'Their Morals and Ours', dedicated to his son Lev Sedov, who had just died in Paris following successive operations.

'Their Morals and Ours' is a curious work. Its language shifts from angry invective to a more reasoned discussion of successive philosophical trends, including the Jesuits, Herbert Spencer and Immanuel Kant; from a calm advocacy of 'dialectical materialism' against 'philosophical idealism' to a rabid denunciation of 'petty-bourgeois theoreticians and moralists'. The chief intention and the recurrent theme, however, were to refute the suggestion that Trotsky, Lenin and Stalin were moral equivalents. For Trotsky, to equate Bolshevism and Stalinism was to commit the gravest of errors, to ignore the contradictory ends that each served at various stages of the class struggle. Thus, for example, it was permissible for Trotsky to decree the taking of (White officer) family members as hostages in the midst of the Russian Civil War, for it served the revolution in its ascendancy. The GPU's employment of the same tactic against (Marxist) opponents was, on the contrary, worthy of condemnation because Stalin was seeking to demolish the revolution and the Bolshevik Party. For Trotsky, there could be no eternal laws of behaviour suitable for all circumstances. Rather, 'moral evaluations, along with political ones, flow from the inner needs of the struggle'.[10]

Dewey responded several months later. For him, Trotsky's answer to the thorny issue of moral conundrums was based on a brand of 'absolutism'. Trotsky had simply sidestepped the issue of how to judge which means really do lead to the liberation of mankind by referring to the exigencies of the class struggle as the supreme law of history. Dewey could not comprehend how this took matters beyond a contested arena of disputes as to who really represents progress in history. Trotsky claimed such a status for himself and the Fourth International, but there were no obviously objective grounds or criteria for deciding if he was right. It was simply an issue of faith. Trotsky did not pen a counter-response to Dewey's concerns, preferring to leave this task to one of his secretaries. In this way the debate simply fizzled out. As matters stood, Trotsky could be satisfied that he had exploited one more setting to serve the political imperative of exposing Stalinism as a betrayal of Bolshevik Marxism.

The outbreak of the Great Purges not only motivated Trotsky to engage in a defence of the ABC of Marxism; he also became more receptive to publishers' requests for a biography of Joseph Stalin. It was a project that he was unable to finish. Research was ongoing at the time of his assassination, the story completed to the author's satisfaction only to 1917. There was sufficient material to hand, however, for the posthumous publication of a book of several hundred pages.

Of all the biographical sketches and essays penned by Trotsky, one might think that the portrait of Stalin presented the most difficulties. After all, Trotsky admitted that he came to know of Stalin only after 1917, and then in mainly negative contexts. Would not the history of their personal and political relations severely cloud Trotsky's judgement? Elsewhere Trotsky had written that he felt no hatred for Stalin as a person. His anti-Stalin tracts were strictly political in nature, based upon an appreciation of 'objective conditions'.[11] In introducing the biography, Trotsky reassures the reader that he had not overlooked 'a single fact, document, or bit of testimony redounding to the benefit of the hero of this book ... if all of this is not objectivity, then, I ask, What is objectivity?' At the same time, however, there is a clear indication of a likely bias in the book. In a brief discussion of political leadership, for example, Hitler is described as an 'orator'; Marx, Engels and Lenin as 'thinkers and writers'. Stalin is seen as unique:

> [He] is neither a thinker, a writer nor an orator. ... Stalin took possession of power, not with the aid of personal qualities, but with the aid of an impersonal machine. And it was not he who created the machine, but the machine created him. ... Stalin did not create the machine but took possession of it. For this, exceptional and special qualities were necessary. But they were not the qualities of the historic

initiator, thinker, writer, or orator. The machine had grown out of ideas. Stalin's first qualification was a contemptuous attitude toward ideas.[12]

The biography's primary concern was therefore to outline the influences in Stalin's career through which 'a personality of this sort was formed'. There was thus a pre-existing thesis to be confirmed. The suspicion remains that Trotsky would find in Stalin's life what he was looking for. The chapter 'Family and School', for example, considers conflicting evaluations of the young Stalin, from a hardworking and able boy devoted to study and song, to a rude, vengeful and cynical character. Trotsky always finds reason to favour the latter interpretation, emphasising how social, family and school environments combined to produce a blend of 'grit, shrewdness, craftiness, and cruelty ... a clever schemer, a cynic, a person capable of the lowest sort of conniving'. In his youth Stalin developed, we are told, a negative psychology, obsessed with the 'bad side' of human nature. It was this that made of him a likely hero of an 'epoch of reaction, which crystallises egoism and perfidy'. Periods of progress dominated by lofty idealism had no place for a man of Stalin's mould.

Already in the first main chapter, then, the biographer has resolved that his subject possessed no great intellect or ability, nor a redeeming character. The subsequent account of Stalin's political career to 1917 tells of failures, disappointments and a hurt sense of pride. It presents the Georgian revolutionist as an 'unknown figure' in the party's history, one who remained 'on the sidelines, sullen, alarmed by the flood of nature at springtide and, as always, malevolent. ... His hurt provincial self-satisfaction must inevitably have been coloured with envy, mitigated only by cautiousness'.[13] It did not escape the attention of contemporary reviewers that the book was marred by a profound dislike of its main actor.[14] It is the least satisfactory of Trotsky's forays into the art of biography.

INTERNATIONAL RELATIONS AND WORLD REVOLUTION

International affairs of the mid- to late 1930s were hit by several crises. In late 1935 Italy sought by military means to consolidate a position in North Africa. In 1936 what turned into a three-year civil war began in Spain as General Franco's nationalist army attacked the Republican government. Most troublesome of all, however, was the pressure put upon the post-World War One settlement in Europe, largely by a resurgent and rearming Germany. Czechoslovakia, Poland and Austria numbered amongst Hitler's targets for revision. There was an unseemly scramble for security and gain. It proved impossible to forge a united anti-Hitler coalition. Czechoslovakia was a notable victim, partitioned as a result of an agreement between Great Britain, France, Italy and Germany at the Munich Conference of September 1938. No other power was willing to fight for its defence. Hitler's demands were not satisfied by such concessions, as the policy of appeasement hoped, but led to another world war following Germany's invasion of Poland in September 1939. Trotsky continued to criticise Soviet foreign policy for being unable to cope with the demands of these troublesome times.

The charges levelled at Stalin were familiar. The Kremlin, Trotsky accused, was betraying the world revolution by poor leadership, subordinating the Comintern to the narrow national interests of the ruling bureaucratic elite. The specific target of Trotsky's chagrin was a fresh turn in the Comintern's tactics towards the so-called Popular Front, or the readiness of communists to join broad anti-fascist coalitions to save countries from fascist takeovers. This idea was first elaborated by French and Czechoslovakian communists after Hitler had come to power in Germany. It took a further two years of discussion and persuasion before it was approved by the Comintern's Political Secretariat in January 1935 and by the Seventh Congress later that summer.

Although the initiative for the Popular Front lay with the national sections – particularly the large anti-fascist strikes in France in February 1934, in which socialist and communist workers collaborated quite successfully – Trotsky discerned only Stalin's malicious hand behind the new orientation. It was, he thought, part of Soviet diplomatic efforts to woo the bourgeois, non-fascist powers into a collective security agreement to contain Nazi Germany. In order to reassure the bourgeois West that the USSR was a reliable ally, the Popular Front policy had been thrust upon national communist parties as a way of saving the bourgeoisie from revolutionary possibilities. This was evident above all for Trotsky in France and Spain. Both countries were, he was convinced, in the midst of a revolutionary situation. Above all, the masses were radicalised and ready for action, while capitalism was in terminal decline. For the people to stage a triumphant socialist revolution, however, the communists would have to mount a vigorous, extreme left-wing campaign. It was time to hoist a programme of radical social change, including the call to establish soviets, for land to be transferred to the peasants, and for workers' control of the mills and factories. Instead, the Stalinists had proposed collaboration with the bourgeoisie in Popular Fronts as a way of protecting private property and the capitalist order. In the French context it was a policy designed, according to Trotsky, to kill 'the faith of the masses in the revolutionary road and to drive them into the arms of the Fascist counter-revolution'.[15] Assessing the lessons of the Spanish Civil War, Trotsky entertained no doubts as to who was most to blame for the fall of the Republican regime:

> Franco needed help from the opposite side of the battlefront. And he obtained this aid. His chief assistant was and still is Stalin. ... The Spanish proletariat gave proof of the extraordinary capacity for initiative and revolutionary heroism. The revolution was brought to ruin by petty, despicable, and utterly corrupted 'leaders'. ... Moscow feared above all that the disturbance of private property in the Iberian Peninsula would bring London and Paris nearer to Berlin against the USSR. ... All the actions of the Moscow agents in Spain were directed toward paralysing any independent movement of the workers and peasants and reconciling the bourgeoisie with a moderate republic. ... Under the label of the Popular Front, they set up a joint stock company. Under the leadership of Stalin, they have assured the most terrible defeat when all the conditions for victory were at hand.[16]

There is some merit in Trotsky's biting critique of the Comintern's record in France and Spain. The Spanish communists' attacks on the Trotskyist sections in Spain, for example, undoubtedly diverted resources away from the struggle against the nationalist forces. Overall, however, Trotsky's thesis of a Stalinist betrayal of the world revolution is as one-sided as it is unconvincing. It ignores, for example, the positive aspects of the Popular Front tactic, evident in the expansion of the communist parties' support and influence. Recent studies of Comintern thinking reveal a lack of consensus over the exact meaning of the Popular Front. Many activists, including Stalin, remained distrustful of bourgeois parliamentarianism and saw the Popular Front as useful only insofar as it improved the prospects for socialism. This was a far cry from Trotsky's version of the Popular Front as a means of subduing the revolutionary tide so as to produce an image of an unthreatening USSR for bourgeois consumption. In actual fact, reformist socialists and pro-capitalists became still more wary of communism given the rise in communist popularity in the Popular Front era. If the Popular Front was to serve the ends of Soviet diplomacy as defined by Trotsky, then the tactic was counterproductive. There is also no evidence to confirm Trotsky's contention, however, that Comintern tactics were dependent on the demands of Soviet diplomacy. In the 1930s there was no certainty that the policy of collective security would bear any fruit, and the option of an agreement with Germany remained open.

Presenting an overly simplified account of the relationship between Soviet security needs and Comintern policy, Trotsky also tended to over-estimate the efficiency of a line of command running from the Kremlin to operatives on the ground. Despite a network of advisers in Spain, for example, a combination of factors, from uncertain lines of communication to the fragmented and confused nature of regional circumstances, allowed a strong Spanish Communist Party to take numerous initiatives of its own accord. The ferocity of the Spanish communists' move against native Trotskyists had as much to do with local rivalries, it has been suggested, as with orders from Moscow.[17] Finally, the accusation of betraying the world revolution, which Trotsky threw at incompetent left allies as well as outright Stalinists, is hard to uphold if there was little chance of a successful communist uprising in France and Spain in the 1930s. In this context, one should note that even commentators sympathetic to Trotsky admit that he continually overestimated revolutionary possibilities.[18] Indeed, isolated and deprived of much information, it is hard to see how Trotsky could become a reliable guide to complex and fluid international events.

A stern critic of Stalin as leader of the world communist movement, Trotsky also perceived no merit in the Kremlin's diplomacy in the lead-up to World War Two. Trotsky did not doubt that another world war was in the offing. It would arise, he argued, out of the self-same imperialist antagonisms that had produced the previous conflict of 1914–18. It was on this basis that Trotsky refused to make a distinction between the hostile camps, say between fascist and anti-fascist armies. All of the capitalist powers were to be condemned as predatory and imperialist. In an era of monopoly capitalism, in which economic survival and growth

was predicated upon controlling colonies, a resurgent German capitalism could not help but seek world domination. The countries in
decline, chiefly France and Britain, could equally not help but resist
German attempts at global supremacy. If the great powers were nothing
but pawns of underlying economic trends demanding the abolition of
national frontiers, Trotsky was understandably sceptical about the
attempts to satisfy Hitler's appetite by the policy of appeasement. The
division of Czechoslovakia in Germany's favour merely gave Berlin a
better base for unleashing a future war, he warned, and did not guarantee 'peace in our time' as the British prime minister, Neville
Chamberlain, thought.

The only uncertainty about the looming war, for Trotsky, was how
German strategy would unfold. He identified German militarism,
driven by an expanding economy, as the likely aggressor. But even the
rearmed German army would not wish to begin a war on more than one
front. A choice had to be made between striking first to the West or to
the East. In making this tactical decision, Trotsky was certain that
Berlin could expect support from Stalin should it decide to begin its
offensive in the West. Trotsky thought that the overriding aim of Soviet
diplomacy was to keep the USSR out of a war. The Soviet bureaucracy
feared a conflict, he argued, because it would be unlikely to withstand
the strains of modern warfare. Not only had it undermined the Red
Army's fighting capacity in the purge of its leading military commanders, but the people would welcome the war as an opportunity to overthrow the hated bureaucracy. Trotsky interpreted the Nazi–Soviet Pact
of September 1939 not as a bolt from the blue, but as the favoured
option of a Soviet leadership willing to sign any humiliating agreement
to save its privileged position within the USSR.

Thus far, one can congratulate Trotsky for damning appeasement but
must question both his characterisation of the great powers and his
account of international diplomacy in the years immediately preceding
September 1939. Although it made sense in Trotsky's terms to dismiss
each capitalist power as imperialist, it was surely blind of him to deny
that the question of who won the conflict was no more than a matter of
indifference. For Trotsky, whoever the victor was, humanity would be
the loser in both a material and cultural sense. Yet, at the time and subsequently, it was clear that there would be a profound difference, if only
on the racial grounds that Trotsky discounted as an important part of

Nazi ideology,[19] to the fate of Europe and the world should Hitler prevail. It was for this reason that American public opinion rightly preferred Stalin to Hitler, even while it condemned the many crimes committed in Moscow.[20] Trotsky was also wrong to claim Stalin as Hitler's best friend. Recent studies suggest that the Nazi–Soviet Pact was the outcome of a last-minute decision and was largely a response to the Paris and London governments' unwillingness to make a firm commitment to Moscow. The collective security line may not have borne the intended results, but it is a gross error to claim that the USSR always preferred an alliance with Germany.[21] Finally, Trotsky clearly underestimated the capacity of the USSR to withstand a German declaration of war, which eventually occurred in June 1941. Stalin proved himself a capable war leader, standing firm at the helm in the initial confusion surrounding the first moments of the German attack.[22] More generally, the Soviet government was able to maintain the loyalty of its citizens in the aptly named Great Patriotic War. Rather than succumbing to an ignominious defeat, as Trotsky predicted, Stalinism was if anything strengthened by World War Two, extending its hold over Russia and expanding into Eastern Europe.

If Trotsky was content to interpret the causes of World War Two through the prism of a Marxist analysis of events in 1914, he also thought that the internationalist tactics of 1914–18 would hold good for the battles of 1939 onwards. In World War One the internationalist left, while initially in a minority, had eventually led a revolution in Russia and created the Third International. Now, he argued, the internationalist left had to renew old campaigns, but under the banner of the Fourth International.

Trotsky was highly optimistic about the future fortunes of the Fourth International, despite the fractious and splintered nature of the small bands of supporters he was able to attract in his lifetime. He thought that a bankrupt and decaying capitalism would no longer be able to prop up reformist socialist parties and trade unions by welfare programmes. The workers would face an impoverishment not experienced for over a century. They would be hungry and angry, but at least prepared by the war, most especially in military training, for an all-out attack on capitalism. Fortunately they would have an exemplary vanguard leadership in the Fourth International. For Trotsky, the Fourth International could pride itself on being the only political body that had correctly foreseen the march of history, and the one political force that had elaborated a revolutionary programme for a just and plentiful order. Under the guidance of the Fourth International, Trotsky envisaged the world proletariat establishing pan-continental Soviet regimes across Europe, the Americas and Asia as stepping-stones to the creation of a world socialist federation. The dreadful alternative was more capitalist misery, with its inevitable rounds of further wars of destruction.

Trotsky thus placed mighty tasks before his followers. It was obvious even to him that at the time of writing the Fourth International was not equal to its historic mission. Indeed, in a review of *The Revolution Betrayed* the scholar Bertram D. Wolfe had correctly identified the Fourth International's weaknesses as mirroring those of the Third: 'As to bureaucracy, is his "Fourth International" any more democratic, any less a one-man show, any less dominated by its "Russian faction" and factional considerations?'[23] The prospects of the small and divided Fourth International deteriorated still further when it lost its guru in the assassination of August 1940.

ASSASSINATION

In the opening months of 1940 Trotsky was concerned that his death, when it came, would arise out of natural causes. Troubled by bouts of high blood pressure and convinced that a fatal brain haemorrhage was an imminent threat, he composed two drafts of a brief Testament, to become public knowledge after his demise. Here he thanked loyal friends and paid special tribute to his wife. Indeed, Trotsky was fortunate in his choice of a life partner. Natalia's political interests matched those of her husband. A less politically committed wife may not have stuck with him through the twists and turns of his political career. Yet Trotsky did not acknowledge an intellectual relationship, highlighting the emotional support he had derived from her 'love, magnanimity, and tenderness'. The Testament's main message was, as ever, political and concerned Trotsky himself.

> If I had to begin all over again I would of course try to avoid this or that mistake, but the main course of my life would remain unchanged. I shall die a proletarian revolutionist, a Marxist, a dialectical materialist, and, consequently, an irreconcilable atheist. My faith

> in the communist future of mankind is not less ardent, indeed it is
> firmer today, than it was in the days of my youth. ... Life is beautiful.
> Let the future generations cleanse it of all evil, oppression, and vio-
> lence and enjoy it to the full.[24]

If pessimism regarding his health continued to worry Trotsky, then
at the end of May 1940 he received a rude reminder of an alternative
form of death. Given the execution of leading old Bolsheviks who had
made no public critical remarks about Stalin, there was no reason to
assume that the Kremlin's leading opponent would be spared by virtue
of his exile. Indeed, Stalin's longstanding desire to have Trotsky eliminated may have been heightened by the effectiveness of Trotskyist
propaganda in the world communist movement. A recent study of the
Communist Party of Great Britain on the eve of World War Two, for
example, shows Soviet operatives worried about the threat posed to
Moscow's domination of rank-and-file hearts and minds by Left
Opposition activists.[25] Furthermore, Stalin may have wanted to bring
Trotsky's work on his biography to an abrupt end before the manuscript
was complete. Whatever the exact motivation, at some point the neces-
sary orders were given to the People's Commissariat of Internal Affairs
(NKVD) for Trotsky to be assassinated.

A first, unsuccessful, attempt was made in the early hours of 24 May,
when the Soviet security services tried to murder Trotsky in Chicago-
gangland fashion. A group of around twenty armed men, masquerading
as police officials, tied up the guards at the front of Trotsky's house
without resistance. Once in the main courtyard, the would-be assassins
fired rounds of ammunition into the main rooms, including Trotsky's
study and bedroom. By sheer good fortune, and much to Stalin's annoyance, the intended victim survived. For Trotsky, the attack could
equally have been the work of Hitler's Gestapo as the USSR's NKVD.
However, he considered that since he was more of a political threat to
Stalin the Kremlin was the more likely sponsor. The fullest account of
the assault as experienced by Trotsky was published in early June 1940,
in the article 'Stalin Seeks My Death':

> The attack came at 4 a.m. I was fast asleep, having taken a sleeping
> drug after a hard day's work. Awakened by the rattle of gunfire but
> feeling hazy, I first imagined that a national holiday was being cele-

brated with fireworks outside our walls. But the explosions were too close, right here within the room, next to me and overhead. ... The shooting continued incessantly. My wife later told me that she helped me to the floor, pushing me into the space between the bed and the wall. ... Splinters of glass from windowpanes and chips from walls flew in all directions. A little later I discovered that my right leg had been slightly wounded in two places. As the shooting died down we heard our grandson in the neighbouring room cry out: 'Grandfather!' The voice of the child in the darkness under the gunfire remains the most tragic recollection of that night.[26]

Trotsky was convinced that one failure would not prevent the NKVD from making further attempts on his life. Indeed, the efforts to kill him would no doubt be redoubled since only a successful elimination would restore the security services to good standing with their master. Furthermore, Stalin needed the murder of 'enemy number one' to 'demonstrate his power'. With an eye on future risks to their leader, funds were raised, chiefly by followers in the United States, to upgrade the security arrangements at Trotsky's house. What the best-laid security plans could not account for, however, was a fatal blow coming from a member of the household itself.

Even before the events of 24 May, the NKVD had managed to infiltrate Trotsky's closest circles. One agent had provided a detailed plan of the house and the use made of its rooms. Another operative, the Spanish communist Ramon Mercader, from a family known for its loyalty to Moscow, had established a love affair with one of Trotsky's secretaries, Sylvia Agelof, as early as September 1938. By May 1940 Mercader, who also went under the names of Jacques Monard and Frank Jacson, was familiar to the Bronsteins as a charming friend of Sylvia, a businessman who occasionally rendered kind services, such as taking Natalia and Sylvia on shopping excursions in his car. When Trotsky's close friends Alfred and Maguerrite Rosmer left Mexico after a stay of several months, it was Mercader who drove them to their ship. The Soviet agent in charge of operations in Mexico, Naum Eitingon, decided that Mercader offered the next best chance of killing Trotsky. Mercader used the excuse of a growing interest in Trotskyism to seek a private audience. On 17 August 1940 he presented Trotsky with a brief article on American Trotskyism. Three days later he returned, unannounced, with a typewritten version. Trotsky invited him into the study. Mercader seized the opportunity of taking Trotsky unawares. He crushed an ice-pick, previously concealed in a raincoat, into his victim's head. In the assassin's words:

> Trotsky gave a cry that I shall never forget. It was a long 'aaaa', end-lessly long, and I think it still echoes in my brain. Trotsky jumped up jerkily, rushed at me and bit my hand. Look, you can still see the marks of his teeth. I pushed him away and he fell to the floor. Then he rose and stumbled out of the room.[27]

Trotsky survived the immediate blow, but not its consequences. He soon fell into a coma, from which he did not awake. Death occurred on the evening of 21 August at a local hospital.

In arranging a spectacular death for Trotsky, Stalin guaranteed his rival a return to headline news. In a replay of Lenin's lying in state, but on a smaller scale, thousands of visitors filed past Trotsky's body. The American government may have refused a request that he be laid to rest in New York, but in the event large crowds watched the funeral proces-sion in Mexico City. An obituary in the London *Times* paid tribute to Trotsky's life. It noted his role as Lenin's 'principal associate', pointing out that, contrary to the statements of the 'official historians' who belit-tled his significance, it was Trotsky who organised the October Revolution and 'brought the Red Army into being'. Although the *Times* saw Trotsky as posing no political threat to Stalin or to capitalism, it admitted that he 'remained a name' around whom 'communists who opposed the opportunistic policy of Stalin' gathered. Finally, the obitu-ary mentioned Trotsky's 'outstanding literary abilities', evident above all in his autobiography and *The History of the Russian Revolution*.[28] Such thoughts were an early indication of Deutscher's subsequent argument that Trotsky experienced a form of 'victory' in death. The circumstances of his death also helped him to gain a more enduring fame. This is evi-dent not only in the films, books and popular songs mentioned at the start of this book. Trotsky was once even described, in a perverse and unjustified claim, as the 'greatest Jew since Jesus Christ'. To be fair, however, Trotsky would not have appreciated the reference to race or to religion.

CONCLUSION

Death has an obvious advantage. It permits us to consider a life in its entirety. It is a vantage point that none of us can enjoy whilst alive. We conduct our lives in a state of imperfect knowledge, with little or no clue as to outcomes and ends. Small wonder that circumstances often make a fool out of even the wisest of people. In a fundamental sense, Trotsky felt himself to be different. He believed that if one possessed an adequate framework of analysis for comprehending history and, more importantly, if one could apply this analysis appropriately, then one could have certainty in the victory of the socialist revolution, resulting ultimately in the liberation of humanity. It was this certainty that Trotsky carried within him from the time of his conversion to Marxism to his assassination in Mexico. In what turned out to be a timely Testament, he could therefore express no regrets about his chosen profession, despite a series of personal tragedies and public setbacks. Trotsky's was about as political a life as one can imagine. He formed friendships and loved his family. He could enjoy other pursuits, most especially hunting, walking and literature. But what mattered above everything else was the battle of the international proletariat to overcome global capitalism. On several occasions Trotsky took up a diary, but this most intimate form of communication was filled with accounts of revolutionary struggle. Reading a diary begun in France in 1935, even Trotsky himself noted the domination of political themes, for 'politics and literature constitute in essence the content of my personal life'.[1]

In actual fact literature came a poor second to political concerns. In Trotsky's infrequent forays into literary criticism, literary texts were analysed from a political point of view.

There were very simple reasons why Trotsky was willing to dedicate his not inconsiderable talent to the socialist cause, why he denied himself much of a life outside politics. Of course he believed in the goal. Should the workers of the world fail to establish communism, he believed that humanity was condemned to suffer capitalism and its want and wars. The choice was actual and stark: either socialism or barbarism. It was therefore reasonable to countenance the loss of life, both actual and personal, in the service of progress. No great historical change had been achieved, he reasoned, without sacrifices. Furthermore, Trotsky saw himself as making a historic contribution to a historic cause. As a theoretician, for example, he had developed and expounded the theory of permanent revolution. Trotsky did not doubt his standing as a practitioner of applied Marxist analysis. No one else was capable, he thought, of 'arming a new generation with the revolutionary method over the heads of the leaders of the Second and Third International'.[2]

For all his self-confidence, however, Trotsky lost most of his major political struggles, whether before or after the October Revolution. In the period to 1917 his major concern was to reunite Russian social democracy around an agreed programme of action. But he failed to heal the rift that had occurred at the party's Second Congress of 1903, largely because of genuine differences in outlook. Even Trotsky engaged in polemics with Mensheviks and Bolsheviks alike, finding the former too conciliatory with the bourgeoisie and the latter overly sectional. These debates were heated and to some outsiders incomprehensible. They also had longer-term consequences. Not everyone was able, like Trotsky, to put the concept of a Russian social democrat above factional loyalty and therefore to be willing to co-operate with a Marxist of whatever background when circumstances dictated. After he joined the Bolsheviks, Lenin's lieutenants, accustomed in the period to 1917 to thinking of Trotsky as a leading antagonist, found it difficult if not impossible to forgive and forget the pre-October polemics.

Trotsky's conversion to Lenin's brand of party politics may have been dosed with heavy reservations in 1917 itself. He protested that he could not call himself a Bolshevik until Bolshevism had 'internationalised itself'. Such doubts were soon forgotten. The fact that Lenin's party managed to maintain power was accepted by Trotsky as sufficient proof of its efficacy as a revolutionary force. He went on to argue that a revolutionary vanguard of the Leninist type was the essential factor in the success of a workers' revolution. He became proud of Lenin's remark that there was 'no better Bolshevik' than Trotsky and devoted the rest of his political life to defending his reputation as a Bolshevik along with Bolshevism itself. Other members of the party's leading institutions, the Politburo and the Central Committee, were less impressed with Trotsky's self-assessment as a 'super-Bolshevik'. They doubted his ability for sound political analysis. They dismissed Trotsky's prognoses of early NEP bureaucratisation and degeneration, for example, as too dramatic and alarmist. Apart from political differences, they found Trotsky a difficult man to work with. Trotsky admitted that he had little time for fools, and preferred to read novels at sessions of the Politburo than waste his time listening to the banal statements of his all too banal colleagues. Little wonder, then, that a group was formed to prevent Trotsky from becoming Lenin's acknowledged replacement.

Devoid of majority support in the party's upper echelons, Trotsky could not count on sufficient backing from elsewhere. He had no talent for building a power base within the key bodies of party and state. Indeed, he had a conception of revolutionary ethics that could make an enemy out of a potential friend. Geoffrey Swain recounts how soldiers who turned to the head of the Red Army to support them in a request for a well-earned break from the front soon found themselves under arrest on Trotsky's orders.[3] Stalin's victory in the 1920s was easy because Trotsky had little standing amongst the party people who mattered. It was for reasons of this sort that one of Trotsky's secretaries in exile justly remarked that his boss did not lose power, for in truth he never possessed it. Furthermore, loyalty to the party kept Trotsky from taking his campaign to broader circles of workers and citizens. How the people would have received him had he done so is, of course, an open question.

Once in exile, Trotsky produced a mound of anti-Stalin tracts attacking the USSR's internal and international policy. For a man deprived of much vital information, the analyses of Soviet domestic life contained much pertinent criticism, evident above all in the classic book *The Revolution Betrayed*. However, there were several profound weaknesses in Trotsky's writings. Above all, his alternative programme contained no guarantees that the USSR would be any the richer or more democratic under Trotsky's guidance. He had only a minimal understanding of economics and a simplistic assumption that all would be well under 'democratic planning'. Given his strong conviction of the correctness of his political viewpoints, it is questionable how free and open debate would have been under Trotsky's leadership. In any case, it is doubtful whether he would have submitted to a majority vote against him. Certainly Trotsky did not have a developed concept of multi-party pluralism under socialism. A one-party system will always find it difficult, if not dangerous, to permit difference of opinion in the media and society more widely.

Trotsky's biggest disappointment was the lack of influence he exerted over the Communist International. He proved incapable of wresting it from Stalin's control, and had to be satisfied with damning the Kremlin for spoiling revolutionary opportunities in China, Germany, France, Spain and elsewhere. But as criticisms these fail to convince. The analysis of events is always reduced to a battle of left, centre and right, with 'truth' residing in the Trotskyist left. There is an unwarranted simplicity in such a classification, and its recurrent repetition in the 1930s renders Trotsky's writings dull and frequently inaccurate; reality was far more complex. Of course, the Comintern's policies deserved to be criticised, and Trotsky presented some thoughtful criticisms. But it seems clear that Trotsky overestimated both the potential for world revolution and the conservatism of Stalin's intentions. Capitalism was saved, not because Stalin desired its rescue, but because it was not as close to death as Trotsky assumed. It is hard to see how a change in the Kremlin's outlook could have manufactured a global revolution when it was not in the offing. There were good reasons why the workers were largely unreceptive to Trotsky's propaganda. The Fourth International has not changed the world as Trotsky hoped it would.

Trotsky, then, was not a great political leader or prophet. He spent the majority of his political life in opposition, the exponent of views commanding minority support. Against a background of political disappointments, there are, however, notable high points in his career. In 1905 he established a reputation as a revolutionary, even if his role was not as great as some would believe. In 1917 it was Trotsky who more than any other leader planned and executed a successful bid for power. He was rewarded with major governmental portfolios, including foreign and military affairs. The debacle over Brest-Litovsk brought his career as foreign statesman to an abrupt end, but as head of the Red Army Trotsky acquired fame both within and outside Russia. It was, after all, Trotsky who led the impressive propaganda and military campaigns to maintain the dictatorship of the proletariat in Russia. Having established a reputation as a decisive military man of intelligence and power, it must have struck observers as odd that Trotsky was so easily banished. But, for services to the October Revolution, Trotsky earned his place in history and the right to be praised and damned. Of course, Trotsky did his best to steer historical judgement towards sympathy. Most especially in the autobiography, Trotsky presented himself as a revolutionary of honour, defeated by a mixture of objective difficulties and unscrupulous scheming. As a man of the revolutionary upsurge, he had to leave the stage during its ebb.

Is there anything of lasting merit in Trotsky's works, or were he and his writing of relevance only to his time and experience? An answer to this question will depend, at least in part, on how one rates Marxism and Trotsky's standing as a Marxist.

To begin with the latter question, it is doubtful whether Trotsky made any lasting contribution to Marxist thought. He may even have been unaware of some of Marx's most basic writings. In *The Revolution Betrayed*, for example, Trotsky several times insists that Marx had nothing to say about Russia, that the master expected a socialist revolution to begin in the countries of advanced capitalism. This ignores Marx's interest in the question of whether 'backward' Russia could bypass capitalism and undertake a direct transition to socialism on the basis of the peasant commune. Marx's response, of evident relevance to Trotsky's theory of permanent revolution, was given in several of his writings, including the Preface to the (1881) Russian edition of the *Communist Manifesto*. Here Marx answered in the affirmative. A Russian Revolution could aim at a direct transition to socialism, but only if it sparked socialist revolutions in the advanced West. If Trotsky had been aware of this and the other texts in which Marx addressed the problem of building socialism in Russia, he would surely have claimed a stronger link between the theory of permanent revolution and Marx, as well as less originality for his conception of the revolutionary process in Russia. If we assume that Trotsky did not know of Marx's concern with Russia, then this points to the conclusion that Trotsky's Marxism was a product of the Russian environment. Such a conclusion would not damn Trotsky to irrelevance. The best example of his applied (Russian) Marxist analysis was the account of why tsarism would give way to socialism and not liberal capitalism. Trotsky could also be credited with explaining why Russian socialism would founder if it was not supported by an international revolution. The causes of the collapse of the USSR in 1991 can easily be found in Trotsky's writings on the Russian Revolution produced as early as 1905. Even if one does not wish to draw such conclusions in Trotsky's favour, his theory of Russian history and the October Revolution should continue to be taught to students.

But to return to the former question, if Marxism has little relevance to the modern world, then surely neither will Trotsky's brand of Marxism. It remains the case that capitalism has not collapsed. Indeed, it seems to be strengthening its grip on the world. Even 'communist' China now accepts profit-and-loss motivation as the driving force of economic expansion. These will be insufficient grounds to persuade Trotskyists that they should abandon all hope. Indeed, it may be possible that Marxism's fortunes will improve following the fall of the USSR. The most thorough study of Marx's work and of its relationship to Russia concludes that:

> Capitalism seems set to become the Universal economic system throughout the world, and to subordinate all spheres of human life to its circulation and reproduction. If it does so then one can expect that it will reach its point of culmination [i.e., to be replaced by socialism] in the way Marx believed.[4]

Academics grouped around the journal *Critique* at Glasgow University claim that, with Stalinism in demise, Marxism can finally rediscover its true revolutionary self. Finally, there are other Trotskyist groupings, including the London-based Socialist Platform which publishes the excellent journal *Revolutionary History*, that still fight for socialism. Even though these forces operate on the margins of society, they are described from time to time in the broadsheets and elsewhere as a genuine threat to capitalist civilisation.[5] Indeed, no one knows what the future holds.

It is not surprising that left-inspired thought sees a modern relevance for Trotsky and Marxism. Even Marxism's detractors might recognise some of Trotsky's words as having a contemporary resonance. At the beginning of the twentieth century Trotsky argued that the major problem of economic management was to legislate for forces of production that had outgrown the confines of a single nation-state. Hence his consistent call for the establishment of a United States of Europe. Trotsky gave this a socialist form, since he thought it impossible to build transnational co-operation on the basis of capitalist antagonisms and hostility. The major powers of Europe may have confounded Trotsky's predictions by engaging in peaceful pan-European agreements, including the establishment of a single currency. But Trotsky was surely right to prioritise the foundation of a United States of Europe as an urgent necessity if the continent was to experience prosperity without war. It may even turn out to be the case that a United States of Europe eventually adopts a more socialist direction. After all, Trotsky always claimed that he was building a policy for the long run.

Even should capitalism flourish, there should be good reason to consider Marxism's, and Trotsky's, criticisms of its injustices and flaws. If there is no such thing as perfect planning, it is also highly unlikely that there is perfect competition. Inequalities in lifestyles and life chances continue to afflict the richest of nations, not to mention the gross differences in wealth across the globe. This may not prove to be a smouldering cauldron of discontent that will produce the world revolution, but there are numerous opportunities for left-inspired activists to seek greater justice in health, education, the workplace, the arts, indeed in every field of human endeavour. Trotsky's battles born of the Russian Revolution may turn out not to have been in vain. The best of today's Marxists seek to learn from the mistakes of the past, and place far more emphasis on democracy and the importance of the independent initiative of the working class rather than on the tutelage of intellectuals. 'Trotsky is dead, long live socialism' may not be an inappropriate conclusion to take from this book.

NOTES

INTRODUCTION

1 C. Sheridan, *Russian Portraits* (Jonathan Cape, 1921), p. 149.
2 The list of essays written in response to Trotsky's 'Lessons of October' and summarised here includes: L. Kamenev, 'Leninism or Trotskyism'; I. Stalin, 'Trotskyism or Leninism?'; G. Zinoviev, 'Bolshevism or Trotskyism?'; N. Bukharin, 'How One Should Not Write the History of October'; G. Sokolnikov, 'A False Exposition of the "German October"'; and 'October and the Komsomol'. These essays are included in L. Trotsky, *Uroki Oktyabrya* (Lenizdat, 1991).
3 J.T. Farrell, 'Leon Trotsky', *Partisan Review*, October 1940.
4 V. Serge and N.S. Trotsky, *The Life and Death of Leon Trotsky* (Wildwood House, 1975), p. 166. This work was originally published in French in 1951.
5 T. Cliff, *Trotsky: The Sword of the Revolution, 1917–1923* (Bookmarks, 1990), p. 94.
6 T. Cliff, *Trotsky: The Darker the Night the Brighter the Star, 1927–1940* (Bookmarks, 1993), p. 384.
7 I. Deutscher, *The Prophet Unarmed: Trotsky 1921–1929* (Oxford University Press, 1959), p. ix.
8 *Ibid.*, p. viii.
9 I. Deutscher, *The Prophet Armed: Trotsky 1879–1921* (Oxford University Press, 1954), pp. 293–4.
10 *Ibid.*, p. 391.
11 D.W. Lovell, *Trotsky's Analysis of Soviet Bureaucratization* (Croom Helm, 1985), pp. 65–7.
12 L. Kolakowski, *Main Currents of Marxism. 3. The Breakdown* (Oxford University Press, 1978), p. 212.
13 L. Kolakowski, *Main Currents of Marxism. 2. The Golden Age* (Oxford University Press, 1978), p. 512.
14 B. Knei-Paz, *The Social and Political Thought of Leon Trotsky* (Oxford University Press, 1978), p. viii.
15 Yu.V. Emel'yanov, 'Poslednie politicheskie programmy i prognozi L.D. Trotskogo', *Sotsiologicheskie issledovaniya* 5, 1990, p. 58.
16 A. Tsipko, 'Esli by pobedil Trotskii', *Daugava*, 1990.

1 THE YOUNG REVOLUTIONARY, 1879–1907

1 L. Trotsky, *My Life* (Penguin, 1971), p. 74.

2 L. Trotsky, 'Ibsen', *Revolutionary History* 7(2), 1999, p. 6.

3 L. Trotsky, 'On the Novel in General and on *The Three of Them* in Particular', *Revolutionary History* 7(2), 1999, p. 27.

4 V.I. Lenin, *Polnoe sobranie sochinenii Volume 46* (Political literature, 1982), pp. 277–8. Elsewhere Lenin sought to help Trotsky by arranging introductions to leading social democrats, including Akselrod (*ibid.*, pp. 240–1). This is ironic as in 1904 Trotsky dedicated his anti-Lenin pamphlet *Our Political Tasks* to Akselrod.

5 *Pis'ma P.B. Aksel'roda i Yu.O. Martova* (Russian Revolutionary Archive, 1924), pp. 79–81.

6 L.D. Trotsky, 'Doklad sibirskikh delegatov', *Trotsky Collection Volume 1* (Trotsky Institute of Japan, 1997), pp. 119–8.

7 See, in particular, Trotsky's article 'Nasha voennaya kampaniya', *Iskra* 62, 15 March 1904.

8 *Perepiska G.V. Plekhanova i P.B. Aksel'roda Volume II* (Europe Printing, 1967), pp. 198–201. Martov thought Trotsky's continued work for *The Spark* absolutely essential. For Martov, if the editorial board conceded to Plekhanov's demands to reject future contributions from Trotsky an important principle of editorial and party independence would have been lost. See, for example, his letter to Akselrod in *Pisma Aksel'roda i Martova*, pp. 101–4.

9 V.I. Lenin, *Selected Works Volume 1* (Progress, 1977), p. 298.

10 L. Trotsky, *Our Political Tasks* (New Park, n.d.), p. 77.

11 V.I. Lenin, *Polnoe sobranie sochinenii 46*, p. 394. See also pp. 389, 395, 408.

12 *Pisma Aksel'roda i Martova*, pp. 110–11.

13 L. Trotsky, 'Open Letter to Professor P.N. Miliukov', *Revolutionary Russia* 3(2), 1990, p. 226.

14 S. Schwarz, *The Russian Revolution of 1905* (University of Chicago Press, 1967), p. 179.

15 S. Witte, *The Memoirs of Count Witte* (William Heinemann, 1921), pp. 270–7.

16 For an appreciation of Trotsky's leading role in the Soviet, see, for example, G.D. Surgh, *1905 in St. Petersburg* (Stanford University Press, 1989), pp. 338–9, 398–401.

17 For these criticisms, see, for example, J.L.H. Keep, *The Rise of Social Democracy in Russia* (Oxford University Press, 1963), pp. 241–2.

18 For more on this, see M. Perrie, 'The Socialist Revolutionaries on "Permanent Revolution"', *Soviet Studies* 24(3), 1973, pp. 411–13, and

the interesting correspondence following this in *Soviet Studies* 25(1), 1973, pp. 153–5, and *Soviet Studies* 26(1), 1974, pp. 145–7.

19 V.I. Lenin, *Collected Works 9* (Progress Publishers, 1972), pp. 236–7.

20 L. Trotsky, *1905* (Penguin, 1972), p. 185.

21 V.I. Lenin, *Collected Works 8* (Foreign Languages Publishing House, 1962), pp. 288–92.

22 See, for example, the excellent summary of post-1945 research into the general structure of the tsarist economy in R.W. Davies, M. Harrison and S.G. Wheatcroft (eds), *The Economic Transformation of the Soviet Union, 1913–1945* (Cambridge University Press, 1994), pp. 1–4.

23 R.B. McKean has studied the issue of Whither Russia? from his PhD at the University of East Anglia (1971) to the present day. For a summary of his latest thoughts on this issue, see, for instance, his essay 'The Constitutional Monarchy in Russia, 1906–17', in I.D. Thatcher (ed.), *Regime and Society in Twentieth Century Russia* (Macmillan, 1999), pp. 44–67. Some of McKean's research has, in turn, been inspired by the work of Leopold Haimson. For Haimson's most recent reconfirmation of his view that tsarism was heading for a revolutionary crisis, see his essay '"The Problem of Political and Social Stability in Urban Russia on the Eve of War and Revolution" Revisited', *Slavic Review* 59(4), 2000, pp. 848–75.

24 Compare, for example, Trotsky, *1905*, pp. 55, 98–9, 235, 255, 263, and A. Ascher, *The Revolution of 1905* (Stanford University Press, 1988), pp. 341, 343. Similarly, Trotsky (pp. 197–8) and Ascher agree that the awakening of the Russian people to political action was one of the most important consequences of 1905.

25 Compare, for example, Trotsky, *1905*, pp. 106, 250, 254, and Surgh, *1905*, pp. 311–12; V.E. Bonnell, *Roots of Rebellion. Workers' Politics and Organizations in St. Petersburg and Moscow, 1900–1914* (University of California Press, 1983), pp. 442–3.

26 Compare, for example, Trotsky, *1905*, p. 188, and V. Andrle, *A Social History of Twentieth-Century Russia* (Edward Arnold, 1994), pp. 64–5.

27 Compare, for example, Trotsky, *1905*, pp. 187–90, and M. Perrie, 'The Russian Peasant Movement of 1905–07: Its Social Composition and Revolutionary Significance', in B. Eklof and S.P. Frank (eds), *The World of the Russian Peasant* (Unwin Hyman, 1990), pp. 193–218. For more on Saratov, see, for example, T. Fallows, 'Governor Stolypin and the Revolution of 1905 in Saratov', in R.A. Wade and S.J. Seregny (eds), *Politics and Society in Provincial Russia: Saratov, 1590–1917* (Ohio

State University Press, 1989), pp. 139–59; T.R. Mixter, 'Peasant Collective Action in Saratov Province, 1902–1906', in *ibid.*, pp. 191–232.

28 Compare, for example, Trotsky, *1905*, p. 40, and J.D. White, 'Moscow, Petersburg and the Russian Industrialists. In Reply to Ruth Amende Rossa', *Soviet Studies* 24(3), 1973, pp. 414–20.

29 Compare, for example, Trotsky, *1905*, pp. 132–9, and the relevant essays in J.D. Klier and S. Lambroza (eds), *Pogroms: Anti-Jewish Violence in Modern Russian History* (Cambridge University Press, 1992).

30 Some recent research shares Trotsky's interest in peasant political activity as a reflection of a modernising process. See, for example, S.J. Seregny, 'A Different Type of Peasant Movement: The Peasant Unions in the Russian Revolution of 1905', *Slavic Review* 47(1), 1988, pp. 51–67.

31 David Moon, *The Russian Peasantry 1600–1930* (Longman, 1999). Some of Moon's themes can also be found in the articles on Saratov cited above.

32 For an account of the rules governing the elections to the various Dumas and a summary of each election campaign and its results, see, for example, I.D. Thatcher, 'Elections in Russian and Early Soviet History', in P. Lentini (ed.), *Elections and Political Order in Russia* (Central European University Press, 1995), pp. 18–22.

33 The summary of Trotsky's views on the Duma is based on the more detailed account given in I.D. Thatcher, 'Trotsky and the Duma: A Research Essay', in I.D. Thatcher (ed.), *Regime and Society in Twentieth Century Russia* (Macmillan, 1999), pp. 27–43.

34 L. Trotsky, 'In Defence of the Party (1907)', *Journal of Trotsky Studies* 2, 1994, p. 73. The points in the following paragraphs regarding Trotsky's views on the workers' congress and unity in the RSDLP are taken from this work.

35 There are numerous summaries of Akselrod's arguments in favour of a workers' congress. See, for example, A. Ascher, *Pavel Axelrod and the Development of Menshevism* (Harvard University Press, 1972), pp. 233–9, 254–65; S. Schwarz, *The Russian Revolution of 1905* (University of Chicago Press, 1967), pp. 230–5, etc.

36 Trotsky included 'There and Back' as an appendix to the later publication of *1905*. The quotes are taken from *1905*, pp. 415, 416, 476.

2 THE FIGHT FOR UNITY, 1907–14

1 *Pyatyi (Londonskii) s"ezd RSDRP* (State Publishing House, 1963), p.

398. Trotsky was to repeat these points in a little-known debate with the Bolshevik Yu. Kamenev. See Yu. Kamenev, 'Londonskii s"ezd Rossiiskoi s-d rabochei partii 1907g.', *Vestnik zhizni* 6, 1907, pp. 101–22; and N. Trotsky, 'Moral Londonskago S"ezda', *Vestnik zhizni* 7, 1907, pp. 65–84.

2 *Itogi Londonskogo S"ezda RSDRP: Sbornik statei* (1907), p. 4.

3 V.I. Lenin, *Collected Works 15* (Foreign Languages Publishing House, 1963), p. 371.

4 For the most recent account of Lenin's polemical inventions, see, for example, J.D. White, *Lenin. The Theory and Practice of Revolution* (Palgrave, 2001).

5 V.I. Lenin, *Polnoe sobranie sochinenii 47* (Political literature, 1978), p. 137.

6 G. Swain (ed.), *Protokoly Soveshchaniya Rasshirennoi Redaktsii "Proletariya" Iyun' 1909* (Kraus International Publications, 1982), pp. xxxv, xxxvii, 109–12.

7 For a translation of the correspondence surrounding the transfer of money to Trotsky, see *Journal of Trotsky Studies* 4, 1996, pp. 125–6.

8 For an account of Trotsky's poor financial circumstances in Vienna, see, for example, F. Keller, 'Trotsky in Vienna', *Revolutionary History* 7(2), 1999, pp. 50–2.

9 V.I. Lenin, *Polnoe sobranie sochinenii 47*, p. 277.

10 For a brief account of the calling of the Paris and Bern meetings of 1911 and for a list of their resolutions, see, for example, R.C. Elwood (ed.), *Resolutions and Decisions of the Communist Party of the Soviet Union 1. The Russian Social Democratic Labour Party 1898–October 1917* (University of Toronto Press, 1974), pp. 141–6. This volume also contains material relevant to all of the conferences and meetings referred to in this chapter.

11 G.R. Swain, 'The Bolsheviks' Prague Conference Revisited', *Revolutionary Russia* 2(1), 1989, pp. 134–41.

12 See, for example, the invaluable R.C. Elwood (ed.), *Vserossiiskaya Konferentsiya Ros. Sots.-Dem. Rab. Partii 1912 goda* (Kraus International Publications, 1982).

13 N. Trotsky, 'Neotlozhnye voprosy' and 'Ot redaktsii. Po povodu stat'i N. Trotskago', *Nasha Zarya* 11, 1911, pp. 116–28 and pp. 128–32.

14 Cited in I.D. Thatcher, 'Bor'ba, A Workers' Journal in St. Petersburg on the Eve of World War One', *The English Historical Review* 450, 1998, p. 101.

15 See, for example, V.I. Lenin, *Polnoe sobranie sochinenii 47*, pp. 296–8.

16 R. Luxemburg, 'Letters on Bolshevism and the Russian Revolution', *Revolutionary History* 6(2/3), 1996, p. 241.

17 For a more detailed account of the relationship between Kautsky and the Russians at this time, see M. Donald, *Marxism and Revolution. Karl Kautsky and the Russian Marxists 1900–1924* (Yale University Press, 1993).

18 Anon., 'Istoricheskaya desyatiletie (1904–1914), *Bor'ba* 1, 1914.

19 See, for example, J. Pallot, 'Did the Stolypin Land Reform Destroy the Peasant Commune?', in R.B. McKean (ed.), *New Perspectives in Modern Russian History* (Macmillan, 1992).

20 See, for example, P. Waldron, *Between Two Revolutions. Stolypin and the Politics of Renewal in Russia* (UCL Press, 1998), especially ch. 3.

21 L. Trotsky, 'Vienna Secession 1913', *Revolutionary History* 7(2), 1999, p. 100.

22 Trotsky's journalism on the Balkans has been conveniently translated into English as L. Trotsky, *The War Correspondence of Leon Trotsky. The Balkan Wars 1912–13* (Monad Press, 1980).

23 G.R. Swain, *Russian Social Democracy and the Legal Labour Movement 1906–14* (Macmillan, 1983).

3 WAR AND REVOLUTION, 1914–17

1 H. Strachan, *The First World War. I: To Arms* (Oxford University Press, 2001), p. 101.

2 Much of the following sections are based on the author's *Leon Trotsky and World War One* (Macmillan, 2000).

3 N. Trotsky, 'Povtorenie proidennago', *Novyi mir* 7 February 1917, p. 4.

4 For example, Lenin was very worried that a liberal government would make Russia far more able to pursue the war, thus delaying the revolution. He therefore attempted to forestall the February Revolution. For this interesting and original argument, see James D. White, 'Lenin, the Germans and the February Revolution', *Revolutionary Russia* 5(1), 1992, pp. 1–21.

5 For more on this, see R.B. Spence, 'Interrupted Journey: British Intelligence and the Arrest of Leon Trotskii, April 1917', *Revolutionary Russia* 13(1), 2000, pp. 1–28; Richard Norton-Taylor, 'MI5 Detained Trotsky on Way to Revolution', *Guardian*, 5 July 2001, p. 6; I.D. Thatcher, 'Trotsky Appeal', *Guardian*, 6 July 2001, p. 19.

6 L. Trotsky, *Sochineniya 3 1917, Part 1: Ot fevralya do Oktyabrya* (State Publishing House, 1924), p. 234.

7 The following section draws heavily on James D. White's brilliant arti-

cle 'Lenin, Trotskii and the Arts of Insurrection: The Congress of Soviets of the Northern Region, 11–13 October 1917', *Slavonic and East European Review* 77(1), 1999, pp. 117–39.

8 J. Stalin, *The October Revolution* (Lawrence & Wishart, 1936), p. 30.

4 DEFENDING THE REVOLUTION, 1917–21

1 A. Bone (ed.), *The Bolsheviks and the October Revolution. Central Committee Minutes of the RSDLP (Bolsheviks) August 1917–February 1918* (Pluto Press, 1974), p. 90.

2 L. Trotsky, *Sochineniya. Volume 3. Part 2. Ot oktybrya do bresta* (State Publishing House, 1925), p. 135.

3 See, for example, L. Trotsky, *The Essential Trotsky* (Unwin Books, 1963), pp. 90–5.

4 N.N. Smirnov, 'The Constituent Assembly', in E. Acton, V.Iu. Cherniaev and W.G. Rosenberg (eds), *Critical Companion to the Russian Revolution 1914–1921* (Arnold, 1997), p. 332.

5 For more on this, see J.D. White, 'Early Soviet Historical Interpretations of the Russian Revolution 1918–24', *Soviet Studies* 37(3), 1985, pp. 330–52.

6 For Luxemburg's brilliant critique of the Bolshevik signing of the Brest-Litovsk Treaty, see her 'The Russian Tragedy', in R. Looker (ed.), *Rosa Luxemburg. Selected Political Writings* (Cape, 1972), pp. 235–43.

7 G. Swain, *The Origins of the Russian Civil War* (Longman, 1996).

8 See, for example, E. Mawdsley, *The Russian Civil War* (Allen & Unwin, 1987); V.P. Butt, A.B. Murphy, N.A. Myshov and G.R. Swain (eds), *The Russian Civil War. Documents from the Soviet Archives* (Macmillan, 1996); and G. Swain, *The Origins of the Russian Civil War* (Longman, 1996).

9 Positive evaluations of Trotsky's role in the Civil War have continued into the recent period. See, for example, A.B. Murphy, *The Russian Civil War. Primary Sources* (Macmillan, 2000), pp. xiv, xvi–ii, 68, 164–5.

10 There are now several excellent essays on the activities of Trotsky's train and how life on board was run along communist lines. See R. Argenbright, 'Documents from Trotsky's Train in the Russian State Military Archive: A Comment', *Journal of Trotsky Studies* 4, 1996, pp. 1–11; R. Argenbright, 'Honour among Communists: "The Glorious Name of Trotsky's Train"', *Revolutionary Russia* 11(1), 1998, pp. 45–66; N.S. Tarkhova, 'Trotsky's Train: An Unknown Page in the

History of the Civil War', in T. Brotherstone and P. Dukes (eds), *The Trotsky Reappraisal* (Edinburgh University Press, 1992), pp. 27–40.

11 V.P. Butt, A.B. Murphy, N.A. Myshov and G.R. Swain (eds), *The Russian Civil War. Documents from the Soviet Archives* (Macmillan, 1996), p. xi.

12 E. Mawdsley, *The Russian Civil War* (Allen & Unwin, 1987), p. 60.

13 V.P. Butt, A.B. Murphy, N.A. Myshov and G.R. Swain (eds), *The Russian Civil War. Documents from the Soviet Archives* (Macmillan, 1996), p. 39.

14 L. Trotsky, *Terrorism and Communism* (New Park Publications, 1975), pp. 109, 75.

15 V. Nevskii in *Krasnaya Letopis* 4, 1922, p. 403.

16 E. Mawdsley, *The Russian Civil War* (Allen & Unwin, 1987), p. 169.

17 G. Swain, *The Origins of the Russian Civil War* (Longman, 1996), p. 251.

18 E. Mawdsley, *The Russian Civil War* (Allen & Unwin, 1987), pp. 200–1.

19 R. Pipes, *Russia under the Bolshevik Regime 1919–1924* (Harvill, 1994), pp. 5–14. See also R. Pipes (ed.), *The Unknown Lenin* (Yale University Press, 1996), pp. 69–73.

20 For an account of the brutal regime imposed by Stalin in Tsaritsyn and how this provides clues to his latter penchant for terror, see R. Argenbright, 'Red Tsaritsyn: Precursor of Stalinist Terror', *Revolutionary Russia* 4(2), 1991, pp. 157–83.

21 F. Benvenuti, *The Bolsheviks and the Red Army, 1918–1922* (Cambridge University Press, 1988), p. 216.

22 J. Channon, 'Trotsky, the Peasants and Economic Policy: A Comment', *Economy and Society* 14(4), 1985, p. 519.

23 V.P. Butt, A.B. Murphy, N.A. Myshov and G.R. Swain (eds), *The Russian Civil War. Documents from the Soviet Archives* (Macmillan, 1996), p. 149.

24 The quotes in this paragraph are from L. Trotsky, *Sochineniya 15. Khozyaistvennoe stroitel'stvo oetskoi respubliki* (State Publishing House, 1927), pp. 368, 387, 389. Trotsky's writings on transport form Section 6 of this volume.

25 A. Heywood, *Modernising Lenin's Russia* (Cambridge University Press, 1999), p. 136.

26 J. Aves, *Workers against Lenin* (I.B. Tauris, 1996), p. 74. Aves' book contains excellent summaries of worker resistance to Trotsky's economic management.

27 There are many summaries of the trade union debate. One of the

most useful, which the next several paragraphs draw upon, is Y. Tsuji, 'The Debate on the Trades Unions, 1920–21', *Revolutionary Russia* 2(1), 1989, pp. 31–100.

28 R. Service, *Lenin: A Political Life 3* (Macmillan, 1995), p. 182.

29 The most accessible source for Trotsky's views during the Soviet–Polish War is L. Trotsky, *How the Revolution Armed 3* (New Park Publications, 1981), pp. 127–243. There is also useful material on this conflict in R. Service, *Lenin: A Political Life 3* (Macmillan, 1995), ch. 5.

30 T. Osipova, 'Peasant Rebellions: Origin, Scope, Dynamics, and Consequences', in V.N. Brovkin (ed.), *The Bolsheviks in Russian Society* (Yale University Press, 1997), p. 173. There are many excellent studies of the protest of 1920–1 against Bolshevik rule. Amongst the most useful are R. Kowalski, *The Russian Revolution 1917–1921* (Routledge, 1997); C. Read, *From Tsar to Soviets* (UCL, 1996); and J.D. White, *The Russian Revolution 1917–1921* (Edward Arnold, 1994).

31 L. Trotsky, *How the Revolution Armed 4* (New Park Publications, 1981), p. 287. For an account of how Trotsky's words fitted a broader campaign by the Bolsheviks to belittle the Kronstadt mutiny, see I. Getzler's excellent study *Kronstadt 1917–1921* (Cambridge University Press, 1983).

5 THE REVOLUTION IN DECLINE, 1921–4

1 For an excellent summary of Trotsky's role in Bolshevik religious policy, see A. Luukkanen, 'The Rise and Fall of Trotsky in Soviet Religious Policy', *Journal of Trotsky Studies* 4, 1996, pp. 31–45. There are many studies that chart the difficulties of early Soviet religious policy. See, for example, W.B. Husband, 'Soviet Atheism and Russian Orthodox Strategies of Resistance, 1917–1932', *Journal of Modern History* 70(1), 1998, pp. 74–107, and the references contained therein.

2 R. Pipes (ed.), *The Unknown Lenin* (Yale University Press, 1996), pp. 148–9.

3 There are numerous summaries of the controversy over foreign trade. One of the best is in R. Service, *Lenin: A Political Life 3* (Macmillan, 1995), pp. 263–8.

4 See V. Kryazhin's review in *Krasnaya nov* 5(15), 1923, p. 405. The so-called Georgian Affair has long been a subject of historical treatment. The most recent and useful account is J. Smith, *The Bolsheviks and the National Question, 1917–23* (Macmillan, 1999). The most recent

research on this topic has also been usefully summarised in E. van Ree, "'Lenin's Last Struggle" Revisited', *Revolutionary Russia* 14(2), 2001, pp. 85–122. For further evidence that Trotsky thought that a Georgia dominated by Mensheviks would act as a bridgehead for international imperialism, see *Trotsky's Writings on Britain 1* (New Park, 1974), p. 116, and *How the Revolution Armed 5* (New Park, 1981), pp. 74–5, 95.

5 N. Harding, *Lenin's Political Thought 2* (Macmillan, 1981), p. 302.

6 L.D. Trotsky, 'The New Course (A Letter Addressed to Party Meetings), December 8, 1923', in V. Vilkova (ed.), *The Struggle for Power in Russia in 1923* (Prometheus Books, 1996), p. 224. This book is a most useful translation of the inner-party correspondence of late 1923.

7 L. Trotsky, 'The Platform of the Forty-Six (October 15, 1923)', *The Challenge of the Left Opposition (1923–25)* (Pathfinder, 1975), p. 398.

8 See, for example, D. Hincks, 'Support for the Opposition in Moscow in the Party Discussion of 1923–1924', *Soviet Studies* 44(1), 1992, pp. 137–52; K. Murphy, 'Opposition at the Local Level: A Case Study of the Hammer and Sickle Factory', *Europe–Asia Studies* 53(2), 2001, pp. 329–50.

9 For the full text of this resolution, see R. Gregor (ed.), *Resolutions and Decisions of the Communist Party of the Soviet Union 2. The Early Soviet Period 1917–1929* (University of Toronto Press, 1974), pp. 209–12.

10 *Ibid.*, p. 221.

11 L. Trotsky, *The Challenge of the Left Opposition (1923–25)* (Pathfinder, 1975), pp. 161–2.

12 The 5 December 1923 Resolution is reproduced in V. Vilkova (ed.), *The Struggle for Power in Russia in 1923* (Prometheus Books, 1996), pp. 206–9. The Trotsky quote is from *The Challenge of the Left Opposition (1923–25)* (Pathfinder, 1975), p. 70.

13 V. Vilkova (ed.), *The Struggle for Power in Russia in 1923* (Prometheus Books, 1996), p. 289.

14 *Ibid.*, pp. 283–4.

15 T.H. Friedgut, *Iuzovka and Revolution 2* (Princeton University Press, 1994), pp. 455–6.

16 M. von Hagen, *Soldiers in the Proletarian Dictatorship. The Red Army and the Soviet Socialist State, 1917–1930* (Cornell University Press, 1990), pp. 198–205.

17 For Lenin's various assessments of Trotsky, see R. Pipes (ed.), *The Unknown Lenin* (Yale University Press, 1996), pp. 67–8, 123–4, 166.

18 R. Service, *Lenin: A Political Life 3* (Macmillan, 1995), pp. 273–4.

19 L. Trotsky, *The First Five Years of the Communist International 2* (New Park Publications, 1974), p. 70.

20 For an account of the problematic nature of Soviet–West relations in the early 1920s, see, for example, the relevant chapters in G. Gorodetsky (ed.), *Soviet Foreign Policy 1917–1991: A Retrospective* (Frank Cass, 1994).

21 For the numerous contradictions in Comintern policy under Lenin, including those inherent in the united front, see, for example, K. McDermott and J. Agnew, *The Comintern. A History of International Communism from Lenin to Stalin* (Macmillan, 1996), ch. 1.

22 For an account of successive communist failures in early 1920s' Germany, see, for example, A. Vatlin, 'The Testing-ground of World Revolution: Germany in the 1920s', in T. Rees and A. Thorpe (eds), *International Communism and the Communist International 1919–43* (Manchester University Press, 1998), pp. 117–26.

23 L. Trotsky, *Problems of Everyday Life* (Monad Press, 1973), p. 62. The ongoing summary of Trotsky's views on everyday life is based upon the articles collected in this volume.

24 See, for example, F.L. Bernstein, 'Envisioning Health in Revolutionary Russia: The Politics of Gender in Sexual Enlightenment Posters of the 1920s', *Russian Review* 57(2), 1998, pp. 191–217; V.E. Bonnell, *Iconography of Power. Soviet Political Posters under Lenin and Stalin* (University of California Press, 1997), especially ch. 2.

25 For a highly critical account of the Communist Party's failings in relation to women, see, for example, V.N. Brovkin, 'Mobilization, Utilization, and the Rhetoric of Liberation: Bolshevik Policy Toward Women', in V.N. Brovkin (ed.), *The Bolsheviks in Russian Society* (Yale University Press, 1997).

26 Yu.V. Got'e, 'Moi zametki', *Voprosy istorii* 11, 1991, p. 151.

27 G. Roberts, *Forward Soviet! History and Non-fiction Film in the USSR* (I.B. Tauris, 1999), p. 30.

28 See, for example, R. Taylor, 'Soviet Cinema as Popular Culture', *Revolutionary Russia* 1(1), 1988, pp. 36–56; D. Youngblood, 'Entertainment or Enlightenment? Popular Cinema in Soviet Society, 1921–1931', in S. White (ed.), *New Directions in Soviet History* (Cambridge University Press, 1992), pp. 41–61.

29 See, for example, the references to Trotsky in E. Naiman, *Sex in Public. The Incarnation of Early Soviet Ideology* (Princeton University Press, 1997).

30 L. Trotsky, *Literature and Revolution* (Redwords, 1991), p. 59.

31 *Ibid.*, p. 153.

32 For further criticisms of Trotsky as literary critic, see, for example, N.N. Punin, 'Literature without Revolution', *Journal of Trotsky Studies* 3, 1995, pp. 47–52. Richard Pipes differs markedly from Trotsky in the evaluation of literary trends. For Pipes, for example, the best traditions in Russian literature survived in exile. For more, see R. Pipes, *Russia under the Bolshevik Regime* (Harvill, 1994), ch. 6.

6 OPPOSITION AND DEFEAT, 1925–9

1 For an account of the falling-out between the members of the triumvirate, see, for example, E.H. Carr, *Socialism in One Country, 1924–1926, 2* (Macmillan, 1959), chs 13, 16, 17.

2 Boris Bazhanov, *Bazhanov and the Damnation of Stalin* (Ohio University Press, 1990).

3 The full text of Trotsky's speeches to the Central Control Commission from which these quotes are taken is in L. Trotsky, *The Stalin School of Falsification* (New Park, 1974), pp. 100–26.

4 For the full text of Trotsky's letter to the Commission for the Study of Party History, see L. Trotsky, *The Essential Trotsky* (Unwin Books, 1963), pp. 183–243.

5 L.T. Lih, O.V. Naumov and O.V. Khlevniuk (eds), *Stalin's Letters to Molotov* (Yale University Press, 1995), p. 135.

6 For a very good account of the pitfalls of the United Opposition's tactics and how Stalin was never really under threat, see, for example, E.H. Carr, *Foundations of a Planned Economy, 1926–1929, 2* (Macmillan, 1971), ch. 39. Recent research has confirmed rather than detracted from Carr's conclusions.

7 Russian Centre for the Preservation and Study of Documents of Modern History, Moscow (hereafter RTsKhIDNI), F. 17, O. 2, D. 329.

8 RTsKhIDNI, F. 17, O. 2, D. 330.

9 J. Hughes, *Stalin, Siberia, and the Crisis of the NEP* (Cambridge University Press, 1991), pp. 34–8.

10 For a brief and recent account of the dangers and difficulties that led ordinary oppositionists to hoist the white flag, see, for example, K. Murphy, 'Opposition at the Local Level', *Europe–Ais Studies* 53(2), 2001, pp. 334–47.

11 For more on this, see, for example, Alan M. Ball, *Russia's Last Capitalists. The Nepmen, 1921–29* (University of California Press, 1987).

12 For more on the contradictions in the economic thinking of the

United Opposition, see, for example, A. Nove, *An Economic History of the USSR 1917–1991* (Penguin, 1992), ch. 5. The obvious problems with Trotsky's assumptions about the kulaks can also be inferred from R.W. Davies, *Soviet Economic Development from Lenin to Khrushchev* (Cambridge University Press, 1998), ch. 4.

13 For a fuller account of these issues, see, for example, I.D. Thatcher, 'Trotsky, the Soviet Union and the World Economy', *Coexistence* 30, 1993, pp. 111–24.

14 L.T. Lih, O.V. Naumov and O.V. Khlevniuk (eds), *Stalin's Letters to Molotov* (Yale University Press, 1995), p. 36.

15 See A. Pantsov's excellent study *The Bolsheviks and the Chinese Revolution 1919–1927* (Curzon, 2000).

16 For more on this, see S.A. Smith's excellent contribution to T. Rees and A. Thorpe (eds), *International Communism and the Communist International 1919–43* (Manchester University Press, 1998).

17 G. Benton (ed.), *Interviews with Wang Faxi on Tang Baolin's History of Chinese Communism* (Leeds East Asia Papers, 1995), pp. 17–19.

18 See, for example, L. Trotsky, *Europe and America. Two Speeches on Imperialism* (Pathfinder, 1971); or Trotsky's speeches, translated by I.D. Thatcher, in M. Cox and H.H. Ticktin (eds), *The Ideas of Leon Trotsky* (Porcupine, 1995).

19 L. Trotsky, *The Challenge of the Left Opposition (1928–29)* (Pathfinder, 1981), pp. 64–5.

20 K. McDermott and J. Agnew, *The Comintern* (Macmillan, 1996), p. 70.

21 L. Trotsky, *The Third International After Lenin* (Pathfinder, 1996), p. 95.

7 AGAINST STALINISM AND FASCISM, 1929–33

1 A. Rosmer, *Trotsky and the Origins of Trotskyism* (Francis Boutle, 2002), p. 148. Other details of Trotsky's daily routine in Prinkipo have been taken from J. van Heijenoort, *With Trotsky in Exile* (Harvard University Press, 1978). Trotsky's enthusiasm for his daily fishing trips is clear from a diary entry he penned just before leaving Prinkipo for good in 1933. See L. Trotsky, *Writings of Leon Trotsky (1932–33)* (Pathfinder Press, 1972), pp. 312–18.

2 S. Kotkin, *Magnetic Mountain. Stalinism as a Civilisation* (University of California Press, 1995).

3 E.H. Carr, 'Stalin', *Soviet Studies* 5(1), 1953, p. 7.

4 L. Trotsky, *Writings of Leon Trotsky (1930–31)* (Pathfinder Press, 1973), p. 282.

5 L. Trotsky, *Writings of Leon Trotsky (1932)* (Pathfinder Press, 1973), p. 274.

6 See, for example, A. Nove, *Studies in Economics and Russia* (Macmillan, 1990), pp. 71–9.

7 L.T. Lih, O.V. Naumov and O.V. Khlevniuk (eds), *Stalin's Letters to Molotov* (Yale University Press, 1995), p. 200.

8 L. Trotsky, *Writings of Leon Trotsky (1930–31)*, p. 205.

9 J.R. Millar, 'Mass Collectivisation and the Contribution of Soviet Agriculture to the First Five-Year Plan', *Slavic Review* 4, 1974, pp. 750–66.

10 The most recent historical accounts of the peasants' adverse reactions to collectivisation include L. Viola's excellent *Peasant Rebels under Stalin. Collectivization and the Culture of Peasant Resistance* (Oxford University Press, 1996).

11 See, for example, Holland Hunter's essay in J. Copper, M. Perrie and E.A. Rees (eds), *Soviet History, 1917–53* (Macmillan, 1995).

12 A. Nove, *Socialism, Economics and Development* (Allen & Unwin, 1986), pp. 135–6. For an appreciation of Nove's contribution to our understanding of Soviet planning, see I.D. Thatcher, 'Alec Nove, Soviet Planning and Market Reform, and the Need for Relevant Economics', *New Political Economy* 5(2), 2000, pp. 269–80.

13 L. Trotsky, *The Struggle against Fascism in Germany* (Pathfinder Press, 1971), pp. 376, 383. All subsequent quotations from Trotsky on the subject of German fascism used in this section are taken from this source.

14 See the pieces by Sam Gordon and Mika Etchebehere in *Revolutionary History* 5(1), 1993.

15 L.I. Gintsberg, 'Fraktsionnaya bor'ba v KPG v kanun prikhoda Gitlera k vlasti. Novye materialy', *Voprosy istorii* 6, 2001, p. 125.

16 See, for example, M. Jones, 'A Comment on Sam Gordon's Reports', *Revolutionary History* 5(1), 1993, pp. 29–32.

17 These and many other valuable points are made in the excellent discussion in K. McDermott and J. Agnew, *The Comintern* (Macmillan, 1996), pp. 98–119.

18 Cited in I. Kershaw, *Hitler. 1889–1936: Hubris* (Allen Lane, 1998), p. 377.

19 For more on this, see I.D. Thatcher, 'Uneven and Combined Development', *Revolutionary Russia* 4(2), 1991, pp. 235–58.

20 See, for example, B.D. Wolfe, *Strange Communists I Have Known*

(1965), pp. 196–206; P. Beilharz, 'Trotsky as Historian', *History Workshop Journal* 20, 1985, pp. 36–55.

21 J.D. White, *The Russian Revolution 1917–1921. A Short History* (Edward Arnold, 1994), p. 88; J.D. White, 'Trotsky's *The History of the Russian Revolution*', *Journal of Trotsky Studies* 1, 1993, pp. 1–18.

22 L. Trotsky, *The History of the Russian Revolution* (Pluto Press, 1977), p. 926.

23 Erik van Ree, 'Stalin's Bolshevism: The Year of Revolution', *Revolutionary Russia* 13(1), 2000, p. 52.

24 See, for example, R. Pipes, *The Russian Revolution 1899–1919* (HarperCollins, 1990), pp. 422, 423, 472, 479, 484, 493, 498, 918.

25 L. Trotsky, *The History of the Russian Revolution* (Pluto Press, 1977), pp. 81, 115.

26 Peter Waldron, *Between Two Revolutions: Stolypin and the Politics of Renewal in Russia* (UCL Press, 1998), p. 185.

27 Compare L. Trotsky, *The History of the Russian Revolution* (Pluto Press, 1977), pp. 781, 787–8, 804, and R. Kowalski, *The Russian Revolution 1917–1921* (Routledge, 1997), p. 80.

28 L. Trotsky, *The History of the Russian Revolution* (Pluto Press, 1977), pp. 873–5.

29 O. Figes, *A People's Tragedy: The Russian Revolution 1891–1924* (Jonathan Cape, 1996), pp. 600, 365.

30 Compare L. Trotsky, *The History of the Russian Revolution* (Pluto Press, 1977), p. 1024, and J.E. Marot, 'Class Conflict, Political Competition and Social Transformation: Critical Perspectives on the Social History of the Russian Revolution', *Revolutionary Russia* 7(2), 1994, p. 156.

31 L. Trotsky, *The History of the Russian Revolution* (Pluto Press, 1977), p. 1079.

8 THE FINAL EXILE: THE FOURTH INTERNATIONAL AND WORLD EVENTS, 1933–40

1 See, for example, C. Ward (ed.), *The Stalinist Dictatorship* (Arnold, 1998).

2 S. Fitzpatrick, *Everyday Stalinism* (Oxford University Press, 1999), pp. 226–7.

3 S. Kotkin, *Magnetic Mountain: Stalinism as a Civilisation* (University of California Press, 1995), pp. 363–4.

4 E.C. Helmreich, *The American Political Science Review* 31, 1937, p. 967.

5 L. Trotsky, *Writings of Leon Trotsky (1937–38)* (Pathfinder, 1970), p. 72.

6 'Telegrams in Brief', *Times*, 20 December 1937, p. 11.

7 'Malaise in Moscow', *Times*, 29 September 1937, p. 13.

8 See, for example, the comment made in J. Arch Getty and O.V. Naumov, *The Road to Terror* (Yale University Press, 1999), p. 63.

9 J.T. Farrell, 'Dewey in Mexico', in S. Hook (ed.), *John Dewey: Philosopher of Science and Freedom* (Greenwood, 1976), p. 351.

10 L. Trotsky, *Their Morals and Ours* (Pathfinder, 1973), p. 52. Dewey's response is also contained in this edition.

11 L. Trotsky, *Writings of Leon Trotsky (1936–37)* (Pathfinder, 1978), p. 67.

12 L. Trotsky, *Stalin* (Harper & Brothers, 1946), p. xv.

13 *Ibid.*, pp. 182, 161.

14 See, for example, P.E. Mosely, 'Trotsky and Stalin', *The Review of Politics* 11(1), 1949, pp. 116–17; W. Gurian, *American Historical Review* 52(2), 1946–7, pp. 321–4.

15 L. Trotsky, *Whither France?* (New Park, 1974), p. 117.

16 L. Trotsky, *The Spanish Revolution (1931–39)* (Pathfinder, 1973), pp. 330–1, 350.

17 See the essay by T. Rees on Spain, in T. Rees and A. Thorpe (eds), *International Communism and the Communist International 1919–43* (Manchester University Press, 1998).

18 See, for example, A. Durgan, 'Trotsky, the POUM and the Spanish Revolution', *Journal of Trotsky Studies* 2, 1994, p. 46.

19 As this may be controversial, let me quote Trotsky:

> The struggle for 'living room' is nothing but a camouflage for imperialist expansion, that is, the policy of annexation and plunder. The racial justification for this expansion is a lie; National Socialism changes its racial sympathies and antipathies in accordance with strategic considerations.
>
> (L. Trotsky, *Writings of Leon Trotsky (1939–40)* (Pathfinder, 1973), p. 193)

20 For more on this, see, for example, D. Wedgwood Benn, 'Nazism and Stalinism: Problems of Comparison', *Europe–Asia Studies* 51(1), 1999, pp. 151–9.

21 See, for example, G. Roberts, 'The Soviet Decision for a Pact with Nazi Germany', *Soviet Studies* 44(1), 1992, pp. 57–78.

22 Several textbooks claim that when Germany invaded the USSR Stalin

was thrown into a panic and it would have been possible to over-throw him – see, for example, G. Hosking, *A History of the Soviet Union* (Fontana, 1990); M. McCauley, *Stalin and Stalinism* (Longman, 1995). These claims are convincingly refuted by S.J. Main, 'Stalin in June 1941', *Europe–Asia Studies* 48(5), 1996, pp. 837–9. See also J. Barber's essay in J. Cooper *et al.* (eds), *Soviet History, 1917–53* (Macmillan, 1995).

23 B.D. Wolfe, 'Trotsky's Case', *The New Republic*, 16 June 1937, p. 164.

24 L. Trotsky, *Writings of Leon Trotsky (1939–40)* (Pathfinder, 1973), pp. 158–9.

25 See the essay by Y. Sergeev, in T. Rees and A. Thorpe (eds), *International Communism and the Communist International 1919–43* (Manchester University Press, 1998).

26 L. Trotsky, *Writings of Leon Trotsky (1939–40)* (Pathfinder, 1973), p. 233.

27 Cited in D. Volkogonov, *Trotsky. The Eternal Revolutionary* (HarperCollins, 1996), p. 466. This work contains a very detailed account of the plans to assassinate Trotsky.

28 'Leon Trotsky. The Bolshevist Revolution', *Times*, 23 August 1940, p. 7. For further reports about Trotsky at this time in the London *Times*, see 'Death of Trotsky', 22 August 1940, p. 4, and 23 August 1940, p. 4; 'Trotsky's Assailant Indicted', 28 August 1940, p. 3; and 'Demonstration outside Soviet Embassy: "Stalin murdered Trotsky" on Placards', 31 August 1940, p. 2.

CONCLUSION

1 L. Trotsky, *Trotsky's Diary in Exile 1935* (Harvard University Press, 1976), p. 43.

2 *Ibid.*, p. 47.

3 G. Swain, 'The Disillusioning of the Revolution's Praetorian Guard: The Latvian Riflemen, Summer–Autumn 1918', *Europe–Asia Studies* 51(4), 1999, p. 678.

4 J.D. White, *Karl Marx and the Intellectual Origins of Dialectical Materialism* (Macmillan, 1996), p. 367.

5 The most recent and bizarre demonisation of Trotsky that I have come across is 'Trotsky Recycled', *Association of Jewish Refugees Journal* 1(9), September 2001. This accuses Trotsky's followers of wanting to inflame the race riots that hit certain British cities in 2001.

FURTHER READING

The complicated history of Russian Social Democracy has been outlined clearly and concisely by J.L.H. Keep in The Rise of Social Democracy in Russia (Oxford University Press, 1963), and L. Schapiro in The Communist Party of the Soviet Union (Methuen, 1963). There are several excellent one-volume introductions to the Russian Revolution, including James D. White, The Russian Revolution 1917–1921: A Short History (Edward Arnold, 1994), and C. Read, From Tsar to Soviets. The Russian People and their Revolution, 1917–1921 (UCL Press, 1996). A more detailed account of revolutionary Russia is presented in R. Pipes, The Russian Revolution 1899–1919 (Collins Harvill, 1990) and Russia under the Bolshevik Regime 1919–1924 (Harvill, 1994). R. Kowalski's The Russian Revolution 1917–1921 (Routledge, 1997) contains a wealth of primary sources, together with a useful commentary. E.H. Carr's The Russian Revolution from Lenin to Stalin 1917–1929 (Macmillan, 1979) has the great advantage of covering foreign as well as domestic developments. For the Stalin period, C. Ward has summarised the most recent research in Stalin's Russia (Edward Arnold, 1999). There are also several edited collections of some of the most important studies of Stalinism, including C. Ward, The Stalinist Dictatorship (Edward Arnold, 1998), S. Fitzpatrick, Stalinism: New Directions (Routledge, 1999), and C. Read, The Stalin Years (Palgrave, 2002). The best and most recent studies of the history of international communism include K. McDermott and J. Agnew, The Comintern: A History of International Communism from Lenin to Stalin (Macmillan, 1996), and T. Rees and A. Thorpe (eds), International Communism and the Communist International 1919–1943 (Manchester University Press, 1998).

There are several academic journals in which the very latest research on the Russian Revolution, including Trotsky's role, is published. The most useful of these are Revolutionary Russia (Frank Cass), Revolutionary History (Socialist Platform) and Europe–Asia Studies (Carfax).

INDEX